6/98

Japanese Culture in Comparative Perspective

Japanese Culture in Comparative Perspective

Chikio Hayashi and Yasumasa Kuroda

Foreword by Hayward R. Alker

Westport, Connecticut
London

Library of Congress Cataloging-in-Publication Data

Hayashi, Chikio, 1918–
    Japanese culture in comparative perspective / Chikio Hayashi and
Yasumasa Kuroda ; foreword by Hayward R. Alker.
        p.   cm.
    Includes bibliographical references and index.
    ISBN 0–275–95861–2 (alk. paper)
    1. Japan—Civilization.   2. Comparative civilization.   I. Kuroda,
Yasumasa, 1928–   II. Title.
    DS821.H375   1997
    306′.0952—dc21   96–37728

British Library Cataloguing in Publication Data is available.

Library of Congress Catalog Card Number: 96–37728
ISBN: 0–275–95861–2

First published in 1997

Praeger Publishers, 88 Post Road West, Westport, CT 06881
An imprint of Greenwood Publishing Group, Inc.

Printed in the United States of America

The paper used in this book complies with the
Permanent Paper Standard issued by the National
Information Standards Organization (Z39.48–1984).

10 9 8 7 6 5 4 3 2 1

Copyright Acknowledgments

The authors and publisher gratefully acknowledge permission for use of the following material:

Excerpts from *Faust: A Tragedy* by Johann Wolfgang von Goethe, translated by Bayard Taylor. Copyright © 1950 by Random House, Inc. Used with permission.

Every reasonable effort has been made to trace the owners of copyright materials in this book, but in some instances this has proven impossible. The authors and publisher will be glad to receive information leading to more complete acknowledgments in subsequent printings of the book and in the meantime extend their apologies for any omissions.

To Prince Régent Shôtoku, who contributed

toward the promotion of *wa* (peace) as the central norm

of Japanese culture,

and

in memory of the late Professor Karl W. Deutsch,

in appreciation for his encouragement

to complete our book.

Contents

Illustrations

TABLES

FIGURES

Foreword

Around the world, people are interested in Japanese culture. Chikio Hayashi and Yasumasa Kuroda's *Japanese Culture in Comparative Perspective* presents some of the finest fruits of a sustained, collaborative, comparative, historical, sociocultural, and statistical study of this subject. Their quarter of century of working together, as well as the contributions of other co-workers, make this synoptic, well-integrated, accessible, English-language report a significant scholarly pursuit in several ways.

A first, major reason for attending seriously to the present work is its wise, contemporary, relevant definition of culture in terms of an implicit or explicit, rational, nonrational or irrational, historically created "design for living" involving both worldviews and human selves (their relatively salient social units and the characteristic ways of responding to the world). The diffuseness of Japanese identities and the salience of extended social units are powerfully illustrated in the present work. This contribution fits nicely with the rise of concern with modern and postmodern selves, the awareness of their constructed character, and the plural quality of the flows and forces tugging at and shaping sociopolitical identities in the contemporary world.[1]

Second, I expect that the non-Japanese reader of this book will find both impressive and challenging the way it integrates findings from traditional literary, historical, and philosophical disciplines with those of the contemporary social sciences. It is important that citizens and scholars in this late modern age see such real examples of (necessarily partial) convergences in understanding between traditional philosophic, contemporary humanistic, and modern empirically oriented social inquiry. They, like I, will want to read more from Prince Regent Shôtoku, the Buddhist priest poet Saigyô, Norinaga Motoori's poetic commentaries, and Kenzaburô Ôe's intriguing Nobel acceptance speech, as well as the works of many other classical and contemporary literary and scientific writers cited in these pages. The sources of their insights and innovations need further investigation; why some of their views have been sustained, and others ignored, also begs for further inquiry. Becoming self-aware about one's traditions, the extent of their validity, and the epistemological limits of their contributions allows "traditions" to be more consciously, critically, and selectively renewed; it helps increase human understanding and collective freedom.

Third, this work stands out for its sophisticated primary reliance on a comparative, empirical approach to the challenging issue of cultural studies. In its multidimensional empirical approach—sensitive to modal attitudes, associations, recurring oppositions, and enduring multidimensional configural orientations—this book shows rich and precise ways of studying culture's quantitative and qualitative features. It treats the issue of cultural uniqueness sensitively, but also comparatively. Thus we see how cultural studies need not be considered a realm of ineffable complexities.[2] The remarkable findings about the role of Japanese and American languages in shaping the tolerance of ambiguity and "either/or" qualities (or ontologies) of their respective cultures is one of the most important benefits of this scientific approach; these findings are nicely supported with data from Hawaiian contexts, in which these different orientations can be observed in revealing ways. Adding information from Middle Eastern countries—especially the Semitic languages—will recall for some Derrida's insistence (Ashley, 1989, pp. 260–261) on the distorting consequences of Western "logocentrism"; the difference in perspective here is a richly suggestive, indeed integrative, combination of Western and non-Western analytical and linguistic perspectives.

The importance of a Rashomon-like sense of multiple perspectives and truths is buttressed by the remarkable mixture of religious attitudes that the authors uncover. As they suggest, I too have found especially noteworthy, and recurrent, the Japanese pattern of men and women "baptized" according to one religion (e.g., Shinto), married in another (e.g., Christianity), and expecting, without a sense of contradiction or inappropriateness, a funeral according to the rites of either or some other (e.g., Buddhist) religion. Similarly, I observed recently in Kyoto a moderately large playing field supporting three simultaneous and interpenetrating baseball games (played with slightly less "hard" baseballs than Americans are used to, and outfielders from one game standing in the infield of another). Very few Americans would be able to sustain such divided attentions as such playing circumstances require, but I have found other Japanese (in particular, students with access to only limited playing fields) able successfully to avoid the "absolutizing" of their attentions. As interestingly, Hayashi and Kuroda's data suggest the Chinese and Koreans to be more totalizing in these regards; in my experience, South Asian Indians fit more the Japanese pattern.

But I would not want these distinctions to be too absolutized. Thus the authors exempt important Japanese attitudes toward outsiders, former untouchables, and other ethnic minorities (and thus most of international relations) from their generalizations. They correctly link the quality of Western "either/or" thinking to Aristotelian formal logic and to Aristotle's insistent metaphysical commitment to the avoidance of debilitating contradictions (especially the principle of the "excluded middle"). But, as I have recently argued in *Rediscoveries and Reformulations*,[3] Western thought about social, cultural, and political matters has also been influenced by the belief that they support only partial, contingent, imprecise, and revisable truths. Similarly, Chinese culture, shown in this study importantly to differ from the Japanese on such matters, nonetheless also has a Daoist tradition that allows or tolerates ambiguities, contradictions, and multiple truths.

So I take Hayashi and Kuroda's work to embody a broader challenge to human understanding than even their Japanese focus suggests: the reconciliation or accommodation of absolutist and nonabsolutist elements within any one culture, and among overlapping ones as well. This book suggests a revealing, disciplined, and imitable way of developing further such explorations in non-Japanese cultures as well.

Finally, for many North American social scientists not familiar with Chikio Hayashi's distinguished methodological and substantive contributions to the social sciences, this book will allow them nontechnical access to some of the nicest technical achievements of that work. I find particularly impressive his independently developed multidimensional quantification-scaling approach deployed throughout this book, and also Hayashi's increasingly refined survey instruments for exploring the roots of Japanese culture in a reproducible, comparative, empirical fashion. In my several visits to Japan since the middle 1960s, I have met no other Japanese social scientist who has made such distinguished, innovative, and sustained contributions of both a methodological and substantive sort. Although there have been numerous English-language papers and reports on this work and some of its substantive findings, which were published in Japan (and occasionally elsewhere), Yasumasa Kuroda deserves special thanks for bringing this mature, integrative, and richly collaborative work to the attention of a wider English-language audience.

Hayward R. Alker

John A. Mcone Professor of International Relations
University of Southern California and
Emeritus Professor of Political Science
Massachusetts Institute of Technology

NOTES

1. Two recent international relations books collecting relevant writings on such themes are Yoself Lapid and Friedrich Kratiochiwil, eds., *The Return of Culture and Identity in IR Theory*. Boulder, Colo.: Lynne Rienner, 1996; and Michael J. Shapiro and H. R. Alker, eds., *Challenging Boundaries: Global Flows, Territorial Identities*. Minneapolis: University of Minnesota Press, 1996. A book attempting an integration of Buddhist ideas and contemporary neuro-science on the constructed character of the self is Francisco J. Varela et al., *The Embodied Mind: Cognitive Science and Human Experience*, Cambridge, Mass.: MIT Press, 1991.

2. Cited by Hayashi and Kuroda in Chapter 2 of this book, Anna Wierzbicka is a writer who has begun the exploration of cultural uniqueness and commonalties with an even more linguistic methodological orientation; she has recently begun writing on Japanese culture as well. A good introduction to her overall approach is her *Semantics, Culture, and Cognition: Universal Human Concepts in Culture-Specific Configurations*. New York: Oxford University Press, 1992.

3. New York: Cambridge University Press, 1996, Chapters 1 and 2. The Pre-Socratic Sophist Protagoras developed such a method of principled oppositions, used by Thucydides to telling effect in many of his analyses. Following the lead of Nicholas Rescher, I suggested how Thucydides' reconstruction of the Melian Dialogue could be respected as a partly formalizable mode of arguing in which some versions of innovations-allowing and contra-diction-respecting reasoning can be tolerated. Contemporary law court practice evinces this earlier tradition, with its ceteris paribus mode of arguing, which allows exceptions to a rule. Aristotelian rhetoric and poetics are similarly less precise.

A key point about informal or dialectical logic, as it is understood by Nicholas Rescher, Stephen Touimin, and other contemporary informal logicians, is that it includes the "either/or" logic of the apodictic Aristotelian syllogism as a special case. Hence informal/dialectical reasoning need not be seen as in contradiction with the principle of the excluded middle, even though Rescher-style dialectical logic transcends that principle. Dialectical logic in this sense is thus not totally opposed to standard formal logic, whose dedication to consistency does have the "either/or" quality that Hayashi and Kuroda also rightly attribute to Aristotelian literalism. Their usage of the term *dialectical* is, interestingly, almost the opposite of mine; but the distinction they are making is almost exactly the same.

Preface

We have witnessed the proliferation of *Nihonjinron* (theory of Japanese culture) literature attempting to characterize the nature of Japanese culture. The boom started in the early 1970s and has continued on and off for the past quarter of a century. The interest in things Japanese appeared following the spectacular double-digit economic growth Japan experienced in the 1960s. It was as though the Japanese had no time to reflect on the question of who they were until then. Unfortunately, however, many works, both by Japanese and non-Japanese authors, are based on their personal accounts of what they perceive Japanese culture to be or what they can synthesize from the historical literature.

Hayashi's professional interest in survey research started in 1947 as he became involved in joint research with criminologists to study parolees. Trained as a mathematician at the University of Tokyo, he started to apply his statistical methods in survey research. He finally began his first *Nihonkokuminsei no kenkyû* (a study of Japanese culture) in 1953 at the Institute of Statistical Mathematics, Ministry of Education. He led a team of scholars to conduct the same survey every five years hence until his retirement. His younger colleagues continued the tradition he started. Kuroda's initiation to the study of public opinion was his attempt to gauge the student attitudes toward an annual athletic event in 1949, when he was a high school student. He was trained in survey research at the University of Oregon as he acquired degrees in sociology and political science in the 1950s. He joined Hayashi's team in conducting the first extension of the Japanese culture survey abroad in 1971 (the first systematic sample survey of Japanese Americans in Honolulu).

Following the initial survey in 1971, Hayashi and Kuroda (hence called "we") started to talk about the possibility of jointly writing a book on Japanese culture in English. We finally started to map out and draft chapters in 1994. The basic framework of the book has truly been a joint work, while the actual writing of the book has been Kuroda's task. Hayashi provided the results of data analysis, while Kuroda came up with the language theory of Rashomonesque *Yamazakura* (mountain cherry blossom). Articles and books written in Japanese on the same data are rich in findings but lack theory. However, it was Hayashi whose doubt in the adequacy of translation finally led Kuroda and his other colleagues to conduct a series of language surveys.

This book represents a culmination of our life-long efforts to understand the Japanese. Our objective is to help others understand the Japanese by providing them with a clear model of what Japanese culture is like. The Japanese too may benefit by knowing who they are in relation to Americans.

The chapters have gone through a number of revisions—sometimes drastic—as a result of discussions in Honolulu and Tokyo over the past few years. Karl W. Deutsch, who encouraged us to write the book and promised to write a foreword, passed away a few years ago. His former student, Hayward Alker who was Kuroda's classmate at Princeton in 1962, agreed to write it on Deutsch's behalf. Alker is one of the few American scholars who is familiar with Hayashi's contribution to statistics.

There are many who helped us directly and indirectly in the preparation of this book. Many data come from not only the Institute of Statistical Mathematics but from other Japanese sources as well. We are grateful to the Ministry of Education, the Toyota Foundation, and others who facilitated our sample surveys. There are thousands of Americans, Arabs, Europeans, and Japanese who contributed to this book by providing us with their opinions. We simply have too many people without whose assistance we could not have written the book. We cannot acknowledge them all individually. However, we wish to thank the following individuals for their contribution to our work: Kamilla K. McClelland, Vincent Kelly Pollard, and Jim Burns.

Japanese Culture in
Comparative Perspective

CHAPTER 1

Introduction: Search for the Core of Japanese Culture

OBJECTIVE

A plethora of authors on Japanese culture approach their subjects from a variety of disciplinary paradigms[1]: anecdotal journalism (van Wolferen, 1989), anthropology (Bachnik, 1994; Benedict, 1944; Lebra, 1976), history (BenDasan/Yamamoto, 1971), literature (Keene, 1952), physiology (Tsunoda, 1985),[2] religion (Umehara, 1987), sociology (Nakane, 1967), and statistics (Hayashi, 1988). Each approach has its own strength and weakness, and some are more powerful than others in explaining key Japanese characteristics. This study presents yet another perspective in the search for the essence of Japanese culture. We have based our study on an inference drawn from a cross-cultural data set collected in Japan, the United States, and the Arab world: namely, that language in a crucial way determines what we perceive in, and how we react to, the world—and, therefore, what and who we think we are.

The objective of the study is to present from a sustained theoretical perspective the results of the longitudinal and comparative surveys of the Japanese culture known in Japanese as *Nihonjin no kokuminsei* (Japanese national character). Chikio Hayashi of the Institute of Statistical Mathematics in Tokyo initiated these surveys in 1953 and repeated every five years hence; they include comparable surveys in Hawaii, the U.S. mainland, Brazil, and Europe. When coauthor Hayashi started his initial survey, he was motivated to define the basic nature of the Japanese culture as Japan regained its independence after World War II. However, he came to realize the importance of making his study comparative, not simply chronologically but also cross-nationally. Thus, Hayashi cooperated with Yasumasa Kuroda, the other coauthor of this book. This resulted in the first study of Japanese culture abroad in 1971 among Japanese Americans in Hawaii.

Many books and articles have been published on the Japanese kokuminsei study, but they are mostly in Japanese. There are several article-length studies published in English. The book is aimed at presenting an accumulation of forty years of longitudinal survey efforts on Japanese culture in comparative perspective, specifically for American readers.

GUIDING QUESTIONS

What constitutes the core of Japanese culture in comparative perspective? To answer this question, four major questions are raised:

1. What kind of theory best presents our findings, primarily from our longitudinal study of Japanese culture? First, is there a salient pattern of Japanese culture applicable to our longitudinal data? If so, what is it? Second, is there a dominant factor shaping the salient pattern of Japanese culture? If so, what is it and why? In other words, what is the core of Japanese culture and what shapes it? How should one define Japanese culture both diachronically and cross-culturally to the American reader?

2. What generalizations can we make chronologically by looking through the longitudinal data collected over the last four decades? What aspects of the Japanese culture have changed while others have remained stable as Japan moved from a war-devastated economy to an affluent economy of more recent years? What majority opinions used to be a minority view, and vice-versa? What caused change—generation, time, or aging? We will focus on specific opinions and values as well as patterns of thinking in answering these questions.

3. What are generalizations we can make about the nature of Japanese culture when viewed from a cross-cultural perspective? We will be making use of the survey data collected in China, Brazil, Egypt, England, Germany, France, the Netherlands, Jordan, and the United States, as well as the longitudinal Japanese data. What constitutes the basis of any culture? If it is language, to what extent and in what ways does our mother tongue shape our thinking and our values, and constrain and promote our understanding of other cultures? What basic differences exist between the Japanese and other cultures, especially American culture? In this sense, what makes a Japanese person a Japanese?

4. Finally, we will focus on the question of basic concern: What will become of Japanese culture in the twenty-first century? Will it remain viable, as it has so far in the past, or will the sun set in Japan? We know from written records that empires have risen and fallen in all parts of the world. Islamic arts and science once flourished from Spain in the West to Asia in the East, as did Chinese culture. Japanese culture, too, had experienced high and low periods in its history, but not to the extent experienced by most other cultures. Unlike the Arabs, Chinese, Greeks, Indians, Jews, Romans, and others, who have all had glorious cultures that once flourished, the Japanese never did have such a time in their history. Will Japan be afflicted with the so-called British disease in the years ahead? How can Japan maintain its sun at high noon for generations to come? Will Japan collapse as did so many civilizations in the past?

Viability implies a capacity to adapt under particular circumstances that often contain unfamiliar elements.[3] The history of Japanese culture, unlike others, has been characterized not by its vicissitudes but by its adoption of outside cultures, initially Chinese, Indian, and Korean cultures, followed by Europeans and eventually Americans. Japanese culture has adopted a large number of items from foreign cultures that did not contradict with its basic character, ambiguity, the *tennô* system,[4] and other traditional values. The Japanese have adopted contemporary science in its entirety because it assumes the indeterminate nature of the world. Although the future is not an extension of the past and the present, it will be affected by the past and the present. Hence, we propose first to examine how the Japanese coped with foreign cultures in their history to see if there are patterns we can observe. We suggested at least one already. Are there any more?

Second, we examine how the Romans, Muslims, Indians, and Chinese dealt with problems that come with success. Third, we ask if Japan is different from other cultures with respect to its capacity to adapt to new circumstances. What makes the Japanese culture adaptable to challenges it has met thus far, from the advent of the armed Black ships to the 1973 energy crisis? How did the Japanese keep the sense of alienation to a minimum while Japan successfully and rapidly industrialized itself to be on par with the West in the past century? How did Japan virtually eliminate poverty without socialism? How did Japan develop such a high degree of income egalitarianism while vigorously promoting social inequality—a "vertical society"? Is there any lesson to be learned if Japan is to meet the unforeseen challenges ahead? How does Japanese culture keep its dynamic equilibrium? How will it deal with foreign cultures in the future? Just how crucial are the roles of Japanese parents, especially the mother, mass media, and schools, in the process of the socialization of children?

Fourth, we consider if the world today is different from the world of yesteryear regarding the viability of cultures to continue growing. For example, the world has never been so deeply integrated economically in human history. Will this have any bearing on the viability of cultures? Fifth, before we discuss substantive issues, we plan to review the literature of cultural dynamics to look for an appropriate theory. What are relevant factors in discussing the viability of culture? This and other related questions should be answered by examining the literature.

In conclusion, what kind of challenge will Japanese culture face as it enters the twenty-first century, and will it successfully overcome the difficulties, as it always has so far in its history? Or will it follow in the footsteps of some others and fail to sustain its growth? What are the implications of all these considerations for Americans whose economy has become an integral part of Japan, and vice-versa? These are the questions we address at the end of this book as a way of developing a dynamic theory of Japanese culture in cross-cultural perspective.

How does our study relate to others in the field? From the earlier classic of Ruth Benedict's *Chrysanthemum and the Sword* (1944) to more recent revisionist works on Japanese culture, a plethora of works from various schools of thought exist.

OUR STUDY OF JAPANESE CULTURE

Ours is different from most of the existing works in the following perspectives:

1. It is based on systematic longitudinal data collected over forty years, something unmatched by other studies. It is also supplemented by comparative data gathered in the United States, Europe, Southeast Asia, West Asia, and South America. In other words, the study has both historical depth as well as cross-cultural width. Unlike studies such as Benedict's, our main data set is based on random sample surveys of Japanese adults, which enables us to make generalizations about the Japanese as a whole. Furthermore, many questions were repeatedly asked every five years to examine how the Japanese views have either changed or remained the same.

2. A language dimension of our study sets our study apart from many other attitudinal sample survey reports. The study will incorporate our findings based on a study, conducted in the past ten years, of the role of language in attitudes in Japan, the United States, and West Asia (the study was sponsored by the Toyota Foundation and others). It will look into explicit meanings of words as well as implicit meanings of words cross culturally to demonstrate the complexity of our language and the difficulties any interpreter face as he or she attempts to translate from one language to another. A portion of the data for this purpose is derived from cross-language "focused group interviews" of students.

3. Unlike revisionists, who tend to exaggerate differences between American and Japanese cultures, the present study will try to present a full picture of Japanese culture in motion as much as the English language allows. However, we are keenly aware of the limitations of English-language speakers, who are socialized in Aristotelian logic, to understand the Japanese in Japanese perspective without learning to speak the Japanese language. Not many can totally liberate themselves from their mother-culture constraints in trying to understand other cultures, particularly without bilingual ability.

4. Statistical formulas, tables, charts, and graphs in the main text will be kept to a minimum, but they will be available in the Appendixes so specialists can examine the nature of our findings in full.

5. Our model of Japanese culture, Rashomonesque *Yamazakura* (wild cherry), is built on theories of the Japanese culture developed by *Manyô* (an anthology of 4,516 poems made between the beginning of fifth century and 759 and compiled shortly after 759) poets Saigyô, Norinaga Motoori, Percival Lowell (1888), Ruth Benedict (1944), and more contemporary authors on Japanese culture. What is different from their theories of Japanese culture is twofold: (1) We systematically test the validity of our model by using longitudinal and cross-cultural survey data, and (2) we posit that the cause of what makes the Japanese culture the way it is largely rests with the Japanese language.

These features of our study should contribute to a better understanding of Japanese culture for Americans and enrich the growing field of the study of Japanese culture.

COMPARATIVE THEORETICAL FRAMEWORK

To present systematically our findings of comparative longitudinal data, we propose to compare data by using the theoretical framework discusses in this section.

Unit of Comparison

What do we compare? There are two levels of comparison. First is an attitude or opinion held by a majority of the respondents. Second, we will look at differences in factors that contribute to an attitude and attitudinal patterns, or ways of organizing experiences. For example, we found that the tradition versus modernity dimension plays a significant part among the Japanese in viewing the world, particularly from 1953 to 1973. What appears to have happened since then is that this pattern has gradually started to be diluted, and the trend has become more pronounced from 1983 to the present. Furthermore we found that this was largely a function of the younger age group respondents (age twenty to twenty-four) changing their configuration of attitudes over the past forty years. In other words, the Japanese no longer view the world in terms of what is traditional and modern (the tradition set in the Meiji era to modernize Japan).

Our focus is on the structure or patterns of Japanese attitudes, rather than responses to one particular question as such, since our interest lies in uncovering the core of the Japanese culture or basic ways by which the Japanese go about observing and organizing their life experiences.

Type of Comparison

What do we look for in comparison? Two types of results are sought: similarities and differences. To what extent and in what ways is Japanese culture similar to and different from American culture? Likewise, how are the Japanese in the 1990s similar to and different from the Japanese in 1950s? These are the questions we attempt to answer.

Direction of Comparison

What data do we compare? We compare two types of data over the years (i.e., a set of longitudinal survey data gathered from 1953 through 1993 every five years or the past forty years and a variety of cross-national survey data conducted occasionally in the United States, Europe, Brazil, Egypt, and Jordan from 1971 through present).[5] The former is based on nationwide random samplings of Japanese adults, while latter data is a mixture of nationwide random sample surveys of adults and classroom surveys conducted outside Japan. Although our focus is on the longitudinal study of Japanese culture, it is also our objective to present the dynamics of Japanese culture in cross-cultural perspective. It is with these three elements in mind that we plan to present our findings.

Framework of Comparison

We will report our findings in numerical order, as specified in Table 1.1. First, in Chapter 3 we focus on enduring patterns of salient Japanese values and their relationships to each other. Second, in Chapter 4 we present changing dimensions of Japanese values and their patterns. Third, in Chapter 5 we add cross-cultural data to look for values and patterns Japanese respondents share with American and European respondents. Fourth, in Chapter 6 we concentrate on unique aspects of Japanese values and their patterns not shared by other cultures. In so doing, we will test the validity and usefulness of our theory of Japanese culture. We will start the reporting of our findings in the numerical order specified in Table 1.1: enduring patterns of the Japanese attitudes, changing dimensions, attitudinal patterns shared by other cultures, and attitudinal patterns that separate the Japanese from other cultures.[6]

Table 1.1

Framework of Comparison

		Data	Type
		Longitudinal	Cross Cultural
Comparison	Similar	1. Enduring	3. Shared
Type	Different	2. Changing	4. Unique

Having described the comparative framework of our research design, we are now ready to report on data sources that will be used to analyze the dynamics of Japanese culture in comparative perspective.

DATA SOURCES: HISTORY AND SCOPE

The history of the Japanese culture surveys dates back to World War II, when a young mathematician, Chikio Hayashi, was mobilized to join the Japanese Air Force's operations research team, which was designed to predict when, where, and how often U.S. B-29s might strike Japan and to simulate how the invasion of the Japanese main archipelago by the United States might be carried out. He learned quickly how consequential the quality of the data is to predicting and simulating air raids. An error in sampling or in any phase of data collection could result in the unnecessary deaths of many civilians. The war was chiefly responsible for making Hayashi interested in survey data analysis and its philosophy. Following the end of World War II, Hayashi was asked to study the ability of the Japanese to read and write the Japanese language. This led to his interest in sampling theories, survey methodology, and statistical data analysis.

Following the end of World War II, sampling methods were introduced to Japan. A group of young scholars organized by the National Institute of Japanese Language conducted a survey of the Japanese ability to read and write the Japanese language in 1948 (Yomikakinôryoku chôsa i-inkai, 1951). Hayashi, prompted by the successful completion of the study, thought it might be a good idea to study how the Japanese think and feel by using a sample survey. This led him to design the first nationwide survey of the Japanese way of thinking and feeling (*Nihonkokuminsei chôsa*) in the early 1950s. He formed a committee to gather what different authors have said about the nature of the Japanese culture. The questionnaire was designed and pretested after reviewing the available literature. The first nationwide random sample survey was conducted in 1953, shortly after Japan regained its independence, and was repeated every five years since. The respondents consist of approximately 2,000 to 4,000 Japanese adults over twenty years of age in 200 to 300 geographic areas selected through stratified three-stage random sampling and interviewed face-to-face with a lengthy questionnaire.

Seven categories of items are included in the questionnaire: (1) demographic attributes, (2) religion, (3) family, (4) social life, (5) interpersonal relations, (6) politics, and (7) miscellaneous. Items in the seven categories are selected for several reasons: (1) items assumed to reveal the basic nature of Japanese culture, (2) items adopted from similar surveys conducted in foreign countries, and (3) items on values and topics assumed to share in common with foreign cultures. The Appendix contains several sets of the questionnaires used in the surveys.

Longitudinal Surveys

Several modifications were made as the longitudinal surveys were carried out. For example, Okinawa was included in the survey upon its reversion to Japan from the United States. The Research Committee on the Study of Japanese Culture at the Institute of Statistical Mathematics, Ministry of Education in Tokyo has conducted nine surveys thus far, in 1953, 1958, 1963, 1968, 1973, 1978, 1983, 1988, and 1993.

Cross-national Surveys

As the longitudinal survey progressed, it became apparent that the study of Japanese culture need to be placed in comparative perspective. In 1971, Kuroda joined Hayashi and his research team in extending the study to include Japanese Americans in Hawaii (sample size = 434). How much of their Japanese cultural heritage do Japanese emigrants retain? Following the initial survey, we found a need to study all other ethnic groups in order to understand how Japanese Americans live in Hawaii. Successive surveys in 1978 (751), 1983 (807), and 1988 (499) used the entire list of registered voters in Honolulu as the population. Subsequently, our comparative nationwide surveys continued to expand to include the United States in 1978 (1,571) and 1988 (1,563), England (1,043), West Germany (1,000), and France in 1987 (1,013), Japanese Brazilians (492) in 1992, Italy (1,048) in 1992, and the Netherlands (1,083) in 1993.

Questionnaires used in the United States, England, West Germany, and France incorporated items adopted from the following sources in addition to items from the longitudinal survey questionnaire: (1) the General Social Surveys of the National Opinion Research Center, Chicago, (2) the Institute for Social Research at the University of Michigan, (3) the Centre de Recherche pour l'Étude et l'Observation des Conditions de Vie, (4) the "Eurobaromètre" of the Commission of European Communities, and (5) the Allgemeine Bevolkerung-sumfrage der Sozialwissenschaften Mannheim: Zentrum fur Umfragen, Method-en, und Analysen e.V. Pilot survey questionnaires were designed by translating them into each country's language and then back again to the original language to test their validity and reliability.[7] After making necessary adjustments following the pilot survey, surveys were conducted by survey organizations in those countries on our behalf.

In addition to these nationwide surveys based on random sampling, other studies involving college students conducted in classrooms and other smaller-scale surveys done in Japan and abroad will be used to supplement our findings. For example, a cross-language survey of American, Arab, and Japanese students that was extended to include focused interviews in Amman and Cairo is an off-shoot of this chain of the study of culture that originated with Hayashi's pioneer-ing work in 1953. Although not incorporated in this study, sample surveys were conducted to discover what one might call a study of prefectural culture (*ken-minsei*) within Japan in order to understand the diverse nature of Japanese culture within Japan. What guided Hayashi in his search for the essence of Japa-nese culture is what one might call the "chain-link progression model" (Hayashi, 1989).

Figure 1.1 illustrates how the Japanese culture study evolved over the years from the original longitudinal survey of the Japanese to include Japanese Americans in Honolulu, Americans, Arabs, Brazilians, and Europeans. What we found is that Japanese Americans are closer to the Japanese in values than any other group outside Japan that we studied, followed by non-Japanese American locals in Honolulu, U.S. mainlanders in Honolulu, and Americans at large on the U.S. mainland. Japanese Americans obviously are Americans in just about every aspect, but they possess certain values that are closer to the Japanese culture. In this sense, they constitute an American sub-culture.

All of the groups we studied, however, share certain values, as illustrated in Figure 1.2. At the same time, each group has a set of unique values and attitudes that separate them from one another. Moreover, there are also values that groups A and B share (item 3 shared in Table 1.1) but not C (item 4 different in Table 1.1), while A and C share but not B, and B and C share but not A. We propose that Japanese culture in relation to that of the United States and the Arab world

Figure 1.1

Cross-cultural Surveys in Chain-link Progression

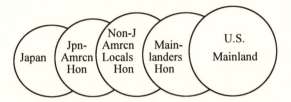

is ambiguous and diffuse because of its language. The diffuse concept of self separates the Japanese culture from the others. As we extended our studies to include the British, French, German, and other cultures, our comparison became not two- or three-dimensional but multidimensional. Hence, when we say that Americans are individually and dialectically oriented, we mean that they are so inclined in relation to the Arabs and Japanese, who are not so inclined. Figure 1.2 shows what the comparison of three cultures is like.

Figure 1.2

Three-dimensional Linkage

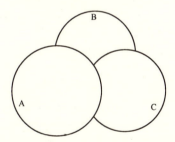

It is from these longitudinal and cross-national comparative survey data that we will draw our inferences in characterizing the dynamics of Japanese culture. We will analyze the data by using common statistical techniques, such as cross tabulation, in addition to quantification III for pattern categorization (correspondence analysis) and other multivariate analysis formulas developed specifically for nonparametric survey data by Chikio Hayashi. Although not well known in the United States, his quantification of response patterns, called quantification method III, is extensively used by mass media and social scientists at large in Japan (Hayashi, Suzuki, and Sasaki, 1992). What are these methods, and why are they useful for cross-national surveys?

GOING BEYOND FREQUENCY DISTRIBUTION: HAYASHI'S QUANTIFICATION METHOD III

Ruth Benedict's concept of culture, as her seminal book entitled *Patterns of Culture* (1934) indicates, is based on an assumption that a culture is an integrated set of values. Culture is not a series of values that are disjointed and disconnected, but instead refers to a set of values that constitute patterns. Implicit in her conceptualization is the notion that a study of comparative culture must go beyond the frequency distribution of items or simple cross tabulation of survey data. We must delve into the structure of opinions or attitudes in order to discern how each value is interrelated to construct an integrated culture. We were made keenly aware of the need to examine the attitudinal structure of the people in different cultures when we analyzed the Japanese American data in Honolulu in comparison with that for the Japanese in Japan. For example, we found that the older the Japanese, the greater the support for adopting a child in order to continue the family name. The relationship between age and the need to maintain the family name was reversed among the Japanese Americans in Hawaii; that is, the older the Japanese American, the lesser the support for adopting a child. In Japan, we found that the older the person, the more he or she believes in traditional values, such as filial piety and *on* (obligation), over the Western values of individual rights and freedom. In Hawaii, we did not find any relationship between age and these values. These items were used in Japan as indicators for the modern/traditional orientation. Obviously, we cannot use the same indicators in Hawaii because of the differences between the respondents' attitudinal structures.

Table 1.2

Frequency Distribution of Two Respondent Groups

	Item 1		Item 2		Total % of
	Yes	**No**	**Yes**	**No**	**Respondents**
Group A	50%	50%	50%	50%	100%
	(500)	(500)	(500)	(500)	(1,000)
Group B	50%	50%	50%	50%	100%
	(500)	(500)	(500)	(500)	(1,000)

How can we effectively ascertain the attitudinal structure in different cultures? Let us suppose that there are two groups of respondents, A and B, and two items in the survey questionnaire, 1 and 2, with Yes and No response categories as shown in Table 1.2.[8]

Let us assume that 50 percent of the respondents (N = 500) in both groups, Group A and Group B, answered Yes and 50 percent (N = 500) No. If we found such a frequency distribution pattern, it is possible for us to conclude that these two groups are the same and that there are no differences between these two items. Is it safe to make such an inference? Our answer is "not always." To see how the responses to the two items in both groups could be similar, we constructed Table 1.3.

Table 1.3

Possible Relationship between Responses to the Two Items in Two Groups

	Group A			Group B		
	Item 2 Yes	Item 2 No	Item 2 Total	Item 2 Yes	Item 2 No	Item 2 Total
Item 1 Yes	100% (500)	0% (0)	100% (500)	0% (0)	100% (500)	100% (500)
Item 1 No	0% (0)	100% (500)	100% (500)	100% (500)	0% (0)	100% (500)
Item 1 Total	100% (500)	100% (500)	(1,000)	100% (500)	100% (500)	(1,000)

The results of a cross tabulation of the responses between the two items for the two groups could be like what we see in Table 1.3 (i.e., although we found 50 percent of Yes and No responses to the two items in the two groups, the relationship between the responses to the two items in the two groups could be as widely different as shown in the table). In other words, 500 respondents in Group A said Yes to Item 1 and No to Item 2 and 500 respondents in the same group said No to Item 1 and Yes to Item 2, while no respondents in Group B said Yes to Item 1 and No to Item 2 and no respondents in Group B answered No to Item 1 and Yes to item 2. The relationships of responses between the two items for the two groups are, thus, diametrically opposed to each other even though the two groups look alike if one looks at only the frequency distribution for the two items in the two groups, as shown in Table 1.2. Admittedly, these two cases represent extreme examples of what could happen. However, it is clear that we must go beyond a simple comparison of percentages to each question for each group if we want to know the way people think in different parts of the world.

Hayashi's quantification III for pattern categorization meets this need to go beyond single-variable-level analysis to examine the ways different people combine their salient values to make them different from one another. When we talk about a way of thinking, we believe we are focusing our attention on our thought processes or the way we think about or combine a set of values. The question, essentially, is how to categorize different combinations of response patterns.

In Tables 1.2 and 1.3, we demonstrated how only two items could be related to one another in the two different groups. We now are going to use four items. Let us limit the number of respondents to twenty and show how

Hayashi's quantification III for pattern categorization works. Table 1.4 shows how the twenty respondents answered four questions, A through D.

Table 1. 4

Responses to Four Items by Twenty Respondents

Respondents	Item A Yes	Item A No	Item B Yes	Item B No	Item C Yes	Item C No	Item D Yes	Item D No
1	x		x		x		x	
2	x		x		x		x	
3	x		x		x			x
4	x		x		x			x
5	x		x		x			x
6	x		x			x		x
7	x		x			x		x
8	x		x			x		x
9	x			x		x		x
10	x			x		x		x
11		x	x		x		x	
12		x	x		x		x	
13		x		x	x		x	
14		x		x	x		x	
15		x		x	x		x	
16		x		x		x	x	
17		x		x		x	x	
18		x		x		x	x	
19		x		x		x		x
20		x		x		x		x

Let us construct from Table 1.4 a table showing the relationship between two items (Table 1.5).

Table 1.5 shows that of ten respondents who answered Yes to Item A, eight said Yes to Item B and two said "No." Likewise, of ten respondents who answered No to Item A, two of them answered Yes to Item B and eight of them "No." What we can infer from entries in the table is that those respondents who answered Yes to Item A and Item B are very much alike. In the same way, ten respondents who said No to Item A and Item B are alike, as are ten respondents who said Yes to Item B and Item C. Conversely, ten respondents who said Yes to Item A and eight respondents who said No to Item B are different. In other words, ten respondents who said Yes to Item B are closer to ten respondents who answered Yes to Item A than ten respondents who answered No to Item B. However, figures as presented in Table 1.5 are difficult for the reader to comprehend without spending considerable time deciphering how the respondents answered the four items. Hayashi's quantification III enables us to demonstrate the interrelationship among the four items in a two-dimensional geometric space, as shown in Figure 1.3.

Table 1.5

Relationship between Two Items

Item	Answer	Item A Yes	Item A No	Item B Yes	Item B No	Item C Yes	Item C No	Item D Yes	Item D No
Item A	Yes	10	0	8	2	5	5	2	8
Item A	No	0	10	2	8	5	5	8	2
Item B	Yes			10	0	7	3	4	6
Item B	No			0	10	3	7	6	4
Item C	Yes					10	0	7	3
Item C	No					0	10	3	7
Item D	Yes							10	0
Item D	No							0	10

The ten respondents who said Yes to Item A are diametrically opposed to the ten respondents who said No to the same item and the eight respondents and the two respondents who answered Yes and No, respectively. We knew from Table 1.5 that the ten respondents who answered Yes to Item A are close to the ten respondents who also answered Yes to Item B. The two groups are, as you can see, both located in the right side of the configuration.

Responses to items C Yes, B Yes, and A Yes appearing in the lower right quadrant are found in opposition to A No, B No, and C No in the upper left quadrant in Figure 1.3. These two sets of item responses appear to constitute two major clusters, while D Yes and D No lie between these two clusters. The way to interpret Hayashi's method of quantification III result is similar to factor analysis. First, dots or responses to items close to each other are assumed to form a cluster or pattern. It is also assumed that they are closely related. Second, we find that responses to items A and C are found close to two ends of horizontal and vertical axes in Figure 1.3. We examine what questions A and C are and find that response item A No signifies a definite and explicit position and A Yes an ambiguous attitude. Likewise, we may find C No to represent group-mindedness or diffuse self, while C Yes indicates a strong sense of individualism. The horizontal axis separates definitive and binary thinking from ambiguous attitudes, and the vertical axis likewise distinguishes collective tendency from individualistic attitude. In fact, that is close to what we found in our comparative study of Arabic, English, and Japanese languages and values. We found Arabic speakers in the left upper quadrant, Japanese speakers (including Americans) in the right upper quadrant, and English speakers (including Japanese nationals) close to the bottom, or the position where C Yes is located. Then we may conclude by naming the upper right quadrant cluster "binary-collective" (Arabic), the upper left quadrant "ambiguous-collective" (Japanese), and the lower quadrant cluster "individualistic" (American English).

Figure 1.3

Configuration of Response Patterns

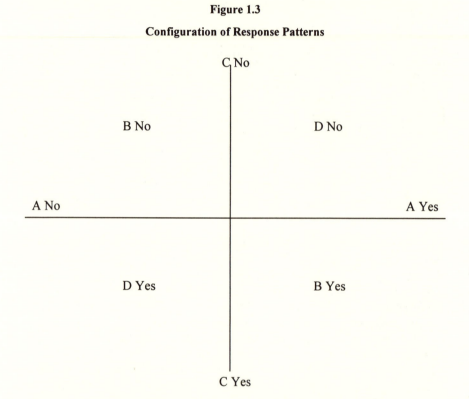

When we apply Hayashi's quantification III technique to cross-national survey data, we often find that we do not find exactly same clusters or patterns. For example, Japanese Americans may resemble Japanese nationals in that similar clusters are found, but only in different quadrants. They may match only if we rotate Japanese American clusters clockwise (let us say 90 degrees). Items that form neat clusters in one culture do not form any cluster in another. In short, we do not think alike in different parts of the world. A series of items that form a tight cluster of thoughts in one society does not form any cluster at all in some cultures. If these two peoples meet, they cannot understand each other as far as these items are concerned. Americans are always willing to give an answer of blue or red and the like to the question of "What color do you like the best?" Britons are likely to respond by raising a further question of "Color for what?" "My blouse or my pet?" Americans think of the color one likes best with a generalized notion of color, while in the British way of thinking, the question must be more situation specific.

Hayashi's method of quantification III (1952, 1956, 1964, 1974a) has been widely used by social scientists and the major newspapers in Japan in analyzing public opinion data since the 60s.[9] In the early 1980s, we discovered that Professor Benzécri (1973) of the University of Paris had independently developed exactly the same method referred to as "correspondence analysis" in English and used in Italy, Eastern Europe, and Latin American countries. The method resembles component factor analysis used in the United States.

The use of Hayashi's method of quantification III on our data will enable us to see how values relate to each other to form principal patterns in a culture. We can go beyond comparison of frequency distribution of values and determine salient ways of thinking in each culture.

SUMMARY

We have outlined the objectives of this book at the outset and introduced the data sources, the comparative theoretical framework, and at least one of the data analysis methods, Hayashi's quantification method III. The next five chapters deal with the introduction of the ambiguous language model of Japanese culture, which we believe best depicts the basic and salient nature of Japanese culture in relation to cultures in the West (Chapter 2), enduring and changing dimensions of Japanese culture (Chapters 3 and 4), aspects of the Japanese culture shared by other cultures (Chapter 5), and finally parts of the Japanese culture that are different from other cultures (Chapter 6). Chapter 7 will deal with the question of what makes a culture viable. What makes culture flourish or plummet and what makes some cultures to be more viable than others? Is Japanese culture viable, or will it fall apart as have so many other ancient cultures? This chapter should give the reader some ideas of what Japanese culture may be like in the future.

How do we propose to analyze the data? Our interest in characterizing the nature of Japanese cultural patterns goes beyond the surface level of attitudes, as described previously regarding Hayashi's quantification III for pattern categorization. We are interested in how the Japanese combine their values to make them different from or similar to others in the world.[10] The next chapter proposes our language model of Japanese culture.

NOTES

1. For the most recent and comprehensive review of the discourse on Japanese culture by 500 authors since the Meiji period, see Minami (1994).

2. For his theory of how language affects our brains in English, see Sibatani (1980).

3. We wish to thank Steve Bog, professor emeritus of anthropology at the University of Hawaii, for his suggestion to approach the question of viability of Japanese culture by

focusing on how Japan might cope with future problems as it enters the twenty-first century.

4. The word *emperor* denotes a commander-in-chief or ruler. Although the Japanese emperor's ancestors may have included the tribal commander-in-chief when he or she first established sovereignty over Japan, the tennô, or emperor, in Japan has not actually ruled Japan for much of its recorded history. The translation of the Japanese tennô as emperor is a misnomer, as Ben-Ami Shillony points out (1986).

5. For those who are interested in the details of data collection, see the Appendix for Chapter 1. It describes when, where, and how the data were gathered.

6. These chapters will draw heavily from Hayashi (1992a, 1992b, 1993) a series of publications by Tôkeisûrikenkyûjô (The Institute of Statistical Mathematics' Research Committee of Japanese National Character).

7. This method is the traditional method used in most cross-cultural sample surveys in the past. However, we found serious inadequacies in this method that need to be addressed to improve the quality of cross-cultural surveys in the future. The central question we came up with is how a questionnaire should be designed properly in countries like Japan, whose people are not accustomed to perceiving the world in binary terms of black and white, Aristotelian logic or dialecticism. There are other questions as well (for example, questions that are relevant in one country but not in others). There are sometimes simply no functionally equivalent categories of experiences matching what one can find in other cultures. For this and other related problems, see Hayashi, Suzuki, and Sasaki (1992, pp. 39–130), Kuroda, Hayashi, and Suzuki (1986), Kuroda and Suzuki (1989a), and the references therein.

8. This section draws heavily from Hayashi (1973), pp. 73–82, and (1988), pp. 169–174; Hayashi and Suzuki (1986), pp. 140–142; and Hayashi, Suzuki, and Sasaki (1992), pp. 237–240.

9. The Japanese mass media, when reporting their results of public opinion data, often go beyond a listing of frequency distribution to show how different variables are interrelated to form patterns by using Hayashi's quantification III for pattern categorization. American mass media, when reporting their results of polling, stop at the listing of percent of people who said this and that, while the Japanese mass media try to show what kinds of views are combined to make some people conservative and some progesive, for example.

10. The way we became keenly aware of the need to go beyond looking at an attitude or an opinion at a time is derived from our own experience of conducting the first sample of Japanese Americans in Honolulu. After the interviewing was completed and the data were entered, cleaned, and analyzed, Chikio Hayashi noted that there is something drastically wrong with the Hawaii data. His first look at responses to each individual item did not surprise him, but he found that the data did not make sense to him in that two sets of values associated positively in Japan sometimes did not show any relationship at all among Japanese Americans. Was the data gathered invalid and unreliable? The puzzle was resolved when Hayashi realized that Japanese and Japanese Americans do not organize or associate values in the same way. In other words, even if a majority of Japanese and Japanese Americans preferred two sets of values, the way they associate these two values could be entirely different, as explained previously.

CHAPTER 2

Rashomonesque Yamazakura: Ambiguous Language Model of Japanese Culture

敷島の大和心を　人間はば　朝日に匂う山桜花

If a person asks me what the Japanese mind is like,
it is a mountain cherry blossom barely visible under the morning sun.

LANGUAGE AND CULTURE: IN THE BEGINNING WAS THE WORD?

We propose a theory that Japanese language embodies the basic characteristics of Japanese culture. Galtung and Nishimura take the position that "a language takes structural and cultural stands . . . predisposing the members of one language community, to act, to think and to perceive the world in certain ways rather than in others. . . . Language predisposes, . . . it does not determine in any unambiguous way" (1983, p. 897). The data analysis of our cross-national language surveys affirmed the validity of cosmology Galtung and Nishimura (1983) proposed (Kuroda, Hayashi, and Suzuki, 1986; Kuroda and Suzuki, 1989a, 1989b, 1991a, 1991b, 1992).[1] How does the Japanese language condition our perception and cognition?

The Japanese language is characterized by ambiguity and diffuseness.[2] In contrast but not exactly diametrically opposed to Japanese culture, American thought patterns are dominated by two key factors: dichotomy in their world-view (propensity to respond to the world in binary terms, as in "Yes" or "No") and individualism, or the view that the individual is the primary or the most salient social unit in a society. The Japanese language espouses a view of the world in nonbinary terms.[3] Likewise the Japanese language predisposes its speakers to pay attention to human relations or the entire social context rather than just to self or the individual. One's own action is a result of what many other people did. American English, on the other hand, encourages its speakers to take responsibility for their actions in the tradition of Archie Bunker. Language is the primary factor that influences the basic nature of a culture, shaping the lens it uses to view the world.

It is written: "In the Beginning was the Word."
Here am I balked: who, now, can help afford?

The Word?. . .
Then thus: "In the Beginning was the Thought." . . .
Is it the Thought which works, creates, indeed?
"In the Beginning was the Power," I write . . .
The Spirit aids me: now I see the light!
"In the Beginning was the Act," I write.
      Johann Wolfgang von Goethe (*Faust*, Scene III, Page 43)

Goethe and Motoori may be correct historically in concluding that in the beginning was the act.[4] However, it is language that distinguishes one culture from another.[5] All of us learn to use a well-established mother tongue. We posit that language affects how we perceive, think, and act today to the world around us. Hence, as Goethe states, "in the Beginning was the Word." If such is the case, it follows that studying a culture requires understanding of its language.

Kluckhohn (1957, p. 124) views each language as "a special way of looking at the world and interpreting experience. Concealed in the structure of each language is a whole set of unconscious assumptions about the world and life in it." Each language, indeed, contains a large set of unconscious assumptions about the world in which we live. For example, the Japanese language assumes that individuals are ranked by social status in a hierarchical social system and that the individual is unimportant within the context of the group (Nakamura, 1964). Furthermore, what one sees in the world is not independent of one's language, which has made one subconsciously look for certain things over others. Conversely, we are all familiar with the fact that we do not hear certain sounds unless we are trained to receive them, or at least we fail to distinguish them from other sounds, such as in the case of *r* and *l* for the Japanese or *b* and for Arabs and Koreans.

So it is with concepts. American students can learn all they can about the proper use of the Japanese *ga, wa, no, ni, and o*. However, no matter how much they learn, they will make errors from time to time, just as Japanese students do in learning to master the proper use of an article before a noun. In both cases, our mother tongue constrains us from seeing the full picture and prevents us from hearing or understanding alien sounds and concepts. Conversely, the implication here is that language is what binds us together as a nation and society, as Miller and McNeill (1969, p. 666) say.[6]

Kluckhohn (1957, p. 125) continues to insist that "Each language is an instrument which guides people in observing, in reacting, in expressing themselves in a special way. The pie of experience can be sliced in many different ways, and language is the principal directive force in the background." Dunn and Dobzhansky (1946, p. 36) also place a premium on language: "By cultural inheritance is meant first of all our language, which is the framework in which we are forced to fit our communication with other humans and even our own intimate thoughts." Kluckhohn considers language as "the principal directive force" in the way we organize our life experience, as Dunn, Dobzhansky, Miller, and McNeill do.

Our surveys of Japanese Americans have uncovered that the core of Japanese American distinctiveness, apart from being an American, is the language (The Research Committee on the Study of Honolulu Residents, 1986, pp. 56–73). The use of the Japanese language, as in writing letters in Japanese or doing mental arithmetic in Japanese, is what makes them identify themselves as being Japanese Americans. Their ability to write or speak the language was the core of their being Japanese Americans—followed closely by their ability to understand the language and their preference for Japanese media entertainment, visiting Japan and attending Japanese-language schools.

If language plays such an important role in culture, in what ways and to what extent does it affect culture, including these elements that Kluckhohn (1957, p. 124) refers to as "unconscious assumptions"? Before answering this question, let us turn to the concept of culture.

After reviewing anthropological definitions of culture, we concluded that Kluckhohn and Kelly (1945, pp. 97–98) probably are the first explicitly to define a culture as including "implicit designs for living" in a way that is most useful to our purpose. They define culture to mean

> all those historically created designs for living, explicit, implicit, rational, irrational, and nonrational, which exist at any given time as potential guides for the behavior of men. . . . A culture is a historically derived system of explicit and implicit designs for living, which tends to be shared by all or specially designated members of a group.

Culture is, then, a historically created design for living shared by members of a group that may or may not be shared by members of other groups. The role language plays in culture cannot be underestimated, for it offers a way of organizing one's life experience in a particular way that is shared by its speakers but not necessarily by people in other cultures.

Linnenberg (1953) calls for a need to demonstrate that some dimensions of language have a direct impact or relationship with a given psychological mechanism, or at least that speakers of different languages differ along certain psychological parameters. That is exactly what we did in our study of Arabic, English, and Japanese languages.[7] Our model of Japanese culture is derived from the findings of a series of student surveys conducted in Japan, the United States, and the Arab world in the 1980s.[8] Our use of Hayashi's correspondence analysis revealed that American English speakers are oriented toward individualism and dichotomism, Arabic language speakers toward collectivism and di-chotomism, and Japanese language speakers toward human relations and ambiguity irrespective of their nationality.[9] We have inferred that language defines the most salient social unit in a society and its basic way of responding to the world, the worldview (*weltanschauung*) or, as Kluckhohn (1957) puts it, the way of slicing the "pie of experience." The next section presents how we define the basic nature of Japanese culture when compared to American and Arab cultures.

RASHOMONESQUE YAMAZAKURA: SALIENT SOCIAL UNIT AND WORLDVIEW

Norinaga Motoori (1730–1801) is cited historically more often than any other scholar by writers trying to define the meaning of being Japanese. He attempted to capture the essence of the Japanese mind by interpreting and introducing the oldest recorded document, called the *Kojiki (Record of Ancient Matters),* for contemporary readers in the nineteenth century (Koike, 1989, p. 126; Koyasu, 1992, pp. 1–4; Motoyama, 1978, p. 137). Although his ideological position includes a firm belief in the emperor's divine right to sovereignty, a doctrine contradicting the *Shôwa* Constitution based on popular sovereignty, he was much more than a mere true believer (Motoyama, 1978, pp. 3–5). His scholarly objective was to capture the core of Japanese culture rooted deep in Japanese history.[10] He went back to the oldest written records of the Japanese people and rendered his interpretation of what Japanese culture is all about.

Motoori was convinced that words (*kotoba*) was an expression of an act (*waza*), beyond which lies *kokoro* (mind or heart) (Koike, 1989, p. 126). His ultimate objective in his study of ancient writings was to capture the core of the Japanese culture, or *Nihon no kokoro*, which we share as the purpose of our study (Motoyama. 1978, p. 137). Furthermore, he firmly believed in what he was searching—how to grasp the pathos of being, the sorrowful nature of things in the world, or *monono aware* as he put it.[11] In this regard, his approach is similar to the way we approach the study of Japanese culture. The major difference is that he only used ancient texts as his data. In contrast, ours is a series of systematically collected and more recent comparative survey data. Motoori successfully revived the Japanese classics, written in Chinese characters, for his contemporaries. His final objective lay in the search for the Japanese identity according to which he wanted to live his life—instead of by the Confucian ethical constraints. We chose to remain Rashomonesque.

The concept of monono aware is derived from the Japanese poem called *waka*. Ôno (1993, pp. 38–42) says that there are roughly two types of waka: (1) those that depict the feeling one receives by viewing the changing nature of the four seasons, and (2) those that express the moaning of changing feelings of man and woman.[12] By monono aware we mean the feeling one gets as spring comes after long winter months, the joy of seeing deep green leaves as the summer approaches, and the sorrow of viewing falling leaves as winter arrives quietly but surely. Likewise, monono aware implies the feeling of a woman who sadly realizes her lover no longer visits her as often as he used to. The ancient and contemporary Japanese effort to express the ever-changing nature of a relationship with nature and the opposite sex, articulated in the form of thirty-one syllables, is waka.

Motoori was not the only person attracted to *sakura* (cherry blossoms) in general and Yamazakura in particular. After all, sakura is the Japanese national flower. Perhaps we should keep in mind the close relationship between Buddhism, on the one hand, and Yamazakura and monono aware, on the other hand. Saigyô (1118–1190), a well-known Buddhist priest-poet, composed about 2,000 *tanka* (Japanese poems) in his life, out of which some 230 dealt with sakura, including Yamazakura.[13] The second most frequently cited subject was the Japanese bush warbler with only thirty-eight citations. The following poem demonstrates how sensitive Saigyô was to monono aware, as manifested in his feelings toward Yamazakura.

Yoshinoyama kozueno hana o mishihiyori	Since I saw sakura in Yoshino mountain my mind has gone out of my body towards Yamazakura
kokoro wa minimo sowazu nariniki.	My heart has gone toward Yamazakura
Akugaruru kokoro wa satemo Yamazakura chirinan inochi minikaerubeki.	Feeling empty in my body I wonder if my mind, which has fallen with the cherry blossoms, will ever come back to me.

Saigyô's attachment to Yamazakura suggests how important it was to him as a poet and Buddhist, and it may well be that his poems are at least in part responsible for Motoori's fascination with Yamazakura. Motoori's best known poem goes like this:

Shikishima no Yamato-gokoro o hitotowaba, asahini niou Yamazakurabana. [If a person asks me what the Japanese mind is like, it is a mountain cherry blossom barely visible under the morning sun.][14]

In short, the Japanese mind is like a faintly visible mountain sakura, or cherry blossom. Motoori appears to point to the temporal nature of life and the way the Japanese view their lives, characterized by their belief that nothing remains the same. He often talked about monono aware. His attitude toward life was not to fight the nature of the world. He accepted the nature of the world as he understood it to be and chose to live as fully as possible while he was alive. Nothing is either permanent or absolute. He did not believe in life after death. He graciously prepared for his own death by directing how his funeral should be organized in detail prior to his death.

Motoori's model of Japanese culture closely resembles our ambiguity-communitarian model of Japanese culture, although there are differences. Ours is similar to the Yamazakura model in that it points to

1. The absence of absolute values.
2. The realistic understanding of the probabilistic world (it is scientific in its worldview without being logical) through the emphasis placed on the implicit (faintly observable) nature of things.

3. The paucity of an individual as a salient social unit.

Cherry blossoms, especially cherry trees on mountains, do not last more than a few days—everything changes, nothing is absolute or remains the same forever. Such a view of the world is realistic in the sense that the world is ever changing and probabilistic. It is not based on inflexible and absolute standards of any sort. Even if we long for permanent beauty of nature or people, regrettably that is not what we are all about in this world. There lies the sense of monono aware.

There are flowers like tulips, roses, or orchids, which one can clearly see and appreciate individually as blossoms, but this is not the case with cherry blossoms. One views a large number of blossoms on cherry trees, not just one blossom. In our interpretation, Motoori's use of Yamazakura as the essence of the Japanese spirit implies the group nature of Japanese culture.[15] Moreover, Motoori is not saying that the Japanese spirit is like mountain cherry blossoms themselves but only those that are faintly visible under the morning sun. Again he is emphasizing that the essence of the Japanese mind is being indirect and implicit rather than logically direct and explicit, as in American culture. The Japanese are like individual particles whose exact location cannot be determined in quantum physics according to Heisenberg's uncertainty principle. The Japanese are observable only as a group, like cherry blossoms.

The absence of absolutism in Japanese society is remarkable in its long history. Some may argue that the emperor's position is absolute, or at least that it was before the Shôwa Constitution. There may have been emperors who actually ruled the country or some portion of it prior to the advent of written records, but not since then. The emperor has enjoyed de jure power as the head of the country for centuries, but not as the actual ruler in reality. Someone else always ruled in the name of the emperor—be it the Tokugawa or Kamakura bakufu (Shogunate). The Emperor Godaigo, who reigned Japan from 1318 to 1339, was not satisfied with being just a titular head and attempted to overthrow the Kamakura bakufu. He was defeated and ended up being exiled to an island. The fall of the Kamakura bakufu later made it possible for him briefly to rule the country, only to be challenged by Takauji Ashikaga, who helped him defeat the Kamakura bakufu.

The Meiji Restoration in 1868 implies the restoration of the emperor to his rightful position. The 1889 Meiji Constitution stipulates sovereignty to be the emperor's domain. However, in reality, Japan was governed by an oligarchy of genrô, or elder statesmen. The New Constitution written after World War II made it official that the emperor was the symbol of the state. Popular sovereignty was incorporated into the Constitution for the first time in history. The emperor has been an organ of the state, as Minobe's theory makes clear.[16] What Japan has had, historically, is a dual system of the emperor system and the ruling body. The difference since World War II is that the ruling body has been made elective.

In our understanding of wartime Japan, 85 out of 466 members of the House of Representatives elected in 1942 during World War II did not belong to the Imperial Household Assistance Association, the only political party officially allowed as a result of the banning of all political parties to maximize the war efforts. Japanese totalitarianism was far from being perfect. The power the military possessed may have been absolute in some cases, however. That may be a reason why Japan was defeated. The military failed to achieve its objective since its attempt at total control clashed with the core of Japanese culture. After living and reporting on postwar Japan for a number of years, Karel van Wolferen complains about the absence of the real leader in Japan. He calls this Japanese trait *The Enigma of Japanese Power* and characterizes the Japanese state "elusive" (1989, p. 42). Despite his intolerable neo-orientalism,[17] it is true that political power is diffuse in Japan as any democracy should be. Hence, either the power of the military, emperor, or the Liberal Democratic Party has never been absolute.

Benedict's incisive study (1944) of Japanese culture is a classic. As the title of her book *The Chrysanthemum and the Sword* indicates the Japanese can be very polite or brutal depending on the situation. The only way Westerners can live with such a logically contrasting pair of characters is to compartmentalize their minds. For the Japanese, however, there are no logical contradictions since there is no absolute standard with which to compare. The Japanese operate with situational ethics.

What these authors on Japanese culture imply consists of two separate constructs that are key to understanding Japan: how one construes (1) the self, as opposed to one's environment, and (2) reality, which makes up one's world. Psychologists, in contrast to anthropologists and sociologists, consider the individual as the most salient unit in understanding human behavior. Markus and Kitayama (1991) successfully argue the importance of the self as the key concept in understanding individual behavior, an "independent" or "interdependent" view of the self. We agree, but equally important, we posit, is another key concept in understanding culture and society—namely, how we learn to construe reality, ambiguously or explicitly and absolutely. The ambiguity model of Japanese culture is composed of two dimensions: (1) the most salient social unit in a society, and (2) the Rashomonesque worldview.

Salient Social Unit: Communitarianism and Individualism

Our model is, first, communitarian in a concept of self opposed to American individualism. The Japanese during World War II used to start their daily life in morning by singing the national anthem. It was replaced after the war by company songs. The loyalty to the emperor, as represented by such wartime slogans as *Messhihôkô* (selfless devotion to the emperor) was transformed to the selfless devotion to the company after the war, to the point of the advent of a new sudden-death syndrome from overwork called *karôshi*.[18]

Hajime Nakamura (1964, pp. 405–417), among others, in his comprehensive work on Asian ways of thinking, rightly characterizes Japanese culture as being preoccupied by social or human relationships "over the individual."[19] He further points out how elaborate honorifics are in the Japanese language structure social relationships to the extent that the individual as an independent and separate entity nearly disappears. He cites Kakinomoto-no-Hitomaro's poem (circa 700 A.D.) and Norinaga Motoori's commentary on the poem to allude to the nonexistence of individual views and the primacy of social harmony. Hitomaro's poem goes as follows (Nakamura, 1964, p. 538; 1968, p. 150):

> In our land covered with reeds and rice-ears,
> people have not argued since the time of the gods.

Moreover, Nakamura attributes the vague nature of the Japanese culture to the language as well. His characterization of the Japanese way of thinking can be summarized as follows:

1. The Japanese language places emphasis on "emotive nuances" over cognitive elements (1964, p. 531).
2. The Japanese language lacks both a "fully established method of composing abstract nouns" and a "fully established method of turning adjectives into corresponding abstract nouns" (1968, p. 145).

In summary, Nakamura essentially concludes that the Japanese language is not inductive to linear, logical, and abstract thinking, the prevailing paradigm of the Western civilization. He correctly adds that it is possible to be logical by thinking in Japanese, however difficult it may be, and does not wish to be thought of advocating any single factor of cultural determinism (1964, p. 543). We agree, but our position is that the language is the single most important factor in shaping the core of the Japanese culture. Another way of viewing what we are attempting to do in the book can be done in Japanese, but we find that writing this book by proposing an abstract model of the Japanese culture is made much easier using English over Japanese. When and if this book is translated into Japanese, the reader will know immediately that the book was originally written in English, for it will sound not as natural in the Japanese as it would had it been written first in Japanese.

Jane M. Bachnik (1994) proposes *uchi/soto* (inside/outside) as the key Japanese organizational locus for "self, social order and language" (Bachnik, 1994, p. 3). She views the organizing of self and society as situated meaning, by the indexing of uchi/soto orientations. We concur with her that uchi is an actor found in a collectivity, not an individual (Bachnik, 1994, p. 26). Soto is a relationally defined concept with uchi. Both are interchangeable depending on a speaker's deictic reference. Where we differ from her lies in our emphasis on relational self and ambiguous, iridescent worldview.

Hiroshi Minami has written a book entitled *Nihonteki jiga* (*The Japanese Self*) (1983).[20] He characterizes the Japanese self as being *jigafukajitsukan* (uncertain individual and collective self). The Japanese self is reactive (i.e., characterized by a lack of independent judgment). It is often other directed and seldom inner directed. Consequently, the Japanese are viewed as reactive and indecisive. In response to the traditional call for wa or harmony, the Japanese are expected to conform to group norms. This proclivity yields situational ethics based on flexible standards. There are no absolute criteria by which one passes judgment. Minami categorizes different types of self to present his concept of self, which is not significantly different from ours. Our approach to conceptualize the Japanese self is to hold that (1) the individual self as the most salient separate unit in a society, as understood in the West, does not exist, and (2) what exists as self is an integral part of the collective self—inseparable from the individual self. We do not wish to convey any notion here that that the Japanese are selfless. They can be selfish, as the term is understood in the West. Conformity to the group to which one belongs is the proper way to meet one's interests.

The pursuit of self-interest is a key dimension of individualism, as well as of human relationism. The difference is that American culture encourages direct pursuit of self-interest without much regard for what happens to others, while such behavior is disallowed or at least discouraged in Japanese culture. One must seek one's self-interest by also satisfying all members of the group to which one belongs. Such behavior can be perceived as self-denial and sacrifice by Westerners; and it is, in a way.[21]

In the words of old proverbs, the squeaky wheel gets the oil in America, while a nail that sticks out gets hammered down in Japan. The Japanese spend a disproportionately large sum of money for socializing, as embodied in semiannual gift exchanges between friends, relatives, and colleagues and after-work drinking of working men and women among co-workers and friends. Likewise, Japanese tourists who visit the United States spend several times as much as other tourists, buying what the Japanese call *omiyage*, or gifts, not only for their family members but for friends and others as well[22] (which contributes to the invisible trade between the two countries).[23]

The pursuit of self-interest and preservation may be a function of genes, but the way we go about satisfying the need for meeting self-interests is culturally shaped. Japanese behavior is shaped in a fundamentally different way by the language the Japanese use, as Americans are by English. The pronoun *I* is very seldom used in constructing Japanese sentences.[24] Lowell (1888) apparently liked the paucity of the use of the first-person and second-person pronouns in Japanese. He says the use of pronouns in Japanese is pleasantly salient by its absence (Saeki and Haga, 1987, p. 56). Credit as well as responsibility for accomplishments are dispersed among people around whom a person comes into contact.

The Japanese are less likely than Americans to believe that whether one is successful or not is one's own doing.[25] Responsibility is diffuse in Japan, while Americans are more likely to attribute their success to their own credit. Many Japanese television detective stories depict the culprit when he or she is found to be someone who committed the crime not for his or her own sake, but for others, so that the viewer is left wondering who is really responsible. It is precisely this characteristic of Japan that prompts Western authors such as Karel van Wolferen (1989) to accuse Japan of being a country in which no one is responsible.

Another perspective of Japan in which the self plays a less significant part is that Japan is a closed society. Katherine Gordon Slingsby Sansom, who followed her husband-to-be, George Sansom, to Tokyo in 1928 from London points out (1936), after praising Japan, that the worst part of Japan is that its society is closed. Of course, more recently, Karel van Wolferen (1989) wrote about what he refers to as the "Japan problem." If *I* is diffuse, it follows that there is no one in charge of running Japan, as van Wolferen would put it. This dimension of Japan points to the ubiquitous existence of groups to which all Japanese belong, from family, school, and workplace to professional associations. The strength of group cohesiveness formed to protect and promote its members' interest has its beneficial and as well as maleficent effects. The rate of crime is low and the sense of alienation is remarkably low in urbanized and industrialized Japan, but it is difficult for newcomers to be accepted into any group.[26] Honda and Sony are two prime examples of Japanese corporations that received high visibility and acceptance in the West before they were accepted by the Japanese corporate world.

We posit that what social psychologists, philosophers, and others label as the Japanese concept of self—be it diffuse self (Kuroda and Hayashi, 1995), the paucity of individuality, uncertain individual (Minami, 1983, p. 1), dependency (Lebra, 1976, p. 50), or collective self (Minami, 1983, p. 10)—relate closely to Doi's *amae* theory (1966, 1971), the Japanese traditional concept of *giri* (obligation) and *ninjô* (human feelings), *mochitsu motaretsu* (support and being supported, or interdependence), and the like. The Japanese often claim themselves to be "wet" in relation to other nationals, whom they assume to be "dry" in that they do not get easily involved with others emotionally. We propose further that these concepts, theories and traditional notions stem from the Japanese concept of self, which is diffuse with ambiguous boundaries and interdependency designed to reward mutually within a group.

Ninjô or amae is a form of diffuse self that blurs the boundaries of the self by emotionally getting involved with others. We realize that Doi claims that the concept of amae is absent in the English-speaking world. He cites a British mother of an Eurasian child switching from English to Japanese to tell him of the lack of her amae relations with her child (Doi, 1974, p. 123). As one interacts with others in the process of growing up, one develops emotional attachment with others that is deep in emotion and lasting in duration. That is perhaps uniquely Japanese. Cliques Japanese develop among their playmates and school-mates often last a lifetime. The Japanese depend on one another for support in many ways, from jobs to family matters, as they go through their lives. This contrasts with the West, in which such an extension of the dependency syn-drome is unacceptable. Individuals should become independent in the West. Peter Pan could live only in a fantasy world and not in the real life of adults.

There are two types of social organization that result from this Japanese propensity: (1) mutual dependency relations, such as in a married couple, and (2) vertical relations (Nakane, 1967) or a hierarchy, as in *oyabun-kobun* (boss-follower) relations (Ishino, 1953). The former refers to what the Japanese tradi-tionally call mochitsu motaretsu relations. The latter requires one party to be assume the role of a leader, which requires one to be pathenogenetic, as Dore (1967, p. 120) describes it. The dependency relations characterized by primary group relations are maintained through the exchange of gifts and frequent visits. The manifestation of these traits is found in several institutions the United States considers nontariff barriers—namely, *keiretsu* (company grouping), dangô (con-sultation = bid rigging), and *sei-kan* relations (close politician-bureaucratic rela-tions). Individuals or companies form a group to pursue mutual interests by helping each other. Hence, in dangô a bidding may be fixed to allow a company in financial trouble to get the government contract while others will refrain from bidding until their turns come.

Where else can we find giri-ninjô in Japan today? The themes of giri-ninjô are found in *kabuki* plays, *jôruri,* (storytelling accompanied by *shamisen,* a three-string Japanese musical instrument), *naniwa-bushi* (chanting and reciting) storytelling, popular *enka* (ballad) and other Japanese songs, and TV soap ope-ras. In other words, they continue to be found in so much of Japan's popular culture today. They make their viewers and listeners cry and laugh or otherwise enrich the everyday life of the average Japanese.

Giri, or a form of obligation one incurs in Japan, is probably somewhat unique in Japanese society. For example, we used a question in which respond-ents were asked to decide what they would do if their father was gravely ill. At the same time there is an important company meeting one must attend that decides whether or not one's company must file for Chapter 11 bankruptcy protection. If one decides to go to see one's father, one opted for ninjô over giri. However, if one decides to attend the meeting, one is trying to enhance one's financial position. Another possible motivation is that one is doing it because of one's giri or obligation to one's employees. The employer is responsible for the employees' welfare. There is no definitive answer if one chooses the latter. Our interpretation must remain Rashomonesque in that different interpretations, some of which may contradict one another, are accepted as realities for the time being.

In short, the Japanese self, characterized by its diffuse nature or collective orientation, represents a self who lost its space to be free of the omnipresence of the giri-ninjô social network in Japanese society in return for being taken care of by its group. The strong sense of belonging to one's company and family assures one materially a comfortable life at the individual level and stability and safety at the social level, making Japan relatively free of violent crimes. Such a life is stifling and meaningless to Americans even if they must pay a high price of alienating from the rest of society. Japan managed to keep a sense of alienation to a minimum as it industrialized and urbanized by maintaining its virtually "village" mentality and social network.[27] The price of Japanese self, to the Americans as well as some Japanese, is the loss of individuality. However, the value the Japanese gain by observing the traditional code of conducts, the giri-ninjô, is material and psychological welfare, which is provided to members of Japanese society more or less equally and fairly at the individual level, and public safety, which is provided at the collective level in Japan today.

In 1888 Percival Lowell published a book entitled *The Soul of the Far East*, in which he claims that individualism is strongest in America and gets weaker as you move toward Europe, toward India, and finally toward Japan. He says that if *I* constitutes the essence of spirit, then the soul of the Far East, Japan, is "impersonality" (Saeki and Haga, 1987, p. 55). He apparently posited this dimension of Japanese society to be the most salient in contrast to American culture, for the first chapter of his book is entitled "Individuality." His interpretation of the Japanese mind is remarkably discerning.

Obviously, Lowell (1888) is not alone in pointing out the strength of individualism in America. Nearly a century later, Hofstede (1980) finds the United States, Canada, and Western Europe to be most individualist oriented (he surveyed 117,000 IBM employees in sixty-six different countries) and Japan to be among the least individualist oriented. Bellah, Madsen, Sullivan, Swidler, and Tipton (1985) provide systematic empirical evidence for the centrality of individualism in American culture. Inkels (1983) points out the historical roots of American individualism. There is now enough empirical and historical evidence to generalize that Americans are probably the most individualistic people on earth.

Over the past two decades, psychologists have devoted considerable attention to the question of self. The self as understood in the West and, in particular, in American culture is rational and self-centric (Shweder and Markus, 1995).[28] Rational-choice theorists even go so far as to believe that every society is basically rational. Their theory assumes that everyone is rational and self-interested, a very parochial paradigm.[29]

We find four different categories of views on the self or individual versus collectivity dichotomy in the literature:

1. Triandis (1989) proposes a socioeconomic development perspective for the individual collectivity dichotomy. As a society becomes affluent, individualism will rise.

2. DeVos (1985) and Greenwald and Pratkanis (1984) view the self in terms of social growth. The former (DeVos 1985, p. 178) says that, at least for American males, "liberation of the self from external authority" is "part of social growth." Greenwald and Pratkanis (1984, p. 158) say that a "pre-self" represents a state of mind not clearly distinguishing self and others, guided by emotion rather than reasoning.[30]

3. Marsella (1985, p. 290) claims that an American who does not develop autonomy is pathological.

4. Yang (1988) and Kâgitçibasi (1994) see a covariation between modernity and individualism.

We found these characterizations of the self incompatible with our survey data as well as our observations of Japan, although there are some relationships between modernity and the preference for individualism. Japan is not the most affluent society, but certainly it is not much behind the United States and Western Europe in the material well-being of its people. Our data also suggest that the Japanese are not as individually oriented as the Chinese and possibly Koreans. The data demonstrate that there has been no significant change in the Japanese orientation toward the self as opposed to the collectivity. As we posited earlier, the difference at least between the Japanese and Americans and Westerners in general is affected significantly by the language in use, not by how economically advanced a nation becomes or whether a person is ill or not. However, we agree that adults being psychologically dependent on others for survival in the West is seen as pathological, and all four characterizations may be correct in much of the world even if they are not applicable in Japan.

Kim, Triandis, Kâgitçibasi, Choi, and Yoon (1994, pp. 6–8) attribute individualism to liberalism in the West and collectivism to Confucianism in Asia. We find it difficult to apply his generalization to Japan. It is true that what Nakane (1967 and 1970) refers to as the vertical nature of Japanese society is attributable to Confucianism. However, Japanese vertical relations place priority on human relations as the criterion for leadership, as demonstrated in Chapter 6, while the Chinese and other East Asians are more likely to place priority on the individual ability to excel at tasks to be performed and how much the leadership can benefits its followers.

We find Kâgitçibasi's approach to the understanding of the self useful. The focus in analyzing the Japanese self must involve "such concepts as personal boundaries and dependence/independence" (1994, pp. 61–65). Dependence/independence relations indeed appear to be overlapping in boundaries of the self to the extent that it is often difficult to distinguish dependent relations from that of independence. Boundaries are blurred. Hence, we consider both Araki (1973), who criticizes the Japanese for being too dependent on others, and Hamaguchi (1977, 1982), who claims that people conform to a group to be rewarded even if their reward may be delayed, simultaneously correct in part.

The Japanese indeed are too dependent on others amae or otherwise from the Western perspective, but they do so because they know that such behaviors are rewarded, as Hamaguchi's human relationism would have it.[31]

After reviewing psychological works on the self, Markus and Kitayama (1991, p. 248) conclude that understanding the self is crucial to understanding individual behavior and other related concepts. We could not agree more with their conclusion.

An anthropologist, Takie Sugiyama Lebra, reports the permanent nature of Japanese dependence relations even if one becomes "independent" by owning one's own company (Lebra, 1976, pp. 50–66). In this sense, others as well as social contexts are found within the boundaries of the self. Lebra, too, characterizes the dependent nature of the Japanese self, which, unlike the Western self, never grows out of a dependence on others.

Thus even if we regard individualism/collectivity as though the two opposing concepts were clearly distinguishable, their boundaries are unclear and overlapping among the Japanese. Many Japanese people in this sense are what the Japanese call amae.[32] Other terms used to describe this propensity are collateral, diffuse, and unindividuated from the Western perspective. However, this is not to deny that even the self in the West is not an "encapsulated" and isolated being, but it is an "intersubjective unit" (Johnson, 1985, p. 129).

Just how do these modern concepts developed by social scientists relate to the traditional Japanese concept of giri-ninjô? Doi reasons that giri and ninjô are deeply rooted in amae (Doi, 1973, pp. 33–35). We agree that they are related, but we propose that both these traditional concepts, as well as modern psychiatric and psychological concepts relating to the self, are rooted in different construals of the self, including others and environments found in different cultures.

When Western observers claim that the Japanese have no individuality or are group oriented, are they not referring to the diffuse and interdependent nature of the Japanese self? By defining the core of Japanese culture through the proposed model of Rashomonesque Yamazakura, we will demonstrate that giri-ninjô is related to the Japanese tendency to prefer the interdependent nature of the self over the individually based rational self, and that these traditional attitudinal structures and proclivities have not significantly altered over the years from 1953 through 1993 despite the radical transformation of the Japanese economy.

We posit that the most salient social unit in the United States is the individual while the Japanese are more diffuse in their choice of the most salient unit to the extent that we may call it communitarian or human relationism.[33] The point here is that the most salient Japanese social unit is diffuse. We should not interpret this characteristic as the exact opposite of individualism as such, a difficult task for those who are accustomed to perceive of everything in dichotomous terms. In short, the individual is relatively independent in American culture, while an individual in Japan is tightly and intricately embedded into a complex of social network human relations.

In summary, our model is composed of two elements consisting of a self and worldview. First, we point out that how one places oneself in relation to others and how one views the world constitutes the key to understanding the core of culture. Second, we posit that one's view of self and the worldview are a function of the language in use. However, we recognize the role one's mother tongue plays in speaking any foreign language.

Worldview: Rashomonesque and Aristotelian Literalism

Second, our model is ambiguous in expression and makes greater use of the implicit meanings of words, avoiding extremes. Kenzaburô Ôe, in his Nobel Prize speech (1995, p. 117), describes the impact of the Japanese ambiguity on him as a writer; it is so powerful that it is like a "deep scar." We are certain that as a foremost master of the Japanese language and its culture and his familiarity with Western languages and literature, he is keenly aware of the preponderance of ambiguity in the Japanese language. It was not an accident that he chose to call his Stockholm lecture "Japan, the Ambiguous, and Myself." It was a deliberate choice. However, he departs from us when he urges the Japanese to free themselves from ambiguity. The irony is that he himself is incapable of divesting his Japanese heritage of ambiguity. The average Japanese reader of his writings finds him so ambiguous that he is impossible to understand.

The American worldview is the opposite of the Japanese in both of these regards. Americans pride themselves in being decisive, explicit, and logical—true of many Westerners.

After examining the nature of several languages and cultures, we decided to postulate that American and Japanese cultures are as shown in Table 2.1.

Table 2.1

Rashomonesque Yamazakura and Logical Individualism

Worldview/Self	Separate/Independent	Diffuse/Dependent
Logical Dichotomy	United States	Arab World
Nonlinear Ambiguity		Japan

Japanese culture is characterized first by the concept of self that is diffuse and inseparable from others, while American culture is historically well known for its premium on individualism (as depicted in the writings of Alexis de Tocqueville, a self that is clearly separate and independent). Second, the Japanese do not always think in logical terms, which prompted early Americans to conclude that they are inscrutable. They do not live in a world defined by computers, structured in binary terms. They think ambiguously, often in nonlinear ways. They may come up with seven different answers in the tradition of the Rashomonesque world instead of the one required in American culture.

Perhaps one of the best indicators of the Japanese public's ambiguous mindedness and other directedness is a typical dish on restaurant menus referred to in Japanese as *omakase ryôri* (literally, "leave-it-to-us dish"). A customer does not know what the restaurant will serve for this dish, which might vary daily. One's expectation is that the restaurant will fix something nice, nothing more, nothing less. However, while other countries such as the United States may have a "daily special," it is always defined so the customers know what they are ordering. You probably will not find such an omakase dish on the menu anywhere else in the world. Ochs (1993, p. 454) cites a bicultural student's comments in drawing an inference that international school pupils frequently recognize behavioral alternations associated with language in use: "In my opinion English is a 'linear' language. . . . When using English, therefore, I often find myself perceiving the world in a more logical and systematic manner than with Japanese or French. I find that Japanese is ambiguous."

Americans are often frustrated with the Japanese, who never say explicitly no to anything Americans request from the Japanese. Americans and Westerners in general are conditioned by their language dialectically to view the world in binary terms or dichotomous categories. To the extent that Western approaches to problem solving do not work in Japan, revisionists are essentially correct that the Japanese are basically different from Westerners.

We found that Arabs thinking in Arabic are least likely to choose middle response categories, such as "it depends," followed, in turn, by Arabs thinking in English, Americans and Japanese responding in English, Americans thinking in Japanese, and, finally, the Japanese answering questions in Japanese. The Japanese responding to our questions in English are almost as decisive in their choice of one or the other dichotomous answers as Americans answering questions in Japanese are reluctant to select either one of the dichotomous answer categories. On certain questions, our findings clearly demonstrate the greater importance of language than the nationality of respondents (Kuroda and Suzuki, 1989a, 1991b).[34]

Our findings are in agreement with other authors' comments on the same subject. For example, a prominent Palestinian scholar says, "If language structures thought, classical Arabic structures it in a decisive way. . . [in] its inherent tendency. . . to impose its own patterns and structures on all linguistic production" (Sharabi, 1988, p. 86). Ben-Ami Shillony, a popular professor of Japanese history at the Hebrew University, informs us that Hebrew shares the same characteristics with Arabic. In fact, what he says about Arabs, Japanese, and Jews coincides with Anna Wierzbicka's observation (1994, p. 79). She reports that Jewish culture induces its speakers bluntly to say "No!" whereas Japanese speakers are discouraged from saying "No!" in disagreement because of culture.

She places English speakers in the middle of these two extremes by saying that they would say "Well, no."

Masumi Muramatsu, who is labeled the "father of simultaneous interpretation," says the nature of the Japanese language is ambiguous and equivocal "out of habit—and often by design" (*Japan Economic Survey*, April 1989, p. 1–6). We concur further with him on the necessity to learn the language and its culture together, for they are indeed indivisible.

Perhaps in the past, this dimension of Japanese culture led Westerners to label the Japanese as inscrutable, dubious, or, at best, ambiguous. Through further use of Hayashi's quantification method III (correspondence analysis) in analyzing the data, we found that so-called the neutral responses, such as "it depends on . . . " do not at all represent a midposition between two polar response categories. What the Japanese language does is predispose its speakers not to approach the world in a dichotomous or dialectic fashion. Japanese speakers just do not think of the world in terms of, say, religious believers and nonbelievers. To them, questions as such defy any yes or no response. That is perhaps what makes it possible for the Japanese to accept more than one religion at the same time, an unthinkable option for monotheistic people of the West and West Asia, accustomed as they are to dialecticism. The Japanese approach the world in a diffuse fashion or inclusively. (The notable exceptions are their attitudes toward outsiders, former untouchables, and other ethnic minorities.) Hence, we propose that language is a basic determining factor of the Japanese culture, the language theory of Rashomonesque Yamazakura.

We posit that the Japanese culture is basically ambiguous or diffuse compared to American culture and that it is the Japanese language that contributes most to the way Japanese view the world. A culture is based on its language, which, in turn, probably is the product of genes and environment. Language certainly reflects the natural and social environments in which it is developed.

Our model of the Japanese culture enables us to explain why most of the Japanese did not accept Christianity or Marxism (as, for example, the Chinese and Koreans have) and why Prince Shôtoku emphasized the importance of harmony in his seventeen-article "constitution" in the seventh century A.D.[35] Over 20 percent of South Koreans and a large number of Chinese in Taiwan and China are Christians and Muslims, while others adhere to Marxism, another absolutism based on dialecticism or binary thinking. No more than 1 percent of Japanese are Christians. Takie Sugiyama Lebra (1976) points to the social-relativistic nature of Japanese culture. Semitic languages predispose their speakers' minds to choose from alternatives—to be a believer or not a believer or to be a Christian or a Jew—while a Japanese speaker is encouraged to add and adapt whatever fits into his or her diffuse culture. The Japanese today marry in Christian or Shintô ceremonies and have their funerals in Buddhist temples. Two-thirds of the Japanese claim to have no religious faith. A majority of the remaining one-third are elderly citizens. To them, religion is something one develops an interest in as one grows older, but is not something one is born with. Absolutism, be it in the form of Christianity or Marxism, requires one to think in terms of dialectics, which the Japanese refuse to do because they perceive the world diffusely. Harmony in a society is impossible if one takes a dialectic position.

Mushakôji (1972) aptly labels the Japanese culture as the culture of *awase* (cultures that adjust) and the Western culture *erabi* culture (cultures that select). The model also helps to explain why the Japanese never experienced a revolution like what the Americans, French, Russians, and Chinese went through. The Japanese are not prone to choose one form of government over another to the point of wanting a revolution. Their overriding concern, instead, is with improving the existing system without totally destroying it. In such a culture, one cannot expect radically new and original ideas to be developed, and Japan has not and probably will not. Most of the Japanese Nobel Prize winners either studied abroad or continue to work abroad. However, Japan excels in improving existing technologies, as evidenced in the Japanese dominance of many of the latest electronic consumer goods in the world. The United States has dozens of Nobel Prize winners in economics, but Japan has none. Japanese culture is not designed for denying or creating new ideas. Its propensity is to design a better living but not the best. The creation of new ideas requires one to think dialectically by denying everything that has been said about a given subject and coming up with an alternative.

SUMMARY

In this chapter, we attempted to construct the ambiguous language theory of Japanese culture. We have identified Japanese language as the key to under-standing the core of Japanese culture. Although we agree with an increasingly large number of psychologists, who claim the self as the key to understanding culture (Kim, 1994, and the references therein; Markus and Kitayama, 1991), our position is that it is equally important how one construes one's reality. Another aspect of our model that separates us from these psychologists is that while many of them categorize Chinese, Japanese, Koreans, and others into one group (e.g., Markus and Kitayama, 1991), we have empirical evidence, present-ed elsewhere, that suggests that the Japanese concept of the self is considerably different from that of the Chinese, despite the fact that both may be influenced by the Confucian doctrine, as many authors claim (e.g., Kim, 1994, pp. 6–8).

To summarize our model, we have placed culture in the property space concept in Table 2.1. The United States falls into the top left cell and Japan in the bottom right cell in the table. American culture gives priority to the individ-ual as the primary social unit, and its worldview is dominated by dialectical thinking. Japan logically is found diametrically opposed to the United States in that the salient social unit in Japan is human relations and its worldview is filled with diffusiveness. This is precisely what we found in our three language studies when we performed quantification method III (correspondence analysis) to see where each language group is found along the two primary dimensions (i.e., diffuse-dialectic and individual-human relations dimensions; see Kuroda and Suzuki, 1991b). Arab culture shares with the Japanese on emphasis on human relations over individuals but departs from the Japanese in its dialecticism. Semites developed the three greatest monotheistic religions of the world: These became the foundation of Western civilization and the development of the ancient Greeks' writing system. We hasten to add that what Arabs and Japanese share in common is a rejection of the individual as the salient social unit over family or other groups. However, what they consider their primary social unit may not be the same in the two cultures. Again, language proved to have a greater impact on the respondents than their nationality.

Having developed the Rashomonesque Yamazakura model of Japanese culture, we are now ready to present our findings on Japanese culture in comparative perspective (i.e., diachronically and cross culturally).

NOTES

1. They define cosmology as follows: "Languages are carriers of cosmology. . . languages condition thought in the language community; they do not determine thought. . . . And culture/structure conditions languages—weaving all of this together, not seamlessly, but into a family, a scheme of things. And that is what cosmology is all about" (Galtung and Nishimura, 1983, p. 919). Their theory appears to be based on the Sapir-Wharf proposition that language provides the means for perception, thought, and *weltanschauung* (Sapir, 1921; Whorf, 1956).

2. There are a number of authors who mention these characteristics of the Japanese language (e.g., Holden, 1983, and the references therein).

3. Kindaichi (1978) claims that Japanese is characterized by "its lack of logicality and of precision of meaning." Our position is that it may lack "logicality" from the Western paradigm, but it makes more sense to view it from cross-cultural perspective—that it has a logic different from that of the West.

4. Norinaga Motoori believed that the word is an expression beyond which lies an act. His primary objective of studying ancient writings was to search for dominant behavioral patterns of the Japanese people (Koike, 1989, p. 126).

5. Benjamin Lee Whorf hypothesized that a person's experience of the world is shaped by the language in use. His hypothesis has been supported by some and rejected by others (1956). Our findings suggest strongly that he was essentially correct. Anthropologists often point out that Aleuts have no word for snow in the generic sense, but there are a number of expressions to describe different types of snow. Our position is derived from a series of surveys conducted among Arab, American, and Japanese students. The study represents an effort to establish a meaningful relationship between attitudes and language in use (Hayashi, Suzuki, and Sasaki, 1992, pp. 39–118; Kuroda, Hayashi, and Suzuki, 1986; Kuroda and Suzuki, 1989a, 1989b, 1991a, 1991b, 1992).

6. "The fact that language contributes to nearly all the phenomena that engage the attention of social psychologists is obvious to the point of banality. Any social psycholo-

gist inclined to doubt the importance of language for his subjects could reassure himself by imagining a society in which individuals had no names. . . . Communication holds society together. Language is the form of communication that above all others best supports the intricate workings of our social institutions."

7. With the support of the Toyota Foundation, a series of surveys among university students in Japan, the United States, and the Arab world was conducted to see how students, many of whom are familiar with English, respond to certain questions in different ways depending on the language in use. We discovered that students, indeed, respond differently on certain kinds of questions depending on the language in which they are thinking more than on their nationality. In other words, language plays a greater role in structuring their response more than their nationalities. For details, see Hayashi, Suzuki, and Sasaki (1992), Kuroda, Hayashi, and Suzuki (1986), and Kuroda and Suzuki (1989a, 1989b, 1991a, 1991b, 1992).

8. Kuroda was project leader of a study entitled "Mother Culture as a Constraint in International Understanding." We wish to acknowledge our appreciation to the Toyota Foundation for its financial support for our research in the United States and the Arab world.

9. Three nationalities (American, Arab, and Japanese students) responding in their native tongues and English or Japanese are grouped into three clusters, basically by the language in use. The first axis separates Arabic speakers from Japanese speakers, with English speakers in the middle along contextualism and ambiguity, on the one side, and, on the other, decisiveness, binary thinking, and rationalism. The second axis separates Arabic and Japanese speakers of American and Japanese nationalities from English-speaking Americans, Arabs, and Japanese. The second pattern consists of the contextual-rationalistic pessimist, on the one side, and the individualistic-optimistic paternalist, on the other. We further analyzed the data by placing each language and nationality group on the first and second patterns. We found three clusters grouped on the basis of language in use. The first (Japanese) cluster consists of Japanese students thinking in Japanese and Americans thinking in Japanese. Both groups are found in the upper right-hand corner of the configuration, suggesting their propensity to be nonbinary in their thinking, ambiguous, and to see the image of self diffuse with others. The second (American) cluster is composed of English-speaking Americans and Japanese who are found slightly closer to the Japanese cluster. The second cluster is found in the bottom of the middle in the configuration, implying its strong sense of individualism and optimism and in the midposition between binary-oriented Arabs and ambiguous Japanese. The third cluster is observed in the upper left location, implying a strong binary orientation and collectivism or contextualism. It consists of Arab speakers. English-speaking Arabs are found in the midposition between the American and the Arab clusters. For more detail, see Kuroda and Suzuki (1991b).

10. Motoyama (1978) points out that this view of Norinaga Motoori existed even during the war by citing Muraoka (1942) and Kobayashi (1977). He was not just an advocate of the imperial sovereignty but a great scholar as well.

11. Monono aware certainly means more than what is translated literally, as done here. It contradicted with the prevailing Confucian moral and ethical constraints imposed on the people by feudal Japan. Motoori often placed a premium value on emotion over rationalism. He wanted the Japanese to liberate themselves from Confucian moral constraints by, for example, tolerating Buddhist priests' yearnings for love and passion as inherent in being human. He pointed out that the ancient Japanese lived more freely

and fully. His main theme of monono aware also meant knowing what is good and bad and being sensitive about what is just and unjust.

12. Saiichi Maruyama, while agreeing with these two themes prevalent in ancient poems, goes further to state the primary motivation for sexual love. To him, the Japanese elevated the ancient affirmation of love into "an exquisite and highly refined form" (1994, p. 3). We would posit that the Japanese love for changing seasonal scenes is genuine and intrinsic though related closely to human passion. In this regard, however, his hypothesis on the difference between the Chinese and Japanese is correct. Chinese consider literary works on love and passion between man and woman as being of extremely low literary quality. *The Tale of Genji* would never have attained acclaim in China.

13. Saigyô's waka appears more frequently (94 poems out of about 2,000 poems) than anyone else's in the *Shin-kokinshû*, compiled in 1205 (Yamaori, 1982, p. 103).

14. Originally the meaning of *niou* referred to brilliant red, but it was later changed to mean the sense of something that is only faintly observable. See Ôki Hayashi, 1986, p. 1753, and Fumihiko Ôtsuki, 1956, pp. 1502–1503.

15. Nakamura notes "the tendency of social relationships to supersede or take precedence over the individual. [There is] . . . heavy stress upon the relations among many individuals rather than upon the individual as an independent entity. . . . The Japanese language has already been mentioned as one of the phenomena ascribable to such a trait" (1964, p. 409).

16. Professor Tatsukichi Minobe of the Tokyo Imperial University developed the "organ theory of the emperor" in 1911. Minobe contended that the emperor is not a transcendent being but nothing more than another organ of government.

17. His view of Japan is a contemporary example of how the Western colonial mind operates. He strongly recommends at the end of his book, entitled *The Enigma of Japanese Power*, that Japan should increase the number of lawyers to promote individualism. If his recommendation is not cultural imperialism at its worst, what is?

18. Motoori was popular during WWII because of his firm belief in the Japanese emperor system. His scholarly achievement was recognized again as the Japanese started to seek their identity after recovering from a war-torn economy and moral confusion.

19. Nakamura says the Japanese "think of things in terms of human relationships rather than as separately existing facts in the objective world. . . . To lay stress upon human relationships is to place heavy regard upon the relations of many individuals rather than upon the individual as an independent entity" (Moore, 1968, p. 559).

20. See also his earlier work, entitled *Psychology of the Japanese People* (1971, pp. 3–33).

21. This aspect of the Japanese culture fits nicely with Buddhism, which emphasizes the importance of nothingness, freedom from want by learning to deny all worldly self-interests (which is one way of satisfying one's self-interests).

22. Takeshi Umehara (1987) claims that the Japanese word *miyage* is derived from an Ainu word *mi-yange* (delicious meat—to offer). The Ainu worldview is that all living things from humans, animals, to plants, go through circles by going through heaven and the earth. Bears come to the earth by bringing *mi* (delicious meat) *yange* (to offer) to humans. Contrary to earlier studies by German anthropologists, who classified the Ainu as proto-Caucasoid, recent studies by University of Tokyo physical anthropologists clearly revealed that the Ainu are Mongoloid, resembling nonagricultural Jômon people (ca. 1000 B.C. to ca. 300 B.C.).

23. The purchase of gifts by Japanese tourists in Hawaii, for example, is not included in calculating trade balance figures: hence the expression, "invisible trade." They spend several times more per day per capita than tourists from the mainland U.S. and Canada because of their habit of taking gifts home for their relatives, friends and coworkers. Since some 5,000 to 8,000 tourists arrive in Honolulu every morning from Japan, the annual amount of money they spend adds up to billions of dollars a year, contributing to the U.S. economy.

24. For example, the Japanese are more likely to say that the flower on the table is beautiful rather than to say "I like the flower on the table."

25. This generalization is derived from the results of correspondence analysis of the three language surveys of American, Arab, and Japanese students (Kuroda and Suzuki, 1991b).

26. The closed nature of Japanese society has its beneficial effects: keeping the rate of social disorganization and alienation to a minimum, resulting in the low rate of violent crime and divorce, as well as making Japan the most egalitarian society (in terms of income distribution) in the world. The *dangô* (consultation = bid rigging) as an institution, for example, is what made it possible for a number of small, independent contractors to survive as *Daiten-hô* (the large-store law] and small business firms. However, this form of social institution contradicts with the American notion of a market-centered open system. Hence the revisionists' thesis that Japan is fundamentally different from the rest of the industrial powers of the West. Whether it was because of American demands or not, Japan is restructuring away from the traditional form of businesses helping each other to survive through such systems as the dangô. The Daiten-hô is on its way out gradually and deregulation is under way. The question is what new institutional arrangements are likely to appear as these old institutions go out since the core of Japanese cultural values is likely to survive through this crisis, as it has in the past.

27. We do not wish to give the impression that the paucity of alienation found in the postwar Japan is a result of the Japanese tradition, for it was the product of complex of social and official government policies accompanied by rapid economic growth. Rapid economic growth is normally associated with a widening gap between the rich and poor, intensifying the sense of alienation. However, the opposite was a consequence of Japan's experience. Japan found that it was much easier to achieve economic democracy while the nation's economic pie was rapidly growing larger. For more details on this point, see Kuroda (1991).

28. For some of these works by psychologists, see recent works by Banaji and Prentice (1994); Kim, Triandis, Kâgitçibasi, Choi, and Yoon (1994); Markus and Kitayama (1991, 1994); Marsella (1985); and the references therein. Triandis (1989, pp. 47–49) summarizes his conceptualization of the self based on his dichotomous categories of idiocentrics and allocentrics. His definition summarizes most variables associated with individualism and collectivism (I/C).

29. Their conviction is so strong that it made it unbearable for Chalmers Johnson, a well-known Japan revisionist, to stay at the University of California at San Diego. He retired from the University system and established a private research organization, Japan Policy Research Institute. For more detail, see Johnson and Keehn (1994) and Clemons (1994).

30. It is probably in this sense that General Douglas MacArthur characterized the Japanese as being twelve-year-old boys during the Allied occupation of Japan.

31. The title of Hamaguchi's book (1982) "kanjinshugi" refers to the focus he places on the human relations dimension. The Japanese self is found in neither the individual nor the group, but in the relationship between people.

32. Caudill's emphasis on dependence on others (1962) and Doi's concept of amae (1966, 1971) point to this paucity of autonomy, often observed in daily behavior of the Japanese.

33. Masahiro Yasuoka (1993, pp. 195–206) points out a similar difference between the East and West. The most salient difference that he claims between the two is that the West is self-oriented while the East is selfless-oriented. The self is so merged in community living that self is not an important separate unit. We are in basic agreement with him, but we would posit that the Japanese are, in relation to the Chinese or Koreans, significantly less self-oriented than their neighbors. See also Feldman (1990) and the references therein.

34. For more on the methodological aspects on this point, see Kuroda, Suzuki, and Hayashi (1987).

35. Its first article states, *Wa o motte tôtoshi to nasu* (let harmony be held in high respect). It was not exactly a constitution but what is today called an "administrative guidance" in Japanese political parlance. Japan's first administrative guidance had immeasurable and lasting impacts on Japanese history, as Sakamoto (1993, p. 11) says:

> The word "harmony" (wa) came later to represent the name of the Japanese state (Yamato). Japanese people called themselves "people of harmony" (wajin), naming their poems "verses of harmony" (waka), and their apparel "clothing of harmony" (wafuku). In other words, the word wa, after it was imported from China, was used to express unique Japanese meanings not found in the original.

CHAPTER 3

Enduring Japanese Cultural Traits

ENDURING PREDOMINANT ATTITUDES

The first part of our findings centers around enduring predominant attitudes (Table 3.1), which possess two characteristics. First, they must be persisting in the sense that the same findings are found in one survey after another at least over twenty years. Second, predominant opinions must be held by two-thirds or more of the people irrespective of age, education, and gender. Predominant opinions to be presented here represent views shared widely by Japanese of all ages and educational levels, men and women alike, for several decades in the last half of the twentieth century. One might characterize these views as typically Japanese attitudes. We found only five items that meet the stringent criteria specified. As you will note, four out of the five items fit our Rashomonesque Yamazakura model.

1. Employment Exam Score or Your Relative?

The first item is a question on whether or not an applicant who scored the highest mark in an employment examination should get a job or a relative who scored the second highest average.[1] The rule stipulates that either of the top two persons can be hired. We asked the respondents to decide on the question as if they were the employer. It is a normative question. A high 67 to 78 percent of the Japanese chose the applicant with the highest score, while 17 to 24 percent chose the relative. The percentages remained intact over the years regardless of age, education, and gender.

Regardless of how one might act if this situation was real, what led our respondents to choose the applicant with the highest score is derived from giri in opposition to ninjô. Giri-ninjô is a struggle between emotional attachment and rationality. The significance lies not in which way the Japanese prefer but rather whether this giri-ninjô thinking constitutes an important component of our model of the Japanese culture, Rashomonesque Yamazakura.

Table 3.1

Enduring Predominant Opinions

Item ID # Subject	1 #5.1c–1 Employ- ment Exam	2 #9.3 Garden	3 #5.6 Manager Type	4 #5.6b Work- place	5 #3.1 Faith	6 #3.2 Religion
Survey Year	High Grade %	Japanese %	Paternali stic %	Friendly %	No Faith %	Importa nt %
1953	—	79	85	—	—	—
1958	—	78	78	—	65	72
1963	75	84	82	—	69	77
1968	78	91	84	—	70	76
1973	73	90	81	74	75	69
1978	72	—	87	78	66	74
1983	70	—	89	—	68	80
1988	70	—	87	—	69	72
1993	67	—	82	65	67	72

We must, of course, keep in mind that this question solicits a normative value held by the Japanese. Answers we received may very well represent their *tatemae*.[2] We are all aware that what we should do is not always what we actually do. Nevertheless, it is remarkable that this view on the employment exam question has been held by so many people for so long. Also, we must note that this question can be considered an integral part of giri-ninjô since it deals with the question of choosing between a socially just response and a response that comes from emotion.

Despite the rapid economic and social transformation Japan went in the 1950s through the 1990s, the Japanese people cling to their old giri-ninjô tradition. In fact, we will present findings in Chapter 5 demonstrating the entire attitudinal structure that makes up this human relations pattern. The giri-ninjô index has remained intact over the past forty years, although there have been some changes in the weight given to individual items.

The first item relates to basic values incorporated in our Rashomonesque Yamazakura model in that it deals with ethical dilemma in human relations. The next item, on the Japanese garden with tea houses, more directly represents an integral part of the Japanese basic values embodied in the model.

2. Japanese or Western Garden?

We showed a picture of the Katsura Imperial Villa in Kyoto, one of the best-known Japanese gardens, and a Western garden at the Versailles Palace in Paris, both of which are beautiful in their own way. Then we asked the respondents for the preference of Japanese people. Despite over a century of modernization and Westernization efforts by the Japanese to learn from the West, there are things the Japanese do not accept. Apparently the preference for

Japanese gardens is one such an example.[3] This question was asked only in the first five surveys from 1953 to 1973. Since then it has been discontinued in order to include some new questions, unfortunately. However, we have no reason to doubt that Japanese attitudes have changed over the past twenty years on this question. The percentage choosing the Japanese garden has remained at an extremely high 79 to 91 percent from 1953 to 1973.

The Versailles garden is beautiful, especially in spring, when many flowers are in bloom. One is awestruck by its splendor, charm, openness, and elegance. It clearly represents a thoughtfully structured piece of art, a result of talented human endeavors. The Katsura garden, with its pounds, on the other hand, gives its viewers a sense of serenity, peace of mind, and the impression of subtle elegance of nature untouched by humans. It provides its viewers with a moment of respite from day-to-day life.[4] The Japanese apparently prefer a sense of serenity in an ever-changing garden scene to that of the splendor of spring flowers. The former certainly depicts the sense of monono aware more than geometrically designed flower beds, confirming the validity of our Yamazakura model of the Japanese culture.

The remaining three items are, in our views, typically representative of Japanese basic values as outlined in the model. In fact, they are directly related to two core dimensions of the Japanese culture—namely, their relativistic worldview (ambiguous) and salient social unit (communitarian).

3. Paternalistic or Impersonal Department Chief?

The Japanese prefer a department chief who "demands extra work in spite of rules against it, but who, on the other hand, looks after you personally in matters not connected with the work." A large majority (78 to 89 percent) of the Japanese consistently from 1953 to 1993, irrespective of their age, education, and gender, chose the paternalistic department chief over one "who always sticks to the work rules and never demands any unreasonable work, but who, on the other, never does anything for you personally in matters not connected with the work." Only about 10 percent would choose the latter. The Japanese consider the workplace to be governed by the rules of primary group relations under a familylike atmosphere. In fact, they often refer to the workplace as *uchi*, meaning my family or household. Their sense of belonging to their company is so strong that the Japanese respond to the question on occupation by saying that they belong to Toyota, Sony, and the like. It is not the job itself that is salient in their mind but rather which company one works for that is most important. One of the characteristics of Japanese corporations is that most employees are generalists who are asked to perform a variety of jobs during their lifetime employment. Reportedly, this sense of belonging is being lost among younger generations in recent decades. There has been more job or company switching in recent decades. We have yet, however, to detect any change in this particular question.

The Arabs, in contrast, see a workplace governed by the rule of secondary group relations. They would rather see all workers treated equally without favoritism. Our focused interviews in Amman and Cairo have revealed that they would rather find friendship in places other than the workplace. Americans are closer to the Japanese in this regard. About half of them prefer the paternalistic chief over the rational chief.

4. Higher Wage or Familylike Firm?

The next item is very closely related to the last item. Seventy four percent, 78 percent, and 65 percent of the Japanese in 1973, 1978, and 1993, respectively, said that they would prefer to work for a "firm with a familylike atmosphere that organized outings and sports days, even if the wages were a little bit less" over another firm with a higher pay. The Japanese definitely consider the place of their employment as a place of their primary group association. Unfortunately, this question was asked only twice in the 1970s but not in the 1980s. We decided to include this item in our report since it falls within our theory of Japanese culture and is so closely related to the last question discussed. The last two items demonstrate how the Japanese define their workplace as an important part of their primary group relations.

The next two items deal with the worldview of the Japanese based on religious traditions radically different from the monotheistic West as well as Chinese and Koreans.

5. Personal Religious Faith?

We asked the respondents about their religion. Do Japanese have any "personal religious faith?" The overwhelming answer was negative. Sixty-five to seventy-five percent of them responded negatively over the years. About a quarter to a third of the Japanese claim to be religious in the sense that they have a faith (shinkô). Perhaps we should mention that if we asked respondents to specify, nearly 100 percent of them would say they are Buddhists and in many cases Scientists as well. The Japanese are, of course, not religious in the sense that they believe in God. Christians constitute about 1 percent of the total population. Most Japanese are not very concerned with religion. They celebrate the birth of children in accordance with the Shintô rituals and bury their dead with the help of Buddhist priests. Meanwhile, they may get married in civil ceremonies, Christian churches, or other facilities.

We made an exception in including this question. The number of Japanese with a religious faith increases with age. Fewer than 10 percent of the Japanese in their early twenties (age twenty to twenty-four) and about 50 percent of Japanese senior citizens over sixty years of age are religious. The older one becomes, the more religious one becomes. Our cohort analysis of the question reveals that religious faith is associated with the aging process (Sasaki and

Suzuki, 1987). The same pattern is repeated one generation after another over the years. Otherwise, the basic finding remains the same regardless of education and gender.

It is interesting to note that Chinese and Koreans are more willing to embrace absolute values, be it Marxism, Christianity, or Islam. China and North Korea are led by Marxists, while many Christians and Muslims are found in both countries. Over 20 percent of the South Koreans are Christians. In recent centuries the Japanese have shown little interest in accepting any absolute doctrine, from Communism to Christianity. Some may raise a questions about wartime Japan. We would respond by pointing out that Japanese totalitarianism was far from perfect. Over 80 Diet members elected in 1942 did not belong to the Imperial Household Assistance Association, the only political party allowed then. Also, those groups who led Japan's belief in its divine mission fell apart, suggesting that such a belief was not suited for Japan. Likewise, Japan never had any revolutions such as experienced by China, France, and the United States. Revolutions are carried out by those who believe in the total destruction of the old regime and the establishment of a radically different doctrine. The Japanese seem to be incapable of totally denying their past. They are always interested in improving (*kaizen*) their existing system—be it via fax machine, Buddhism, or television sets. This is their worldview. This is one basic aspect of the Japanese culture that sets them apart from other peoples in our view.

6. Is Religion Important?

Prior to 1983, we asked the question of whether or not religion was important of those who professed no religious faith, since we, the social scientists and statisticians involved in the survey, assumed that those who profess to a faith consider religion important. The rational or logical view would have it that if the Japanese have no religious faith, it follows that they do not consider religion important in their lives. An interesting finding is that 69 to 77 percent of those without any faith *do* consider religion important. The Japanese as a whole (72 to 80 percent of them) consider religion to be important. They do not see any incongruency between not having any religious faith now and considering religion as being important.

It makes sense if religion is perceived as an instrument to demonstrate a deep respect for one's ancestors. The Japanese also know that they will become religious as they grow older. Hence religion is important even if they do not have any religious faith now. In other words, Japanese are definitely not religious in a monotheistic sense.

The majority of the Japanese do not take religion very seriously from the Western perspective. They remain skeptical of any absolute truth in the tradition of an elderly man at the *Rashomon* (*Rashô* gate)—"Don't understand." The renowned movie director Akira Kurosawa ends *Rashomon* with the affirmation of faith in man; the Japanese remain optimistically skeptical of the world.

JAPANESE ENDURING MAJORITY OPINIONS IN CROSS-CULTURAL PERSPECTIVE

Enduring Majority Opinions

Are these enduring Japanese predominant opinions universally found unique to Japan?

Table 3.2

Japanese Majority Opinions and Cross-cultural Surveys

Item #	1 #5.1c–1[5]	2 #5.6	3 #3.1	4 #3.2
Subject	Employ. Exam	Dept. Chief Type	Religious Faith	Religion Important
Survey Site/Year	Highest Grade %	Paternal- istic %	Yes %	Important %
Jpn-American Hawaii 1971	68	58	71	90
Jpn-American Hawaii 1978	62	63	66	91
Jpn-American Hawaii 1983	64	58	66	82
Jpn-Brazilian 1991	77	68	89	91
Non-Jpn-American HI 1978	62	57	73	88
Non-Jpn-American HI 1983	73	54	77	83
USA 1978	72	50	93	85
USA 1988	66	51	85	87
UK 1987	73	57	64	59
Germany 1987	45	69	75	58
France 1987	59	64	64	63
Japan 1988	70	87	31	72

Table 3.2 presents a summary of questions asked in the United States and Europe in the 1980s. Unfortunately, we do not have longitudinal data sets from other countries. However, entries in the table give us some idea of how these Japanese views are shared or not shared with the developed nations of the West.

We can draw several inferences from data found in Table 3.2. First, the enduring and dominant Japanese attitudes are, by and large, shared by a near majority of Westerners, with the notable exception of religion. A great majority of Westerners have religious faith, while only a third of the Japanese profess a faith. Only 45 percent of Germans, as opposed to 60 percent or more Americans, Europeans, and Japanese, would choose to select the applicant with the highest score in the employment examination. Germans probably tend to demonstrate less restraint in saying what they have on mind than others.

Second, Americans consider religion more important and professed to have religious faith more often than Europeans. There are definite differences between Americans and Europeans, although the British tend to be closer to Americans than continental Europeans.

Although Americans and Europeans may share some of the Japanese majority views on human relations at work, their views toward their religions are radically different from those of the Japanese. The Japanese polytheistic religious views are totally alien to Westerners. The Japanese attitudes toward religion are also different from those of their neighboring Chinese and Koreans, who are more willing to accept monotheistic religions as well as absolutist ideologies, including Marxism. The Japanese have adopted many foreign ideas, including Buddhism and Confucianism, as long as doing so did not require the acceptance of absolutist values. The Japanese accepted and incorporated many elements of Confucianism from the Chinese, with the notable exception of the Mandate of Heaven concept since it contradicts their belief in the emperor. Ever since Prince Shôtoku during his reign (593 A.D.–622 A.D.) as the regent for his aunt issued the seventeen-article Constitution in seventh century exalting the virtue of wa or harmony with Buddhism in particular and Chinese and Korean civilization in general, the Japanese have upheld the principle of social harmony as the highest norm of the Japanese society (Reischauer, 1977, pp. 40–41).

In summary, we find that the majority responses of all six items[6] are indicative of the validity of the Rashomonesque Yamazakura model. A logical conclusion is that all of these opinions must be held by a typical Japanese. Entries as summarized in Table 3.3 suggest that nearly but not quite half of the Japanese hold all of these five opinions.

Table 3.3

Percentage of the Respondents Holding All Five Views

	1963	1968	1973	1978	1983	1988	1993
All Five Views	46%	52%	44%	—	—	—	—
Four Views[7]	—	—	47%	53%	52%	47%	41%

Although the Japanese people are said to be homogeneous in many ways, there are not too many opinions they share in common. What they share to the extent they do as found in Table 3.3, however, suggests the salient attitudes as embodied in the Rashomonesque Yamazakura model. What they share widely consists of those items that largely deal with the Japanese sensitivity to the nature, trees, flowers, pounds, and ground covers (such as cider moss and rocks), as symbolized in Japanese gardens, Yamazakura, and the like. In addition, they share the Japanese high sensitivity to human relations and the paucity of the sense of self in contrast to Americans.

What then is the Japanese sense of human relations? Many students of Japanese culture learn Japanese words that describe Japanese concepts that are difficult to translate properly into English due to a lack of equivalence in American culture. One such concept is giri-ninjô. The last part of the concept, ninjô, refers to passion or emotion we as human beings feel more or less naturally (Lebra, 1976, p. 46). It is the first part of the concept that requires an explanation. It literally means the right or correct way, which probably was the original meaning of the word. However, an additional meaning was attached during the Edo or Tokugawa period (1600–1868). It incorporated elements that are contrary to human passions or emotion (Ôno, 1993, p. 49). For example, one is forced to take one's relationship with family and the society at large into consideration in making decisions that may contradict with one's feelings (Reischauer, 1977, p. 153). This dilemma is referred to as monono aware and was discussed in Chapter 2. To know giri-ninjô is to know how to act and how to balance between what one is socially expected to do and what one feels inside. In general, one's feeling is to be disregarded in favor of social obligation, communitarianism. Hence, the first question discussed previously, on the employment examination, can be viewed as an integral part of giri-ninjô attitudes.

Another pair of terms often used in discussing Japanese culture is *tatemae* and *honne* (Lebra, 1976, p. 136). The former refers to the proper role expectation as defined by society and the second to one's real inner feelings, however irrational they may be. Often, to act in accordance with giri is to act in conformity with the norm of a community (tatemae).

If giri-ninjô represents a traditional way of life among the Japanese, as said by so many authors of Japanese culture, has their concept of giri-ninjô changed any in the past four decades? There are seven questions regarding interpersonal relations that have been asked repeatedly in our longitudinal data. How can they be analyzed best for our purpose?

We used two methods: the construction of an index of ninjô and Hayashi's quantification III for pattern categorization or correspondence analysis on a series of seven questions dealing with giri-ninjô situations. (We have placed all statistical tables and figures presenting the results of data analysis along with a list of items used in the data in the Appendixes rather than within the text. We are including in the text only those tables and figures that are understandable to general readers without training in statistics. Those readers interested in operational definitions and details of the data analysis are welcome to examine the Appendixes.)

The results of the index construction as displayed in Figure 3.1 in the Appendix for Chapter 3 illustrate two major findings: (1) The same distribution of points in the index over the years demonstrates the stable nature of the extent of giri-ninjô-orientation among the Japanese. Nearly all of the lines are identical. Fewer than 10 percent of the respondents scored four or five on the index. Those who scored three points comprised about 20 percent, one or two points comprised about 35 percent, and those with zero were less than 10 percent. (2) The Japanese are giri-ninjô-oriented, but not in all situations. The mode is found in the index value of only one or two points. We found only a few who scored zero or four or five points. The Japanese professed to act on the basis of emotional affection for loved ones, but not always. In fact, there are only a few who always do so. There are also 7 or 8 percent who never act on the rule of giri-ninjô. Obviously, for the Japanese the giri-ninjô criterion is one of the factors that enters into making decisions.

Second, we used Hayashi's correspondence analysis called quantification III for pattern categorization designed for nonparametric data like ours.[8] It enables us parsimouniously to bring out attitudinal structures that underlie a series of seven interpersonal relations questions (i.e., how each response is related to others among all items included in the analysis). The method is similar to principal component analysis, developed by Hayashi in the 1950s (1952, 1956, 1974a). Benzécri (1973) independently came up with exactly the same method a couple of decades later.

Figure 3.2 in the Appendix for Chapter 3 presents the results of Hayashi's quantification III for pattern categorization done on the survey data for the past thirty years (1963, 1968, 1973, 1978, 1983, 1987, and 1993). The configuration of patterns to the seven items as shown in Figure 3.2 clearly demonstrates the stable nature of the giri-ninjô structure over the years. The first axis (horizontal) beautifully separates ninjô-oriented answers (O) on the left from non-ninjô or modern responses (●) on the right side. The second axis separates what the Japanese tradition calls for the textbook cases of two items in the top left quadrant consisting of two circles in bold ("2x3" and "4x5") from other giri-ninjô items in the bottom left quadrant. Giri-ninjô is a complex concept in that there are times when one is forced to choose between giri and ninjô and these two items represent such cases. The two items represent two different situations, resulting in the choice of ninjô in the first instance and the selection of giri in the second instance. The remaining items do not involve the choice between the giri and ninjô but rather the choice is between rational and individualistic values on the one side and on the other the traditional giri-ninjô response items. We are awe-struck by the ability of Hayashi's quantification technique to make such a fine distinction and the stability of the tradition of giri-ninjô concept that has remained structurally in tact for the thirty-years study period during which time the Japanese have attained an unprecedented economic prosperity.

Many observers of Japan have correctly pointed out that younger Japanese are different from older generations in many ways, even to the point that some younger people are called "new Homo sapiens." Are their ideas applicable to the traditional giri-ninjô orientation?

We divided our data into five age groups: (1) twenties, (2) thirties, (3) forties, (4) fifties, and (5) sixties and over. As shown in Figure 3.3 in the Appendix for Chapter 3, the pattern configuration for the youngest age group, consisting of those who are in their twenties, is different from the rest in that the whole pattern is tilted by 90 degrees to the right direction although the basic structure remains the same as other groups. Something happens to the Japanese as they grow from their twenties to their thirties. We decided to further bifurcate respondents in their twenties and analyze them. The results are reported in Figure 3.4 in the Appendix for Chapter 3. We learn that the youngest age group, consisting of those between twenty and twenty-four years of age, is off 90 degrees from the older age groups. However, as they grow older into their late twenties, their configuration is off by only 60 degrees instead of 90 degrees. We would infer, then, that as the Japanese graduate from high school or college and obtain jobs, probably away from home settings, they begin to change their orientation toward giri-ninjô. We posit that it is most likely that their work setting acts as the most salient agency of socialization to instill the traditional giri-ninjô perspective to young employees. Hence, by the time young adults start heading a section to have younger recruits working under them, they acquire a traditional giri-ninjô orientation similar to that of their older cohorts.[9]

Our response to those who claim that younger Japanese are different from the traditional older Japanese is as follows: While young adults may act differently from mature adults, they will grow out of nontraditional behavioral patterns and become mature adults who know the rules of social relations in accordance with the tradition of giri and ninjô. Of course, the giri-ninjô concept is not the only rule of social interaction in Japan. The Japanese adults over thirty years of age have not changed their giri-ninjô orientation even an iota in the past three decades if not longer. Probably there have been changes in other areas of their attitudes, but not as far as the giri and ninjô principles are concerned. Hence, our conclusion is that what you see among young adults constitutes a temporary deviation from the traditional orientation and that as they mature they become like their older generations in their giri-ninjô orientation.

Having discussed the stability of giri-ninjô orientation among the Japanese over the past three decades, we now turn to another question: Is this orientation unique to the Japanese among other nationalities?

Giri Ninjô in Comparative Perspective

The giri-ninjô index discussed earlier is used to compare non-Japanese attitudes toward the seven items. Table 3.4 summarizes our findings of how much giri and ninjô Americans, Hawaii residents, Japanese Brazilians, and Europeans have.

Entries in Table 3.4 make it abundantly clear that the giri-ninjô orientation is a unique character of the Japanese. The Japanese Brazilians scored closer to the Japanese than any other nationality. Another point is that the Giri-ninjô index values have not changed much in the past three decades.

Table 3.4

Giri-ninjô Index Values in Comparative Perspective (%)

Index Value	Japanese 1988	Jpn-Braz 1991	NJH* 1988	Jpn-Americn 1988	American 1988
0	6	20	34	25	34
1	35	46	50	43	47
2	38	25	14	27	17
3–5	22	9	3	5	2

Index value	Dutch 1992	English 1987	French 1988	German 1987	Italian 1992
0	16	24	21	21	33
1	65	50	47	54	46
3-5	18	21	25	21	18
2	2	5	7	4	4

*NJH = Non-Japanese Americans in Hawaii.

Scale values for the Giri-ninjô index as shown in Table 3.5 demonstrate the stability of traditional Japanese values from 1963 to 1993. Ninjô, or human feelings, relate closely to other often-cited Japanese values, such as Doi's amae and our concept of diffuse self. The Japanese, who score over three points on the scale, are significantly higher (about 20%) than the Westerners, whose scale values range from 2 to 7 percent.

Table 3.5

Japanese Giri-ninjô Index Values in Historical Perspective (%)

Index Value	1963	1968	1973	1978	1983	1988	1993
0	7	6	8	6	5	6	8
1	35	38	37	34	33	35	39
2	36	35	34	36	38	38	35
3–5	23	21	21	24	24	22	18

To see how Japanese Americans in Honolulu compare with Japanese Brazilians, we constructed Figure 3.5 (see the Appendix for Chapter 3) for further comparative purposes. Figure 3.5 reveals that Japanese Brazilians are closer to the Japanese in Japan than Japanese Americans, who lag behind their Brazilian counterparts. Americans in general are even farther from the Japanese, as Figure 3.5 illustrates. The mode index value for the Japanese is about 2, while it is 1 for the rest of the groups. The Japanese Americans lie between Americans as a whole and the Japanese in Japan. Our data analysis of the first Honolulu survey conducted in 1971 and the Japan survey of 1973 indicate that younger Japanese are less giri-ninjô-oriented than older Japanese Americans in Honolulu, as shown in Table 3.6 (Kuroda, Hayashi, and Suzuki, 1978).

Table 3.6

Giri-ninjô Index by Age and Nationality

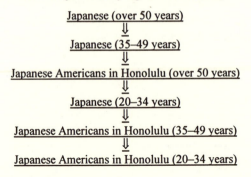

Japanese (over 50 years)
⇓
Japanese (35–49 years)
⇓
Japanese Americans in Honolulu (over 50 years)
⇓
Japanese (20–34 years)
⇓
Japanese Americans in Honolulu (35–49 years)
⇓
Japanese Americans in Honolulu (20–34 years)

Table 3.7 shows how the Japanese rate on the giri-ninjô orientation is stable and predictable in relation to others.

Table 3.7

Giri-ninjô Index by Nationality over Time

Index Value	Japanese 1963	Japanese 1968	Japanese 1973	Japanese 1978	Japanese 1983	Japanese 1988	
0	7	6	8	6	5	6	
3+	23	22	21	24	24	22	

	HI Jpn-Am 1988	HI Other 1988	Jpn Brazl 1991	US conti 1988	English 1987	German 1987	French 1988
0	25	34	17	34	24	21	21
3+	5	3	12	2	5	4	7

Three sets of Japanese data, consisting of the 1963 survey (K3), the 1973 survey (K5), and the 1988 survey (K8), in relation to American and European survey data are used. The Japanese Americans (1971: H0; 1978: H2; 1983: H4) and Honolulu residents as a whole (1988: H8) are scattered in their configuration from year to year, indicating the unstable nature of their attitudes toward the giri-ninjô orientation. The Japanese nationals, on the other hand, remain stable and were found in the left middle without exception. Interestingly, even though Japanese Americans vary in their position from time to time, they are still always found between Americans on the mainland and the Japanese in Japan.

SUMMARY

In this chapter, we tried to characterize the Japanese by focusing on two dimensions of the Japanese culture. First, we found five common views held by the Japanese irrespective of age, gender, and schooling for several decades at least in the past half of the twentieth century. Two views dealt with human relations, another two with religion, and the remaining one with the Japanese preference for the Japanese garden. Second, we attempted to look for the dynamics of attitudinal structure, with special attention paid to the giri-ninjô perspective. We found the Japanese concept of giri-ninjô structurally intact despite the fact that Japan has gone through drastic changes in the past forty years. We also, not so surprisingly, discovered that this giri-ninjô perspective is unique to the Japanese culture and is not observed among Europeans and Americans as far as our comparative data can ascertain.

In defiance of a common belief that the Japanese are homogeneous in their thinking and views, we found only five items among over 150 items that qualify as enduring views shared by a large majority regardless of gender, age, and education. All of these five beautifully fit the Rashomonesque Yamazakura model in the following perspectives: First, the Japanese are not religious in the sense that they believe in the absolutist notion of God or even "religious faith" as such, but they do believe religion is important—a very Rashomonesque Japanese position, incomprehensible from strictly logical perspectives.[10] Second, the Japanese find beauty in *shibui* gardens that provide a moment of respite from everyday life. The Japanese prefer monono aware feelings (Yamazakura) over the feelings of awe from the splendor of spring flowers in the Versailles garden. There are hardly any flowering plants in the Katsura Imperial garden with a few exceptions, such as the azalea and lily. Plants consist mostly of trees, bushes, and Japanese cider mosses that cover the ground. Third, the employment of the giri-ninjô perspective in social decision making (Item 1) is a uniquely Japanese characteristic. Fourth, the concept of individual is diffuse in the workplace (Item 2). Immediate and material return for the labor is not what one seeks the most in the workplace among the Japanese. One extra item included in the discussion although it did not meet our criteria for the commonly shared enduring attitudes, Item 4, also dealt with the question of the choice between an individual-oriented rational workplace and a familylike workplace, in which the individual becomes integrated with the entire workplace.

We failed to find any item among the five that contradicts our model of Japanese culture. On the contrary, all five of them fit charmingly with our Rashomonesque Yamazakura model.

NOTES

1. Specific questions (Table 3.1: #5.1c–1; #5.1c–2) asked in the survey questionnaire are reproduced in Appendix for Chapter 1.

2. The word *tatemae* refers to an expected pattern of normative responses. The antonym is *honne*, or one's honest and real opinion.

3. The Katsura Detached Palace is not open to the public, except on a limited basis for those who are willing to wait for more than several months. Non-Japanese visitors have

easier access than the Japanese. However, they too must apply for entrance (security clearance) in advance and receive a written permit from the Imperial Household Agency. Visitors are watched discreetly by security agents and are allowed access in small groups of about two dozen at a time. In other words, the Katsura Detached Palace garden has not been seen by many Japanese people. It is a beautiful garden designed in such a manner that one can view its beauty from anywhere within the compound.

4. The characterization of the two gardens is personal and may not be shared by others. This is Kuroda's reactions to the two gardens he personally saw in Paris and Kyoto.

5. #5.1c–1 and other numbers in the row refer to questionnaire item numbers that are reproduced in the Appendix for Chapter 1. Those who wish to know the exact questions asked may see the Appendix for Chapter 1.

6. The item excluded is item 4 on the two types of firms, one that pays good wages and one with a familylike atmosphere. It was excluded because it was asked only twice, in 1973 and 1978.

7. The item on the Japanese garden was excluded.

8. The method known in Japanese as *Suryôka IIIrui* (quantification III) is used by most major mass media and social scientists in Japan in reporting their public opinion survey data. It enables us to present response patterns to a series of questions most parsimoniously in a graphic manner. For more detail as well to see the use of the same method on some of the same data, see Hayashi, Suzuki, and Sasaki (1992, pp. 241–259).

9. The place of employment in Japan acts as a more important agency of socialization, including the skill-acquisition process, than in the United States. Japanese companies hire college graduates not for their specialized knowledge or skill. Many of them are hired for their potential talents and ability. The Japanese companies do their own training after young employees are recruited. Many employees are not expected to do the same thing during their tenure in their company since all industries go through industrial restructuring from time to time. Lifetime employment is impossible if one sticks to one's own special job. Many Japanese workers are trained to perform many different jobs. Many companies maintain much more elaborate orientation programs for their young recruits than their U.S. counterparts. In short, the Japanese employers act as very important agencies for young adult employees.

10. Of course, this is not unique to Japanese culture. Public opinions often indicate internal consistencies in many other cultures as well.

CHAPTER 4

Changing Japanese Culture

The last chapter dealt with unchanging dimensions of Japanese culture in terms of some specific items that met certain criteria and enduring structural patterns observed among Japanese adults over the past forty years. No culture remains the same in all aspects. What specific opinions and attitudinal structures changed as Japan became independent in 1952 and achieved unprecedented economical prosperity over the past several decades? In answering these two questions, we intend to explore the types and possible causes of these changes.

CHANGING OPINIONS DEFINED

We have arbitrarily decided to use 20 percent differences in responses as the cutting point in operationally defining changing opinions.[1] In other words, we consider any item that produced more than a 20 percent difference in response over time as a changing opinion. We found that about a dozen items came under our definition of changing opinions. We have grouped them into two categories: (1) the secularization and democratization process, and (2) social consequences of economic development.

Although our sampling process has remained largely constant, demographic profiles have changed significantly, especially in terms of their level of education and economic well-being. There have been slightly more female than male respondents in recent years, reflecting the improvement in life expectancy of the Japanese and economic development. The level of education has significantly improved, as is evident from the percentage of college graduates, which increased from 6 percent in 1953 to 25 percent in 1993, while elementary and middle-school graduates decreased from 68 percent to 27 percent, respectively, during the same period. We asked no questions about income, but we are all aware of the spectacular economic growth Japan went through over the past forty years from the early 1950s to early 1990s. Perhaps a more remarkable economic miracle than the growth of the gross national product (GNP) is how Japan has virtually eliminated poverty by reducing the gap between the rich and the poor to a minimum (Kuroda, 1991). Urbanization, while minimizing alienation, is another unique change Japan went through during this period. Every industrial nation goes through the process of urbanization, but it is often accompanied by an increased level of social disorganization and alienation, except for Japan (Kuroda, 1995). Respondents living in communities smaller than 50,000 declined from 68 percent in 1953 to only 31 percent in 1993. We need to keep these demographic and social changes in mind while viewing the changing opinions.

Secularization and Democratization

The Ise Shintô shrine is considered Japan's national shrine. The question asked was this:

#3.9 Some Prime Ministers, when they take office, pay a visit to the Imperial Shrine at Ise. What do you think about this practice?[2]

1) Should go	2) Better to go	3) Can please himself
4) Better not to go	5) Should not go	

Table 4.1

Ise Shrine by Year

Response	1953	1958	1963	1968	1973
Should go	7	5	4	3	4
Better to go	50	33	28	28	21
Please himself	23	27	41	33	48
Better not to go	6	12	9	14	10
Should not go	2	5	5	6	5
Sample N	2,254	1,449	2,698	3,033	3,055
Response	1978	1983	1988	1993	
Should go	3	2	2	2	
Better to go	17	19	16	17	
Please himself	51	52	59	64	
Better not to go	7	6	6	6	
Should not go	5	4	4	3	
Sample N	2,032	2,173	1,858	1,833	

In 1953 when the question was first asked, 50 percent of the respondents chose the second response and only 23 percent the third response (Table 4.1). The number of respondents choosing the second response ("Better go") plummeted to 17 percent in 1993 from 50 percent in 1953, while those giving the third response—letting each prime minister decide on his own—shot up to 64 percent by 1993 from 23 percent in 1953. This is one of the typical items that has changed in the sense that traditional views have been declining over the years as those who grew up before World War II pass away. The respect a newly elected prime minister should pay to the Ise Imperial Shrine was the traditional view held because Shintô was the considered the state religion during the war. The separation of the state from any particular religion was made explicit following the end of the war, when the new constitution came into existence.

The effects of this change had less impact on those who were sixty-five or over, according to Yoshino's 1988 data analysis (1992, pp. 92–93). In other words, the prewar generation of the Japanese continue to believe in the traditional view that new prime ministers should visit the Ise Shrine. For the remaining Japanese population, the change in views is probably a result of the dynamic nature of the times.

Another aspect of postwar reform was to democratize not just the formal government structure but to instill the concept of democracy in the minds of all Japanese. It appears to have succeeded at least to some extent, as responses to the next item indicate.

The item here asks the respondent to choose between democracy for the people and democracy by the people (see Table 4.2). Both are important for a democracy to prevail. The question, however, is which is more important. Initially in 1953, immediately following the independence of Japan as a nation-state again, there were more Japanese (43 percent) who believed in leaving everything for politicians to decide than the respondents (38 percent), who disagreed with the idea of letting politicians do so. However, support for the former position started to decline in the 1950s and continued through the 1970s, while those who believed otherwise increased sharply from 38 percent in 1953 to 68 percent in 1993. The percentage difference between the two response categories was 5 percent in favor of the first response category in 1953. The percentage difference between the two polar response categories not only reversed direction but increased to favor the second answer category to 23 percent over 51 percent in 1973.

What has happened over the years as the Japanese economy went through rapid development in the 1950s and 1960s is that the Japanese seemed to have developed confidence in themselves as participants in governing process while developing a healthy political cynicism—a sign of sophistication.

#8.1 Some people say that if we get good political leaders, the best way to improve the country is for the people to leave everything to them, rather than for the people to discuss things among themselves. Do you agree with this or disagree?
   1) Agree   2) Depends on circumstances and person
   3) Disagree   4) Can't imagine there being such an outstanding politician

Table 4.2

Government for or by the People by Year

Response	1953	1958	1963	1968	1973
Agree	43	35	29	30	23
Depend	9	10	12	10	15
Disagree	38	44	47	51	51
Can't say	3	2	4	3	5
Response	1978*	1983*	1988*	1993*	
Agree	32	33	30	24	
Depend					
Disagree	58	60	61	68	
Can't say					

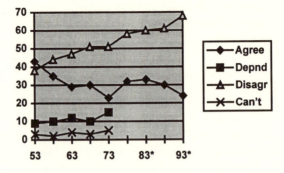

*Response categories for the item were modified in 1978. The new response categories eliminated "2) Depends on circumstances and person" and "4) Can't imagine there being such an outstanding politician." Hence the results of this item are not exactly comparable to the results of the previous surveys from 1953 through 1973. However, the results still give us a sense of the public preference for agreeing or disagreeing with the statement asked.

The general election for the House of Representatives is the most important election since the House is by far a more important legislative body than the House of Councilors. For all practical purpose, it is the House of Representatives that elects the Prime Minister of Japan. How important is it to take part in the General Election then?

#8.1b (Card shown) What do you do during a general election for the House of
Representatives?

1) Let nothing stand in the way of voting
2) Try to vote as much as possible
3) Not much interested in voting
4) Hardly ever vote

Table 4.3

The Sense of Civic Duty by Year

	1953	1958	1963	1968	1973	1978	1983	1988	1993
Let	—	62	53	51	41	45	39	34	40
Try....	—	32	41	44	50	47	48	50	50
Not....	—	3	4	4	6	5	9	10	7
Hardly	—	2	1	1	2	3	3	5	3

Entries in Table 4.3 show that those who are enthusiastic about voting in the general election are declining—from 62 percent in 1953 to a mere 34 percent in 1988. We just noted that the Japanese are becoming more democratic over the years. Is this not a contradiction?

Our response is that democracy is a complex, multifaceted phenomenon. While it is true that, everything being equal, the more democratic the country the higher the voting turnout, it is equally important that voters in a democracy have the right not to take part in politics if they so choose. The sense of civic duty normally reflects voter willingness and self-confidence in politics. Hence, if one is willing to vote, one is considered to be high on the sense of civic duty. However, it is also true that some people in some countries may show a high sense of civic duty not because they are democratic but because of special circumstances. For example, voter turnout in totalitarian states is normally high. The Japanese under the Meiji Constitution, promulgated in 1889, were considered the subjects of the emperor, who was at least constitutionally sovereign. The subjects are expected to obey the imperial order. Voting was considered a national duty as a subject. The new constitution put an end to this imperial sovereignty to declare the establishment of popular sovereignty. However, it takes time for the people to transform themselves psychologically from being a subject to being a citizen with equal rights. Another reason for high voter turnout is conformity. Our hypothesis is that voting after the war was considered a matter of being a good member of a community, where conformity was imposed on its members, and not a sign of a sense of civic duty (Kuroda and Kuroda, 1968).

Democracy cannot be measured only quantitatively. Our inference from entries in Table 4.4 is that the Japanese are becoming more sophisticated citizens of a democracy, which is an improvement in quality. The validation for our inference that democracy is not declining but growing in Japan is borne out in the results of the 1993 survey on the question of acceptance of democracy. The following question was asked first in 1963:

#8.2 What do you think about democracy, capitalism, socialism, liberalism, and conservatism? Are you favorably or unfavorably disposed to these ideas?   1) Favorable   2) Depends on   3) Unfavorable

a) Democracy   b) Capitalism   c) Liberalism   d) Socialism

Table 4.4

The Acceptance of Democracy by Year

	1963	1968	1973	1993
Favorable	38	38	43	59
Depends on	49	52	46	33
Unfavorable	10	7	9	7

Approximately half of the Japanese adults had no strong feelings toward what is enthusiastically espoused in much of the world today, the word *democracy*. Perhaps this is another testimony to our contention that ambiguity is the hallmark of the Japanese culture. The question was first asked in 1963 but discontinued after 1973 until the latest survey in 1993. The latest finding of 1993 suggests that well over half of the Japanese citizens have favorable attitudes toward democracy. This change has taken place in the past two decades while the respondents' enthusiasm for voting declined. Our hypothesis is that the Japanese are no longer voting because they feel the social pressure for conformity, but they vote because they accept democracy as their preferred form of government.

We now move from political questions to what appear to be consequences of Japan's success in the virtual elimination of poverty among its citizens[3] without socialism but with unprecedented affluence.

Social Consequences of Economic Development: Modernization to Internationalization

#4.5 In bringing up children of primary school age, some people think that one should teach them that money is the most important thing. Do you agree with this or not?

   1) Agree
   2) Disagree
   3) Cannot say one way or another in general terms

Table 4.5

The Importance of Money by Year

Response	1953	1958	1963	1968	1973	1978	1983	1988	1993
Agree	65	—	60	57	44	45	43	35	35
Disagree	24	—	23	28	38	40	42	47	45
Can't	9	—	15	15	17	13	13	16	18

The trend is clear. The Japanese started to place lower priority on the teaching that money is the most important thing in life (Table 4.5) as Japan became affluent and more equal in the distribution of income from the 1950s to the 1990s.[4]

> #9.6 Generally speaking, would you say that the Japanese people are superior to or inferior to Western peoples?
>
> 1) Japanese superior
> 2) Japanese inferior
> 3) The same
> 4) Cannot say one way or another in general terms

Table 4.6

Ethnic Superiority Complex by Year

	1953	1958	1963	1968	1973	1978	1983	1988	1993
Superior	20	—	33	47	39	—	53	—	41
Inferior	28	—	14	11	9	—	8	—	6
Same	14	—	16	12	18	—	12	—	27
Can't say	21	—	27	21	26	—	21	—	20

It is clear from entries in Table 4.6 that the number of Japanese who believe in their superiority over Westerners rose dramatically, from 20 percent in 1953 to 53 percent in 1983, while the number who think they are inferior to Westerners has declined sharply, from 28 percent in 1953 to 6 percent by 1993. Those who believe in Japanese superiority declined to 41 percent in 1993 from 53 percent in 1983.

There are several comments we wish to make. First, the question does not specify whether respondents are being asked to judge the innate ability or status of the Japanese versus the Westerners. The respondents probably took both qualities into consideration in answering the question. Second, this type of question cannot be asked in the United States, where the norm for the belief in racial equality in social terms (not in the economic sense) is so strong.[5] Japan is a vertical society, to borrow Nakane's characterization, in that social inequality is promoted energetically (Nakane, 1967, 1970). The Japanese think nothing of ranking individuals, companies, universities, and other institutions in terms of various social terms. If this is difficult for Americans to comprehend, so it is for the Japanese to understand why so many are homeless and poor (particularly among minorities) in America today, where there is supposed to be equal opportunity and everybody is putatively equal. Third, one of the encouraging findings is that we found that the better educated tend to believe that the abilities of Japanese and Westerners are "the same."

One could, of course, point this out as the evidence that Japanese are racists even if they claim to be otherwise. The reality as it exists everywhere unfortunately points to the fact that the difference in racism among peoples lies in its extent and form. Another difference is that the Japanese are reluctant to admit the existence of racism, while Americans are more willing to admit and work openly to improve the situation.

In 1987, we asked the same question in Shanghai, China and Japan to see which nationality the Chinese and the Japanese thought had the best brain. The following was the result: In China, a high 78 percent of the Chinese thought they were the best, followed by the Japanese (16 percent) and the Americans (5 percent). In Japan, 48 percent chose the Japanese, followed by the Chinese (14 percent) and the Americans (8 percent), while a high 30 percent claimed that they could not discern the truth. What is interesting here is that a high one-third of the Japanese refused to name themselves the most intelligent, while the Chinese were more decisive. There were hardly any Chinese who did not know what to say. The Chinese are still more confident about themselves than the Japanese, despite Japan's economic success.

As one of the coauthors pointed out, this finding contradicts Japan's efforts to internationalize the country (Kuroda, 1987). If Japan is to become a member of the international community in good standing, it is incumbent on the Japanese people to work more resolutely toward eliminating racism, ageism, and sexism.

Another interpretation of increasing feelings of superiority among the Japanese is that such feelings simply reflect the extent of economic affluence Japan achieved in recent decades. The Japanese have regained their self-confidence. Of course, the problem is that the extent of their self-confidence is so high that it must be considered overconfidence. The need to be humble is in the Japanese tradition, as one finds in an old *haiku* (a seventeen-syllable poem containing a seasonal word):

みのるほど 頭の下がる 稲穂かな

[The heavier rice ears get, the lower they bow,
or the boughs that bear most hang lowest]

#4.2/#4.10 If you have no children, do you think it necessary to adopt a child in order to continue the family line, even if there is no blood relationship? Or do you not think this is important?

1) Would adopt   2) Would not adopt   3) Depends on circumstances

Table 4.7

Family Line Preservation by Year

Response	1953	1958	1963	1968	1973	1978	1983	1988	1993
Adopt	74	63	51	43	36	33	27	28	22
Not adopt	16	21	32	41	41	48	51	52	56
Depends	7	8	12	9	17	12	15	15	16

At least one aspect of the Japanese concept of family has changed drastically, as shown in Table 4.7. Those who believe in adopting a child to continue their family line has declined from 74 percent in 1953 to 22 percent in 1993. About three out of four respondents wanted to adopt a child to continue the family line in 1953. By 1993, only one out of four or five shared that desire. This is an interesting contrast to what we found in the United States in 1978, when 56 percent of Americans wanted to adopt and 32 percent did not. It is almost the opposite of the way the Japanese answered—33 percent and 48 percent, respectively (Hayashi, 1981, p. 75). In general, we assume that family is more important to the Japanese than to the Americans, but that is not true, at least as far as this aspect of the family life in the two countries is concerned.

We also must note that the percentage of Japanese Americans in Honolulu who believe in adopting a child to continue their family line is also declining, from 52 percent in 1971, 49 percent in 1978, and 49 percent in 1983 to 33 percent in 1988. Comparable figures for the non-Japanese American population among the rest of Honoluluans is as follows: 50 percent in 1978, 58 percent in 1983, and 45 percent in 1988. However, an interesting contrast between the Japanese in Japan and the Japanese Americans is that age has an opposite effect on them. The older the Japanese, the more they believe in the preservation of the family name; whereas the older the Japanese Americans, the less they believe in the preservation of the family line in Hawaii.

Why is the decline in the belief for keeping the family line so drastic in Japan? Our hypothesis is that there are several factors that contribute to the change in this aspect of family life in Japan. First, the abolishment of the primogeniture system after World War II has made the distribution of family inheritance equal among all children. This has resulted in the weakening of the family as a unit. Second, the stiff progressive income tax imposed on inheritance has resulted in children inheriting about a half of what the parents leave. The children, in turn, must divide that half among themselves.

We now move from the family line to a more general preferred way of life (Table 4.8).

This question has been used since 1930 by the draft board for Japanese young men who are drafted (Hayashi, 1981, p. 76). We have added a comparable young male respondents group in Table 4.8b for the purpose of comparison with prewar and wartime draftees' responses.

> #2.4 There are all sorts of attitudes toward life. Of those listed here (card shown), which one would you say come closest to your feeling?
> 1) Work hard and get rich
> 2) Study earnestly and make a name for yourself
> 3) Don't think about money or fame; just live a life that suits your own tastes
> 4) Live each day as it comes, cheerfully and without worrying
> 5) Resist all evils in the world and live a pure and just life
> 6) Never think of yourself; give everything in service of society

Table 4.8a

Preferred Way of Life by Year

Response	1953	1958	1963	1968	1973	1978
Get rich	15	17	17	17	14	14
Name	6	3	4	3	3	2
Own tastes	21	26	30	32	39	39
Live each day	11	19	19	20	23	22
Pure and just life	29	22	18	17	11	11
Social service	10	6	6	6	5	7
Response	1983	1988	1993			
Get rich	18	15	17			
Name	2	3	3			
Own tastes	38	41	40			
Live each day	23	23	26			
Pure and just life	9	9	6			
Social service	5	4	4			

Table 4.8b

Preferred Way of Life for Male Draftees by Year

	20-year-old Male, 1930	20-year-old Male, 1940	20-24-year Male, 1978
Work hard & get rich	19	9	14
Make a name	9	5	2
Your own taste	12	5	52
No worrying	2	1	19
Pure and just life	33	41	6
Social service	24	30	4

Responses to this question reflect the mood of society. Following the infamous Siberian intervention (1918–1923) by the Japanese military, the military suffered significantly by being called tax eaters and other names, to the point that soldiers had to take their uniforms off as they left their bases. Then came the Depression and the gradual rise in military and nationalist forces. The Manchurian affair in 1931 signaled the coming rise of the military in prewar Japan. Obviously, getting rich was important for young men in the Depression era (1930), as indicated by 19 percent choosing the first answer category. The percent of the young men who selected the same response decreased to only 9 percent as World War II approached in 1940. Those who would dedicate their lives to the glory of the country increased also, as indicated in the sharp rise in the percentage of the young men who chose the last two response categories in 1940. A high 71 percent would consecrate their lives to social needs rather than to satisfying their individual causes. One can infer that many young men were socialized in such a manner that they would willingly give their lives for the glory of the nation, an unthinkable option for the young Japanese male today, as the 1978 figures imply.

Returning to our own data analysis, we can see that one-third of the Japanese in 1953 were still willing to dedicate their lives to social service by living a pure and just life (29 percent) or by giving everything in service of society (10 percent). The percentages of respondents who chose these two categories gradually but surely declined since then to 6 percent and 4 percent, respectively, for the two response categories by 1993, a fraction of what they were forty years ago. Those who chose the third and fourth response categories, which may be characterized as being based on individualism, doubled from 21 percent and 11 percent in 1953, respectively, to 40 percent and 26 percent by 1993. A plurality of the Japanese (40 percent) want to live without thinking of money or fame, instead following their own tastes in life. This is similar to the way Honoluluans want to live their lives. We found that 33 percent chose the third response and 36 percent the fourth response of a worry-free life among the Honoluluans in 1988 (The Research Committee on the Study of Honolulu Residents, The Institute of Statistical Mathematics and the University of Hawaii at Manoa, 1990, Appendix 3).

The next item concerns how to deal with a school teacher in trouble (Table 4.9). Should a parent tell the truth or cover up since the teacher is considered a role model for children when one is talking with children? Telling a story contrary to the reality is tolerated in many societies under certain circumstances. In fact, telling a white lie is not only tolerated but encouraged in some cases, for a number of reasons.

What we find here is that the percentage of the Japanese who are willing to admit the truth has increased gradually over the past four decades, to the point that now the ratio is almost 3 to 1 in favor of affirming the truth. Mizuno reports that women are more likely to deny the fact than men, and the older the women, the more likely they deny the fact (1992, p. 99). It appears that the Japanese are becoming more realistic in socializing their children about school teachers' position in society.

#4.1 Suppose that a child comes home and says that he has heard a rumor that his teacher had done something to get himself into trouble, and suppose that the parent knows this is true. Do you think it is better for the parent to tell the child that it is true or to deny it?
1) Better to deny   2) Better to affirm

Table 4.9

School Teacher in Trouble by Year

	1953	1958	1963	1968	1973	1978	1983	1988	1993
Deny	38	38	33	29	31	27	26	23	24
Affirm	42	40	50	52	54	57	59	62	59

Another dimension of Japanese role expectation that has gone through considerable change is that of women. The following question was derived from Cantril (1951).

#6.2 If you could be born again, would you rather be a man or a woman?
    1) Man   2) Woman

Table 4.10

Born Again by Gender and by Year

	1953	1958	1963	1968	1973	1978	1983	1988	1993
M→M	—	90	88	89	89	90	90	90	88
M→F	—	5	7	5	5	4	5	4	3
F→M	—	64	55	43	42	41	39	34	29
F→F	—	27	36	48	51	52	56	59	65

Our assumption here is that woman's position in a society vis-à-vis that of man is not the same and that the intergender relationship is changing. Our effort has been to grasp the process and look for possible causes. Everything being equal, the more desirable the position of either, the more both male and female would choose to be born as a member of the desirable gender next time.

Cantril reports that 66 percent of American women and 60 percent of Canadian women wanted to reborn as women (Takahashi and Shimizu, 1961, p. 256). The Japanese women appear to be fifty years behind North American counterparts in this regard, at least as far as entries in Table 4.10 suggest. Our finding from the 1972 survey of Japanese American women respondents in Honolulu indicates that 73 percent of them desire to be born as women again (The Research Committee on the Study of Honolulu Residents. 1984, p. 58).

We found that Japanese men's position on this question has remained almost unchanged over the years, while women's views have changed radically (Table 4.10). Women who prefer to be reborn as males have plummeted, from 64 percent in 1958 to 29 percent in 1993. Likewise, women who wish to be reborn as the same gender climbed from 27 percent in 1958 to 65 percent in 1993.

The trend clearly reflects the improvement of women's position in Japanese society over the years. Although their position in Japan in many respects lags far behind that of American women, no one can deny the improvement made in the direction of gender equality. The trend is expected to move in the same direction. What interests us is how soon the percentage of women who aspire to be reborn as women will reach the level of the males at 90 percent.

An interesting shift in values regarding gender preference seems to be under way in Japan today. An inference for this comes from a finding that indicates the preference of a girl baby over a boy baby among the Japanese. When the respondents in 1988 were asked to choose between a boy and a girl baby or either one, 37 percent said "either," 32 percent preferred boy, and 29 percent chose girl baby. An interesting change took place in a short span of five years when the same question was repeated in 1993. A plurality of 36 percent of the Japanese chose girl baby over boy baby (33 percent) and 30 percent chose "either." The preference order was totally reversed in the five years. If this represents a trend, then a reason might be found in an increasing number of senior citizens, who came to realize that daughters are more likely to be of assistance to them as they grow older.[6] Most sons leave their homes, while daughters are less likely to do so and are likely to be in a better position to help their parents as they grow older, while a sons' help may be limited to financial assistance.

Nakamura's cohort analysis of the thirty-year period from 1953 to 1988 suggests that aging and cohort effects are minimal and the effects of period the greatest (1992, pp. 124–130). Obviously, it is the nature of times that is responsible for the change. The society as a whole is changing, and with that women are changing their views regardless age or the time of birth.

Thus far we have discussed specific changing opinions on particular items; we have observed consistent changes over the past forty years. Is there any item that has gone through changes other than consistent changes? We found responses for one item that reversed its trend around 1970.

The number of those who regarded nature as something to be conquered was rising for a while, from 23 percent in 1953 to 34 percent in 1968 (Table 4.11). However, as shown in the figure that accompanies Table 4.11, the percentage supporting the cause took a sudden nose-dive to 17 percent in 1973 and continued to decline to 7 percent by 1993. Likewise the "follow nature" option plunged from 26 percent in 1953 to 19 percent in 1968. But the trend reversed itself in 1973, when 31 percent chose this first response category. The upward trend continued rising to 48 percent by 1993.

#2.5 Here are three opinions about man and nature. Which one of these do you think is closest to the truth?

    1) In order to be happy, man must follow nature.
    2) In order to be happy, man must use nature.
    3) In order to be happy, man must conquer nature.

Table 4.11

Nature-Person Relations by Year

	1953	1958	1963	1968	1973	1978	1983	1988	1993
Follow	26	20	19	19	31	33	36	42	48
Use	41	37	40	40	45	44	47	44	38
Conquer	23	28	30	34	17	16	11	9	7

Table 4.11 (Continued)

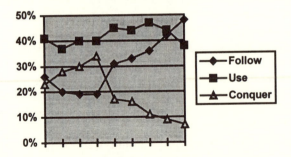

Our hypothesis is that there was a sudden rise in the awareness of environmental problems in the late 1960s through the early 1970s in much of the industrialized world, including Japan. The extend of damage done to the environment as a result of the rapid development of the Japanese economy in the 1960s was so devastating that a huge number of ordinary citizens took to the streets to protest (Kuroda, 1972). The mass media joined in with the citizens' movements. This rise in consciousness for the importance of protecting the environment must have resulted in the change in Japanese attitudes toward nature. Due at least in part to a delayed response to the rising concern voiced by citizens groups, in the early 1970s the Japanese parliament was forced to pass one stringent law after another against large corporations to protect and clean up the environment.

It is possible that those who desire simply to follow nature will surpass those who wish to use nature in the near future. We found no other items where this type of change has occurred. There is a possibility of a trend toward the Japanese returning to their traditional values to some extent, but it is not definitive at this time.

We will now move from individual items to changes in structural dimensions.

CHANGING ATTITUDINAL STRUCTURE[7]

Industrial to Postindustrial Attitudinal Patterns

We discussed the giri-ninjô orientation structure as being stable over the years we examined in the last chapter. We looked for attitudinal structures that have changed over the years and found one. There is a series of questions concerning the Japanese tradition vis-à-vis modern orientation included in the questionnaire. Starting in 1868, Japan has been bent on modernization. Japan succeeded in modernizing itself more quickly than any of its Asian neighbors and, at least economically, it has achieved equality with advanced Western nations. What has come of Japanese efforts to learn from and catch up with the West? An earlier (pp. 61–62) discussion on the Japanese superiority feelings suggests that there must be some change in this regard, and there is.

Hayashi's quantification method III for pattern categorization is used again to look for changes in the configuration of variables relating to the tradition-modern orientation. Six questions appearing in Figure 4.1 (see the Appendix for Chapter 4) are used to perform a quantification III analysis for each survey. Response categories with a bullet (●) indicate traditional, "X" modern, and "Δ" an intermediate position. Figure 4.1 presents our findings.

There are several observations we can make from configuration dynamics as shown in Figure 4.1. First, traditional response variables are compactly concentrated in the midlevel on the left in a rather confined area from 1953 through 1973. Modern response variables are located in the lower right side, while intermediate response variables are found in the upper right side. They remained stable during the first twenty years.

Second, there are no other variables found in the small confined area of the traditional response variables. The first and second points lead us to infer that the Japanese think of what we consider the traditional responses to be in direct opposition to what we assumed to be the modern responses as if they were two different ends of a continuum.

Third, this relatively fixed and stable configuration starts to break down in 1978. We find "3X," a modern response variable, among the traditional responses. Another modern variable, "2X," crossed over the Y axis to the left side in 1978 also.

Fourth, the breakdown goes several steps further by 1983, as "2X" gets closer to the traditional domain. It finally gets into the traditional domain by 1988.

Furthermore, it was safe to assume that younger Japanese are more modern in their views and older Japanese more traditional in their orientation prior to 1973. What started to happen in 1973 and became more apparent in 1978 is that some younger Japanese started to hold more traditional views than older Japanese. The results of the same analysis among only those who are between twenty and twenty-four years old by each survey (not shown here) demonstrate this trend clearly. The traditional domain is widened significantly in 1978 and contained in its pattern two modern responses and one intermediate variable (Hayashi, 1991, p. 202). This trend continues to this date. In other words, the Japanese are no longer structuring their thinking in what used to be considered a diametrically opposed pair of positions. One of the reasons is that those who wish to "follow nature" (traditional) increased, while those who want to "conquer nature" decreased in number. Perhaps this breakdown is caused by Japan's passing the industrial stage and entering a postindustrial age. This certainly is seen in an increasingly larger number of Japanese voters turning away from Socialists and the Liberal Democrats, both of which were founded in the

Industrial Age-based organizational structure, supported by labor unions and industrialists, respectively. Because they are more sensitive to new or postindustrial values, younger Japanese are turning away faster than older Japanese from the Industrial Age configuration. Hayashi's analysis of the 1988 data by age groups makes it clear that the trends are continuing and show no sign of stopping (Hayashi, 1991, p. 205).

Perhaps a more appropriate way of describing this change is transformation of the Japanese attitudes from that of the Industrial Age to a postindustrial age. This marks an end to modernization, at least as far as the industrialization aspect of modernization is concerned, and the advent of a new era of postindustrialization and internationalization.

SUMMARY

In this chapter, we examined changing aspects of Japanese attitudes. We found that some aspects of their opinions as well as attitudinal structures have changed irrevocably over the past forty years. We may be able to classify these changes largely in terms of a transformation Japan has gone through in the past forty years and is still going through as we approach the twenty-first century.

Transformation into a Postindustrial Era

The Japanese attitudes toward nature made a U-turn to the preindustrial era. There has been a rise in the number of the people who wish to follow rather than to conquer nature. Furthermore, the trend toward going "my way" in making decisions used to be considered modern rather than following custom, which is traditional. The trend became murky in the past two decades. The number of those who wish to go their own way has been declining, while following custom has been on a gradual rise over the years. Making money is no longer the most important lesson taught to children. The attitudinal structure probably set in the Meiji era, as Japan launched into modernization to catch up with the West in 1868, came to the end of its road about the time of the first energy crisis in 1973. The increased sense of self-confidence (or racism, as some may prefer to call it) among the Japanese suggests the passing of the era of catching up with the West. Most, but not all, changes we observe among the Japanese seem to reflect the transformation Japan is going through along with other industrialized parts of the world.

Collectivity to Individual Orientation

These changes suggest that the Japanese are moving from a collectivity-centered life to a more individual-centered life. This change is manifested in the family line question, following a preferred way of life, and less interest shown in electoral participation. The Japanese are far from being individually oriented in relation to Americans. But there is no denying that individuals are becoming more important in recent decades vis-à-vis the government, family, company and other entities.

Liberalization: Subjects to Citizens

The Japanese are becoming more democratic in their orientation and transforming themselves out of being subjects to citizens with a full sense of confidence in taking part in politics. Women are beginning to be treated better than ever before, even though Japan has a long way to go toward being on par with the United States.

Possible Causes of Changes

These observed changes appear to be caused by several factors. First, the way the Japanese make a living has revolutionized some of their attitudes. In the past forty years, Japan has moved from an agriculture-based economy (partly as a result of losing a large portion of industrial capacity in World War II) in the early 1950s, to a manufacturing-based economy in the 1960s, and finally to a service-based economy starting in the 1970s. Certainly, Japan's attitudinal change toward nature signals the end of the Industrial Age.

Second, the increased amenities and more affluent economy made Japanese people change their attitudes toward money and assess their own ability or level of self-confidence in relation to others in the world. An increase in the number of Japanese who believe that they must discuss political matters among themselves and not leave everything for politicians to decide may be also caused by the Japanese people's increased self-confidence.

Third, the internationalization of Japanese economy may in part be responsible for further Westernization of Japanese values (such as on the question of women's position and the separation of religion and the state). The liberalization of Japanese values and the movement toward a more individual-centered life style could also be related to further intensified contact with the West.

Which Direction?

Where is Japan headed? Can we anticipate the type and extent of changes the Japanese may go through in the future? Our position is that the basic core character of the Japanese, as described in Chapter 2, is not likely to change broadly even if it is modified. We will return to this point in Chapter 7.

NOTES

1. Although 20 percent is an arbitrary figure, it is the figure considered as a rule of thumb in survey research for assuming that there must be a statistically significant rela-

tionship between two variables when a difference in response varies by at least 20 percent.

2. We normally have a couple of other response categories consisting of "Other" and "DK/NA" (Don't Know/Not Ascertainable), as we do for this item. However, the number of respondents who fell into these answers is not reproduced here. Hence, percentages shown will not add up to 100 percent.

3. We advisedly use the adverb *virtually* to describe the status of poverty in Japan. We realize that poverty continues to exist in some parts of Japan, but it is not a ubiquitous phenomenon in large cities as it is in the West, where one invariably finds slums in all large cities. Social and economic discrimination against the former outcast people, Korean and Chinese residents, persist.

4. The sharp rise in the price of land and stocks in the late 1980s created a deepening gap between those who owned either of the two or both and those who were without either one, at least in terms of wealth. There has also been a slight easing in inheritance tax assessments.

5. In 1978, we translated this question in English for Honolulu voters as follows: "If you could be born again, to which nationality—that is to say, which race or ethnic group—would you like to belong?" For the result by ethnicity, see The Research Committee on the Study of Honolulu Residents (1980), p. 72.

We tried to translate this question in English for Japanese Americans in Hawaii. The ults read as follows: "If you were not a Japanese, which of the following nationalities ld like to be? Choose as many as you like. 1) Chinese, 2) Korean, 3) Filipino, 4) waiian, 5) Portuguese, 6) Local haole, 7) Arab, 8) Jew, 9) Russian, 10) German, 11) French, and 12) English." We obtained some interesting results. See The Research Committee on the Study of Honolulu Residents (1984), p. 51.

6. The change in percentages represents more than sampling errors. However, there are nonsampling errors, not all of which can be measured. We can have more confidence in our findings if the same trend is found in the 1998 survey.

7. This section draws heavily from Hayashi (1993), pp. 75–78, and Hayashi (1991), pp. 198–204.

CHAPTER 5

Common Japanese Culture

SHARED SENSITIVITIES

All humans share certain qualities that enable them to develop culture, which sets them apart from the rest of the creatures on earth. What are some values and ways of thinking the Japanese share with others in Europe and in the United States?[1]

By shared Japanese culture, we mean a shared sensitivity in the tradition of *The Tale of Genji*, which was completed in 1007. The only difference between Murasaki Shikibu and ourselves is that she was referring to what Japan shared with China, its major foreign contact in the eleventh century. Countries in our frame of mind are mostly major industrialized nations in the twentieth century.

As we noted earlier, we can first look at the frequency distribution of questions commonly asked in all five industrialized countries: France, Japan, the United Kingdom (hereafter referred to as the UK), United States (hereafter referred to as the US), and Federal Republic of Germany (hereafter referred to as the FRG). Do Americans and Europeans share the Japanese enduring predominant opinions, presented in Chapter 3? Do demographic factors such as age and gender have the same impacts on opinions that they do on the Japanese?

After examining each factor separately, we will examine the data to see if we can find common threads in viewing the world using Hayashi's quantification method III. In so doing, we decided to include some discussion of how each nation is different even when nations share basic ways of thinking. In other words, do we come up with the same or different results when we think alike?[2] If the results differ, how do we differ even when we view things in the same way?

We divided this chapter into three parts. First, we present the frequency distribution of separate items that are similar in all five countries. Second, we examine age and gender as factors shaping opinions irrespective of cultures. Third, we delve into our shared ways of thinking among the five nations. We discuss what we share and what we do not.

FREQUENCY DISTRIBUTION

In Chapter 3, we pointed out four enduring predominant opinions in Japan for the past forty years and compared them with responses to comparable questions in the five countries (Table 3.2).[3] Our focus in this chapter is commonality and shared values among all five industrialized countries. We know that the Japanese are different from the Westerners in not having a personal religious faith as such, although they consider religion to be as important as Westerners do.[4] We will examine four items in this chapter: (1) the hiring of a person who scored highest in an employment examination (#5.1c1), (2) the preference for working under a "paternalistic" section head (#5.6) over a "rational" section head, (3) the preference for the Versailles garden over the Katsura Detached Palace garden (#9.3),[5] and (4) the importance of religion (#3.2). Do we find the majority of Westerners agreeing with all four items?

Table 5.1

Japanese Enduring Predominant Opinions Shared with the West

Population	#5.1c1 Highest Grade	#5.6 Paternalistic head
Japanese American in Hawaii	68%	59%
Non-Japanese American in Hawaii	67	57
United States	66	51
United Kingdom	73	57
West Germany	45	69
France	59	64
Japan	70	88
	#9.3 Versailles garden	#3.2 Religious mind
Japanese American in Hawaii	66%*	80%
Non-Japanese American in Hawaii	77*	80
United States	85	87
United Kingdom	64	59
West Germany	75	58
France	64	63
Japan	31	76

*1983 data.

We find that the Americans and Europeans (the British, French, and Germans) share four of the six enduring predominant opinions the Japanese had for four decades (Table 5.1). The exception is found in the first column for the Germans, with 45 percent—close, but not exactly a majority. They apparently do not feel strongly about giving priority to the employment test score as much as the other four industrial nationals do.

The Japanese have regard their workplace as an integral domain of their primary group almost the same as their family. In fact, they use the same word to refer to both family and their employer—*uchi*. It is thus understandable that a high 88 percent of them would choose the paternalistic section head over the rational head.[6] It is noteworthy that even in the United States at least a majority would prefer the paternalistic section head.

The Japanese majority obviously prefer the Japanese garden. If we reverse the percentage figure, clearly the majority of the Japanese prefer their garden over the non-Japanese garden, just as the majority of Westerners prefer the Western garden. The size of majority in each country may differ, but the point is that these are views held by the majority in all five industrialized nations.

What is the significance of these four items? First, the five nationals all consider fairness and objectivity in employment as the most important, and not such factors such as personal relations with applicants. Second, workplaces in all five nations are structured in such a manner that human relations play an important part. They all consider their workplace to be the domain of what sociologists call primary group relations.[7] What is considered beauty by the Japanese is not by Westerners, and vice-versa. Westerners love Western-style gardens, and the Japanese Japanese-style gardens. All of them like their own style of beauty. While there are differences among Americans and Europeans or Germans and French concerning the sense of beauty, differences among them are not as radical as the preference for the Japanese garden as opposed to the Versailles garden. Although the Japanese differ from the Westerners in rejecting monotheistic religions and do not consider themselves to have any personal religious faith, that does not prevent them from believing that religion is important. A majority (about 70 percent) claim to have no religion. A question that comes to the mind of the logical Westerner is, Why should they think religion important if so many do not espouse a religious faith? However, religion is not a personal faith as such, but it is a family and community activity the Japanese engage in from time to time. It is important as a way of demonstrating respect for ancestors. Hence, the significance of why the Japanese people think religion is important may differ from the reason Westerners claim the importance of their religion.

So far, we have limited our presentation to the enduring majority opinions. Are there any current majority opinions shared by four Western nations? We found nine out of seventy-four items that attracted over 50 percent of responses from all five nationals[8] (Table 5.2).

Social class identification in our surveys is based on self-assessment. Regardless of one's objective standard of living, we asked the respondents to identify themselves with one of the five classes, ranging from upper, upper-middle, middle, lower middle, to lower. We see from entries in Table 5. 2 that a majority of the respondents in the industrialized world feel that they belong to the middle class. Objectively speaking, there are differences in the distribution of net income, as measured by the Gini index among the five nations in the following order: Japan (0.316), UK (0.318), US (0.381), FRG (0.383), and France (0.414).[9] It is ironic that the French, who prefer a socialist economy more than any other nationals (according the results of our surveys), have the most unequal distribution of income. However, the results of our self-assessment of social class identification indicate that a majority of all five nationals identify themselves as the middle class.

Table 5.2

Shared Majority Opinions in the Five Nations

Item #*	#1.8 Mid-class	#2.82 Aesop	#7.19 Success	#4.4 Teacher	#5.1d Filial piety
JA HI	67%	91%	—%	79%	78%
Non JA HI	54	91	—	76	69
US	55	85	70	90	69
UK	54	83	56	75	63
FRG	54	78	57	58	55
France	61	79	64	64	52
Japan	54	75	53	62	78

Item #*	#5.6h Friendly	#3.3 All religion	#7.87 Coop	#8.8 Reform
JA HI	82%	75%	—%	81%
Non JA HI	77	65	—	71
US	79	57	66	66
UK	85	71	70	70
FRG	78	62	55	55
France	63	58	63	63
Japan	62	63	59	59

*The item numbers correspond to those found in the Appendix for Chapter 1. #1.8 Self-identification of social class 3) "Middle Class." #2.82 Aesop story on ant and grasshopper 2) Shares food. #7.19 Success depends on 1) Ability and effort. #4.4 Teacher in trouble 1) Tell the truth. #5.1d Important value 1) Filial piety. #3.2 All religions are the same 1) Agree: #7.87 Employer vs. Employee 2) Cooperate. #8.8 Attitudes toward social change 2) Improve by reform. JA HI = Japanese Americans in Hawaii.

Aesop stories are told in many parts of the world for their timeless universal appeal, but we know that stories are often told differently even if the main structure remains the same. A story about a diligent ant and idle grasshopper is told in many countries today. The question here is, What should an ant do if an idle grasshopper comes asking for food in winter? Should the ant share or not share food? A large majority of all five nationals would share food with the idle grasshopper after encouraging the grasshopper to work harder next summer. All five nations are major donor countries for aid to developing nations. We see from our survey results that the public in these nations is supportive of aid programs.

If there is a rumor that a teacher is in trouble, should a parent tell the truth to his or her child? The answer is affirmative in all countries, especially in the

United States. This is an opinion that has changed over the years in Japan. The results from the surveys conducted in 1953 and 1958 indicate that only 42 percent and 40 percent, respectively, would tell the truth. This finding suggests that this is one aspect of Japanese attitudes that has changed in recent decades to conform with the common norm, as defined by the major industrialized world.

Filial piety is evidently a common value that we all possess in the industrialized world. It is not just a Confucian doctrine practiced in East Asia. We asked the respondents to choose two of four values: (1) filial piety, (2) on, or repaying obligations, (3) individual rights, and (4) individual freedom. We realize that the concept of on in Japan is not the same as simply repaying obligations, as translated into English, just as the Japanese interpret individual freedom differently from Americans. We may not have succeeded in establishing functionally equivalent response categories used in the survey.[10] Nevertheless, the concept of filial piety is a relatively culture-free concept. We may note that the percentages of the Japanese who prefer the last two Western values had declined somewhat in the 1970s and has not changed much since the late 1970s.[11]

A desirable image of a person is not comprised of being efficient and unconcerned with others, but of being caring and friendly, even if that person is an inefficient worker. A humane quality that contributes to the building of a caring society is apparently what the people in the industrialized world desire. Efficiency is demanded in the modern industrial world, but that is not what is considered desirable. A good citizen in the industrial world is a friendly person who cares for others' welfare. This value, despite the reality, is upheld as a norm in the five nations.

Although different religions take different stands, they all preach the same thing. So say the results of our surveys in all five nations. We know that all three monotheistic religions share the concept of God, but the Japanese are not monotheists. Is this a case of a good misunderstanding? Or is it a sign of not everyone taking religion seriously? We are certain that the majority feel that all religions are essentially the same—an intriguing finding. Further studies would be necessary to explain the significance of this finding.

Labor unions in most industrial societies have been declining in strength for the last few decades. Keeping in mind that the surveys were conducted before the fall of the Berlin wall, a majority in advanced industrial societies apparently feel that labor and management should cooperate rather than fight each other to maximize their interests.

All five nations are relatively stable, as indicated by the large majority of their citizens who feel that they belong to the middle class. They apparently feel no need for any revolutionary change in their society, although they all feel the need to reform and change gradually. Of course, it does not take a majority to cause a revolution. Revolutions are normally carried out by a small group of determined people. This is an interesting finding in that Japan is the only country among the five that has never experienced revolution in its long history.

Japan has had a history of reforms, in its recorded history, but not revolution in the sense that the Americans and the French have.

In every society, some people have certain ideas and others have other ideas. Public opinions often vary by demographic factors. Are there similarities in the way our opinions vary by demographic factors that cut across cultures (for example, the younger the persons, the more they possess types of views irrespective of culture)?

OPINIONS THAT VARY BY DEMOGRAPHICS

Age

Table 5.3

Items That Vary by Age in the Same Direction

Item #	Code*	FRG	France	UK	US	HI	Jpn
#7.31 Future Living Standard	1+2	→**	→	→	→	→	→
#8.80 National Goal: Demo.	2	→	→	→	→	→	→
#2.80 Health: Insomnia	1	←←	←	←	←		←
#5.81F Importance: Religion	6+7	←	←	←	←	←	←
#2.83e Life: Alienation	1	0	0	0	0		0
#8.8 Social Change: No!	3	←	←—	←	←	←	←—
#8.86 Party Support: Strong	1+2	←	←	←	←		←

*Response category for each item.
** → = Higher among younger respondents, ← = higher among older respondents, ←← = strong trend, ←— = weak trend, 0 = no variance.

There are some opinions that vary by age in every society. Our concern here is to discover any item that varies by age in the same direction in all five countries. Table 5.3 summarizes our findings. The first item concerns how the respondents feel about their future living standard. Apparently, the younger the respondents, the more optimistic they are in all five countries, including Hawaii in the United States. This is interesting in view of the fact that the United Kingdom is a mature country, while Japan and Germany have caught up with the Western standard of living only in recent decades.

More say for the people in making important national decisions is what younger generations are asking for in all five nations. Apparently, the younger the respondents, the more they demand to have a government by the people in the industrialized world—an encouraging sign for the future of democracy.

Insomnia strikes a greater number of senior citizens ubiquitously. It may be that they have a greater tendency to be inflicted by insomnia as a result of the aging process, although there are many other causes for insomnia.

Religion becomes an increasingly important part of life for older respondents everywhere. However, there is great variation among different nationals. Those who selected 7 on the scale of importance from 0 to 7 constituted the following percentages in the order of higher to lower: US, 47 percent; Japan and the UK, 14 percent; France, 12 percent; and West Germany, 9 percent. In short, religion as a part of life is far more important to Americans than to people in the rest of the industrialized world. The point is that we are all alike in one dimension of our attitudes toward religion, but there are vast differences as well. Reasons for this spectacular difference in perception among the Americans go beyond the scope of our study.

The sense of alienation has been said, by Marx and others, to be a consequence of industrialization. Their hypothesis is correct in many ways in many parts of the industrial world today. Such indicators of social disorganization as violent crime, suicide, divorce, and children raised without fathers in the West affirm the modern alienation hypothesis. Our findings, as presented in Table 5.3, suggest that this sense of variation does not vary at all by age in all five countries.

The Marxian hypothesis has been borne out in the West, as we see the rising rate of violent crimes and other indicators of social disorganization in the United States today. The exception is postwar Japan, where the rates of violent crime, suicide, divorce, and what the Japanese refer to as *shiseiji* and *shoshi* (natural/illegitimate children) have declined many times over since the turn of the twentieth century.[12] This objective observation does not coincide with how much the Japanese feel alienated from the community in relation to the rest of the industrial world. The percentage of the people who feel alienated in the five countries is as follows, in the order of high to low: Japan, 71 percent; FRG, 68 percent; US, 67 percent; UK, 55 percent; and France, 48 percent. Again, we wish to demonstrate that how the people feel does not always coincide with what exists independently from their perception in aggregate statistics, whether or it is the sense of alienation or the importance of religion.

Defend against destructive violent forces in society is what younger people everywhere believe. The younger the respondents, the more they feel that way ubiquitously. It could be that they feel a greater stake than older respondents, whose years are numbered.

The older the respondents, the more they identify with their political party. The more experience the respondents have with elections and politics, the more they feel they are in the party they want to be in. Apparently, younger respondents feel less comfortable in saying that their ideas are close to those of the party they support, if they have party support at all. There is a trend toward independent voters in many countries today. This could be a reflection of the trend toward an increasing number of voters alienated from the existing parties.

Since we do not have a longitudinal data set for the four Western countries, we are unable to present cohort analysis to discover which one of the three possible factors contributes to the age factor affecting the attitudes of the respondents presented here: aging, generational, or historical period factors. We are thus not able to claim which one of the three age factors is responsible for our findings. The age factor may vary from one nation to another (such as the aging factor in one country and the periodic factor in another). We had no choice but to treat all the countries as if they were the same.

We now show another variation in age affecting the respondents' opinions. Table 5.4 summarizes our findings.

Table 5.4

Items That Vary in Middle Age in Either Direction

Item #	Code	FRG	France	UK
#2.81 Scheduling problems	1	^>*	^>	^>
#5.1b Father at death bed: home	2	∪>	∪>	∪>

	Code	US	Hawaii	Japan
#2.81 Scheduling problems	1	^>		^>
#5.1b Father at death bed: home	2	∪>	∪>	∪>

*^> = High in the middle-age categories and higher among younger respondents than older respondents; ∪> = low in the middle-age categories and higher younger respondents than older respondents.

First, many of us experience scheduling difficulties between our job and individual or family chores in our daily life. Does this type of conflict affect more younger or older or middle-aged respondents? Our focus in this section is on the middle-aged groups. We found that the problems are most acutely felt by the middle-aged groups, followed by younger respondents and then by older respondents in that order in all five nations. We would infer that this may be a consequence of the middle-aged respondents. They are likely to be more occupied with their work than younger or older respondents. In addition, they are more likely to have children, who often also complicate their lives. Older respondents are most likely to be free from parental responsibility, which should reduce their conflicts between their job and family life. Evidently, this is a common trend.

The next items are an opposite case from the first case of scheduling conflicts. The question here is if one should go see his or her father at his death bed or attend a crucial meeting that decides the fate of his or her company. Middle-aged company persons everywhere are most reluctant to go to see their father. The reason for this may lie again in the importance of the job to middle-aged people in every society.

Table 5.5

Items That Do Not Vary by Age

Item #	Code	FRG	Fran	UK	US	Hi	Jpn
#7.24 Job criterion: good pay	1	0	0	0	0	0	0
#5.80b Neighborhood safety	1+2	0	0	0	0		0
#2.3c Family satisfaction	1+2	0	0	0	0	0	0

Next we present cases in which we observed no age effects (Table 5.5). We asked respondents to choose the most important criterion for getting their job: good salary, safety, congenial co-workers, or accomplishment in life. Good pay is preferred by 13 percent (FRG) to 21 percent (US). However, we found no difference by age. In other words, about 20 percent of Americans chose the good pay criterion regardless of age, as did the respondents in the other nations.

Burglary is a problem everywhere to a varying extent. Nevertheless, age is not factor in all five nations. Unlike other discrepancies we found between the objective reality, as demonstrated in aggregate statistics and individual psychological assessment, there seems to be a closer relationship between how safe a respondent feels and aggregate statistics in this case. The following percentages are the total percentage of respondents who felt no problems at all with burglary in their neighborhood by country, in the order of high to low: Japan, 54 percent; FRG, 42 percent; US, 30 percent; UK, 16 percent; and France, 15 percent.

The extent of satisfaction one feels with one's family life does not vary by age in all nations. Furthermore, figures not presented here indicate that a great majority of people everywhere are either completely or at least somewhat satisfied with their family life, with the French respondents giving us the least positive response as follows: UK, 89 percent; Japan, 82 percent; FRG and US, 81 percent; and France, 68 percent. There is a remarkable similarity in the percentages among all nations.

We move now from age to gender to see how men and women share their views with their counterparts in other industrial nations (Table 5.6). Are certain opinions dependent on whether one is male or female?[13]

Gender

Women everywhere are more concerned with possible car, war, and nuclear power accidents than are men, especially when it comes to war. Keeping in mind that all these surveys were taken before the end of Cold War, the threat of war was present then and is still present, but to a much less extent today. Women are more interested in peace and safety than men are universally. There are reasons for this finding derived from their being female. Along with gender-based differences in the extent of worry, some nationals are more worried than others. For example, the French are more worried about everything in relation to others by far. A good example is their fear of car accidents. The following is the percentage of people who said that they worry "very much" about car accidents: France, 44 percent; Japan, 26 percent; UK, 24 percent; US, 22 percent; and FRG, 9 percent. Whatever the reason for some nationals to be more worried, women tend to worry more about car accidents, war, and nuclear accidents.

Table 5.6

Items That Vary by Gender

Item #	Code	FRG	France	UK
#2.30d Anxiety: car accident	1+2	F	F+	F
#2.30f Anxiety: war	1+2	F+	F+	F+
#2.30g Anxiety: nuclear accident	1+2	F	F	F
#7.80a Saving: health care	1	=	=	=
#7.80c Saving: household goods	1	F	F	F
#7.80d Saving: food	1	F	F	F
#7.80e Saving: beauty care	1	F+	F+	F+
#7.80j Saving: cigarettes & liqueur	1	=	=	=
#2.80a Illness: headaches	1	F+	F+	F+
#2.80c Illness: nervousness	1	F+	F+	F+
#2.80d Illness: depression	1	F	F+	F
#2.80e Illness: insomnia	1	F	F+	F+
#7.82 Aesop: ant & grasshopper	1	M	M	M
#5.81a Life: family & children	7	F	F	F
#2.3c Satisfied with family life	1	=	=	=
#7.86d Future: Life in space	1	M+	M+	M+
		US	Hawaii	Japan
#2.30d Anxiety: car accident	1+2	F	F	F
#2.30f Anxiety: war	1+2	F+	F+	F
#2.30g Anxiety: nuclear accident	1+2	F+	F+	F
#7.80a Saving: health care	1	=		=
#7.80c Saving: household goods	1	F	F	F+
#7.80d Saving: food	1	F		F+
#7.80e Saving: beauty care	1	F+		F+
#7.80j Saving: cigarettes & liqueur	1	=		=
#2.80a Illness: headaches	1	F+		F+
#2.80c Illness: nervousness	1	F+		F
#2.80d Illness: depression	1	F		F
#2.80e Illness: insomnia	1	F		F
#7.82 Aesop: ant & grasshopper	1	M	M	M
#5.81a Life: family & children	7	F	F+	F
#2.3c Satisfied with family life	1	=	=	=
#7.86d Future: Life in space	1	M+		M

The next series of questions calls for areas in which the respondents felt they could save. We find that there are two areas of possible savings without regard to gender: health care and cigarette and liquor consumption. Three other areas in which they thought they could save money (but more so among women in the five nations) are: household appliances or goods, food, and beauty care. These areas represent the type of items women are more responsible for buying than men. Women everywhere feel that these are areas where they could save in their family budget.

The next sequence of questions was whether the respondents suffered from any of the following health problems in the past month: headaches, backaches, nervousness, depression, and insomnia. We found that women suffer from more health-related problems than men, especially when it comes to headaches, nervousness, depression, and insomnia. Backaches afflict more women in the four Western nations, except in Japan. Japanese men apparently have weaker backs in relation to Western men, or at least they complain as much as women in Japan. This is an interesting finding because women almost universally (and certainly in the industrialized nations) live longer than men by five to six years. These differences could be a result of the differences in the physical make-up of men and women. They do not seem to be a product of culture.[14]

Although women among the five nations have more health problems, some nationals have more illnesses than others. On the average, the frequency of health problems the respondents had in the past month by nation is as follows, in the order of frequency: France, 38 percent; US, 28 percent; FRG and UK, 26 percent; and Japan, 17 percent. Again we find that the French worry more than the other nationals and suffer from illness more than any other nationals. The Japanese complain of these illnesses less than half as often as the French. The Japanese seem to enjoy better health than the Westerners as far as these five health problems are concerned.

If women are more peace and safety oriented than men, are they more kind and warm? The answer is resoundingly affirmative. Our findings strongly suggest that women in the five cultures are more kind and sympathetic to the idle grasshopper than men are. The differences among the national boundaries are minimal, ranging from Japan's 15 percent (who would send the grasshopper away without giving food) to America's 12 percent. In other words, gender makes a greater difference than culture as far as response to this question is concerned.

Are family and children more important to men or women? Evidently, the answer everywhere is women. They claim that family and children are dear to them more often than men do, especially in Hawaii. If this trend is not culture bound, is it a female instinct? We realize that women are more likely to spend the time with their children than men are in much of the world today. This could be a consequence of custom observed everywhere, even though more than half of married women are engaged in gainful employment in Hawaii (where the cost of living is 40 percent higher than on the mainland United States). This high rate of working women does not seem to stop women in Hawaii from caring more for their children than men do.

We observe that gender makes no difference on the question of the level of satisfaction the respondents have with their family life. On the whole, they are satisfied with their family to just about an equal degree in all five nations. We realize that women in the United States, for example, enjoy greater equality than women in Japan. However, that has nothing to do with the level of satisfaction men and women receive from their family in the two nations. Gender has no impact here.

Men in the five nations are much more likely than women to think future life in space is possible in the next twenty-five years. Is man adventurous or optimistic because of his genes?

We have no sufficient evidence to conclude from any of what we discussed that genes really make a difference in our viewpoints. We do know that there are a number of near-universal trends for men or women to hold certain views. Culture is important in shaping the nature of ideas, but there are values and ways of thinking we share as men and as women with men and women of other cultures, possibly because of our gender.

We now have some idea of what we share in values as far as single factors are concerned. Let us go beyond the single-factor level of discussion and focus on the relationships among different factors.

COMMON THREADS IN THE WAY OF THINKING

Table 5.7

Common Threads of Thought Process in the Five Nations

Item	Common Ways of Viewing Item
Living standard and class identification	Positive, neutral and negative patterns
Anxiety	High, middle, and low patterns
Science and technology	Positive, neutral, and negative patterns
Ancestor, family, alienation, tradition, etc.	Important, neutral, and unimportant patterns
Health and life satisfaction	Positive, neutral, and negative patterns
Money and work orientation	Money and nonmoney patterns
Living standard and future	Positive, neutral, and negative patterns
Trustworthiness of the people	Trustworthy and untrustworthy patterns
Family	Modern, neutral, and traditional patterns
Ideology	Democracy/capitalism, socialism, and "it depends" patterns

There are not too many similarities among the five nations as far as the frequency distribution of responses is concerned. However, we found that all five countries share some basic ways looking at the world today when we go beyond simple comparison of percentages. When we grouped what we thought formed a set of related questions, we found that they are unidimensional, as defined by Guttman (1944).[15] In other words, we can put a set of all answers on a single continuum or line, such as from most negative to most positive. Even if where we stand on a continuum may differ, the way we see the world is more similar than our findings in the last section. We grouped seventy-four questions into ten categories and analyzed them using Hayashi's quantification method III.

Table 5.7 summarizes our findings of common threads or patterns of viewing various items, while Table 5.8 encapsulates each nation's position in different patterns.

Table 5.8

Consequences of Common Threads in the Five Nations

Item	Each Culture Characterized by Cluster
Class & reality	Japan and FRG least association, then UK, US, and France highest association
Anxiety	Japan and US midposition, UK mixed, FRG lowest, France highest level
Science & technology	US, France positive, FRG negative, UK somewhat negative, Japan midposition
Ancestor, etc.	US most important, Japan in mid, followed by UK, France, & FRG least important
Health and life	France negative, Japan, US, & UK positive, FRG midposition
Money & work	FRG & France money oriented, US & UK non-money oriented, Japan unique*
Future prospect	US positive, UK negative, France most negative, Japan and FRG mid & positive
Trust	France distrust, UK, US, & FRG trust, Japan mixed and separate
Family	Traditional to modern patterns: J, US, UK, F, FRG in that order
Ideology	US cap/demo followed by FRG, France socialism followed by UK, Japan "it depends"

*Japan is in the midposition between the two patterns, but it is different from them in that Japan's position is inconsistent. For example, the Japanese are willing to work even if they have enough money to live, but they want to teach children the importance of money and think life is meaningless without work.

Standard of Living and Social Class Identification

Our findings of three questions on the standard of living (7.30b, 7.30a, and 7.31) and a question on social class with which respondents identified themselves (1.8) for five nations show remarkable similarities. The configuration for all five date sets suggests that responses to the four items are clearly grouped into positive, neutral, to negative patterns with some variation. Those who have positive views of living conditions tend to identify themselves with a higher social class for all five countries.

Japan and Germany have the fewest associations between the standard of living questions and social class, followed by UK and US. The closest association between the three standard of living questions and social class is found among the French. Hence our survey research finding coincides with aggregate economic data analysis of economists regarding the distribution of income and wealth in these countries. Japan ranks among the most economically egalitarian state, while France is found as the least egalitarian, as indicated in their Gini index.[16] Although there are no appreciable differences in percentages in the way all five national groups responded to the self-identification of social class (a majority of 54 percent in four countries, except France with 61 percent), those who identified themselves with a higher class and have positive attitudes toward their living standards are most likely to be found among the French respondents and least likely among the Japanese, followed closely by the Germans.

Anxiety

Four items dealing with anxiety are serious illness (2.30), traffic accident (2.30d), unemployment, war (2.30f), and accident at nuclear power plants (2.30g). We found that responses are definitely structured into three patterns: very anxious, neutral, and not anxious at all. In other words, we all approach these items in the same way, consisting of three patterns.

Although we view these sources of worry in the same manner, the Japanese are not worried much. Most important of all, they are in the middle. The French are most worried, and the Germans are least concerned, with Americans and British somewhere between these two extremes. These patterns of the five nations are similar to what we found in the last section.

Views on Science and Technology

Nine items on various facets of science and technology, such as the usefulness of science (7.36), the desirability of computers (7.33), alternative medical treatments (7.83), science of mind (7.84), science of social problems (7.85), safe disposal of nuclear wastes (7.86), cure for cancer (7.86b), cure for senility (7.86c), and space living (7.86d) are found to form a unidimension, except for the alternative medicine question (7.83). All five nationalities in the industrialized world are similar in viewing science and technology from the viewpoint of positive, neutral, and negative. Nearly all responses are categorized into three groups.

We found that the Americans have the most positive attitudes toward science and technology, followed closely by the French. The Germans are most negative toward science and technology, with the British toward the middle. The Japanese, as in other cases, are most neutral.

Ancestor, Family, Alienation, Tradition, and Religion

Eight items on various facets of life, including one's views on ancestor (4.11), family (4.10, 4.80, 5.81e), alienation (7.83e), traditions (2.1), and religion (5.81f, 3.2), are found to share something in common. The responses are grouped into three distinctive groups of those who believe family, community life, and religion are important, neutral and unimportant. The Americans consider all these items most important and are most definite about their belief. Europeans, especially Germans, view them as least important. The Japanese are in the middle and least definite. Japan's position here again demonstrates the prevailing presence of the Rashomonesque character of the Japanese culture.

Views on Health and Life Satisfaction

Despite the large number of items (thirteen) included in this series, we found that the respondents in all five nations approach the thirteen questions in exactly the same way. The thirteen items included in the analysis were 7.18 (outlook on health), 2.30 (fear of serious illness), 7.80a (health care expenses), 2.3g (satisfaction with one's health), 2.3f (quality of life), 7.83 (alternative medicine), 7.86b (cure for cancer), 2.3c (satisfaction with family life), 2.80 (headaches), 2.80b (backaches), 2.80c (nervousness), 2.80d (depression), and 2.80e (insomnia). Their response patterns are clearly divided into three distinctive clusters of positive, neutral, and negative groups, with the notable exception of two items on the possible use of alternative medicine and the cure for cancer. The responses to these two items are separate and independent from the rest of the twelve items.

We found the French alone on the negative side and the British, Japanese, and Americans on the positive side, with the Germans in the middle. This configuration, of the positive cluster consisting of the Americans, British, and Japanese, is different from the rest of the results of analysis thus far. Apparently, these three nationals are alike in their positive outlook on health and life in general in relation to the French, who are pessimistic and negative.

Attitudes toward Money and Work

Eight items on various facets of money and work, consisting of eight questions, are selected for this series: 7.81 (higher income or free time), 2.8 (continue to work), 7.25 (money or work), 7.24 (reason for employment), 2.4 (way of life), 4.5 (importance of money), 2.30d (national goal), and 2.83d (money: end or means). Attitudes toward money, work, and life in the five nations are nearly identical in the way think about choices concerning money and work. All of them are either money oriented or non-money oriented.

Anglo-American cultures are definitely antimoney, while Continental Europeans, French, and Germans are moneyoriented. Again, we found Japan in a unique position of being not only in the middle but taking a position away from the four Western nations. The Japanese are different in that (1) they tend to wish to continue working even if they have money, (2) their life without work is meaningless, (3) they feel the need for teaching the importance of money to children, and (4) they choose to remain neutral. The French and Germans, being most rational, see no reason to work if they have enough money, while the Americans and British feel the opposite. Hence there are differences in what all these nationals choose, but they are alike in the way they categorize and relate their life experiences, (i.e., the way they structure their thinking).

Attitudes toward Living Standard and Future

We asked five related questions on economic conditions and the future: 7.30b (comparison of nation's living standard 10 years ago), 7.30a (comparison of your own living standard ten years ago), 7.31 (future living conditions), 7.18c (future happiness), and 7.18b (peace of mind). The responses are neatly divided into three clusters: negative, neutral, and positive clusters. What is intriguing is that all these five items are interrelated among all five nations even when two analytically different categories of items are included (namely economic conditions and future mental state of affairs). Apparently, we all share our view of these two categories of life experience in the same way among the five countries, although how we feel about these items differs.

We observed that Americans are most positive in their economic outlook and in their expectations for the future. The British are somewhat more negative than the Americans. The French have the gloomiest outlook on life, while the Japanese and Germans are on the side of a positive outlook but remain neutral. We are beginning to get the impression that Americans are the most optimistic, followed closely by the British, while the French are the least positive. The Japanese and Germans are largely positive but are not so sure.

Trustworthy of the People

Are people trying to take advantage of you or are they in general trustworthy? Three questions on interpersonal expectations are grouped into this series: 2.12 (people are helpful), 2.12b (people are fair), and 2.12c (people are trustworthy). All nationals dichotomize their experience with other people into trusting or untrusting. They scaled nicely into positive and negative clusters.

However, as with other series, we found national differences. The French are most distrustful of others, while the Americans and British are most trusting, with Germans following them closely. The Japanese are found on the side of trusting but tend to believe that others look after themselves instead of trying to be helpful. They do not, however, believe that others are trying to take advantage of them, as the French believe. The Anglo-American optimism extends to include their views of other people in general.

Attitudes toward Family

We have five questions on this subject as follows: 4.30 (home is most relaxing), 4.32 (marriage is permanent), 4.31 (women's role for housework and child care), 5.81 (importance of immediate family), and 5.81b (importance of career). We discovered that the respondents in the five nations view these questions from modern-traditional perspectives. In other words, we tend to approach these questions based on whether we think in modern terms or from a traditional perspective. We located three clusters of responses, modern: neutral, and traditional. Family life is a universal experience found in all parts of the world, and these respondents in the five industrialized nations apparently think alike on the question of family life.

The Americans, British, and Japanese are traditional. The Japanese are especially so in their view of the role of women in housework and child care. The Germans, on the other hand, are most modern, followed by the French, in that they tend to think that immediate family members are not as important as the other three nationals do. This is a unique finding in that the Germans are found on the extreme side of being the least traditional.

Attitudes toward Ideology

The last series is on three questions on ideology: democracy (8.2e), capitalism (8.2f), and socialism (8.2g). We eliminated a question on liberalism that is viewed differently in the United States in relation to the other four countries, who are similar in their attitudes toward liberalism. We discovered that all the nationals approach these three ideologies in the same way in that their responses are clearly categorized into three clusters of "democracy-capitalism," "socialism," and "it depends on" clusters. Obviously, that is how we slice our ideas of these political labels in the five countries. We share these, but we differ in what we like about each cluster.

The Americans are definitely enthusiastic supporters of democracy and capitalism, while the Japanese are "lukewarm" ("it depends on the situation") supporters of these ideals. The Germans are closest to the Americans in liking these two ideologies. The French are most socialistic, with the British being located near the French socialism position in the configuration. The Japanese alone proved most unenthusiastic toward all these ideals, though they are on the side of democracy and capitalism rather than socialism.

Shared Ways of Thinking

The ten series of questionnaire items we examined attest to the existence of our shared ways of viewing at least these ten dimensions of our attitudes. However, in all ten cases, we find that each nation finds itself alone or with others, and we did not discover any instance in which all five nationals are found in the same cluster.

Interrelations among Different Sets of Items

You recall the Aesop story of the hard-working ant and the idle grasshopper. A minority of the respondents (12 to 15 percent) in all five nations chose the tough position of not sharing any food with the grasshopper. The majority in all countries would give their food after telling the grasshopper to work hard next summer. How do these two responses to this question relate to responses to the items presented previously such as economic outlook, anxiety level, and views on science and technology? Are the respondents who took the tough position trusting, positive, and less money oriented? Do we find any common relations among all five nationals?

We found several common items associated with the former and the latter positions. We uncovered that the former who refused to share food are (1) money oriented, (2) distrustful of others, (3) alienated from community, and (4) lacking in positive social attitudes. The latter, who would share food with the grasshopper, are (1) low on anxiety, (2) satisfied with life, (3) likely to choose achievement as the reason for employment, (4) likely to attach importance to human relations, (5) likely to hold a positive outlook on life, (6) low on the scale of alienation, (7) for the paternalistic department chief over the rational department chief, and (8) not money-oriented.

Our findings suggest that in every nation we find two distinctively different peoples: (1) the people who are generally positive in their attitudes toward others in the society and have an optimistic outlook, are well integrated in the community, and attach less importance to material values; and (2) the people who are, by and large, negative in their outlook, worry, distrust others, are isolated, and are money oriented. The former constitute the majority and the latter the minority.

SUMMARY

The task of this chapter was to search for common values and ways of thinking that the Japanese share with the West. In so doing, we also demonstrated how each culture finds itself in different patterns even when the cultures share basic patterns of thought.

First, we discovered that the Japanese share their enduring predominant opinions, consisting of four items and nine current majority opinions, with the West to a large extent. These opinions deal with some basic human values, such as religiosity; the importance of human relations, compassion, fairness, truth, and beauty; the need for social reform; and social class identification.

Second, age and gender seem to have similar impacts on the Japanese and the Westerners, as evidenced in the results of cross tabulation between the demographics and seven items in the questionnaire. For example, the younger the respondents, the more optimistic they are in thinking that their standard of living will improve and the more they feel the need for government by the people. Conversely, the older the respondents, the more they have insomnia, the more religious they are, the more they are opposed to radical change, and the more strongly they support their political party. We also reported on items that were uniformly not affected by an age factor in the five nations.

We examined gender as an independent variable affecting various attitudes. The results show that sixteen out of over seventy-four items in the questionnaire are affected by gender regardless of culture. Keeping in mind that we did not control any other variable by keeping the rest of the possible factors constant, we found as follows: (1) Women have higher levels of anxiety (car accidents, war, and nuclear accidents) than men, (2) women know more ways of saving money in their family budget than men, (3) women are more inflicted with illnesses such as headaches, nervousness, depression, and insomnia than men, (4) men are less compassionate than women, (5) women consider family and children more important than men do, (6) men and women are equally satisfied with their family lives, and (7) men are more optimistic about the possibility of living in space in the future.

These findings suggest that age and gender may have similar effects on at least on some items of the industrialized world independent of culture. They certainly point to the fact that culture does not determine everything in society.

Third, our efforts focused on how we relate or associate a set of values to each other in different cultures. We uncovered ten sets of values (188 values in total ranging from 9 to 35 per set) that "hang together" basically in the same ways in the five cultures (Table 5.7). These values are found to be divided into either two or three common clusters in all cases, with minor exceptions. What these imply is that we categorize our life experience in very similar ways as far as these ten sets of values are concerned. In short, we all associate what we observe in the same manner.

Just because we categorize our life experience in the same way does not, however, guarantee that we all believe in the same values. In fact, we do not most of the time, as revealed in our analysis. Japan found itself most frequently—six out of ten cases—in the middle position and in "it depends on" clusters between two extreme clusters in relation to twice by FRG and once each by US and UK. The evidence favors the validity of our Rashomonesque Yamazakura model of the Japanese culture. The US and the UK were found very close to each other in the same cluster in three out of ten possible cases, suggesting a cultural linkage between the two cultures.

It is clear from these findings that each culture has some common elements but also possesses some unique dimensions. The evidence presented plainly disputes both those who claim that Japan is radically different from the West and unique, as well as those who insist that Japan is just like any other country on earth. Japan is unique in some basic ways that separate its culture from those of the West or its Asian neighbors, while it shares a number of thought patterns with others, as demonstrated in this chapter. Our position is that both the revisionists and antirevisionists have no sound rational and empirical basis for their assertions if they insist on the purity of uniqueness or universality.[17] We learned from Chapter 3 that Japanese opinions are also not very homogeneous, as alleged by some.

An inference we draw from these findings is that our culture is an intricate mix of values and ways of grasping reality and generating fantasy. It is not subject to casual generalizations, but it deserves careful observation, analysis, and inferences. By so doing, our objective is to come up with a useful model that helps explain why Japanese culture is the way it is.

NOTES

1. We regret that our comparative data are limited largely to Western Europe and the United States. The data used for our analysis were collected in the late 1980s, prior to the demise of the Cold War. Value changes that occurred as a result of the end of Cold War are not reflected in our analysis. Some data gathered in Brazil, Egypt, Jordan, and other countries are also included.

2. Findings reported in this chapter draw heavily from Tôkeisûrikenkyûjo (1991), pp. 71–340. The reader interested in examining the results of Hayashi's quantification method III and other multivariate analysis is asked to consult the Report. Detailed figures, graphs, and other data are presented in the Report in Japanese, with some parts in English.

3. The data sets used in Chapter 3 are not exactly the same as those presented in this chapter. Our focus was to use the comparative data sets gathered in only 1987 and 1988.

4. Taichi Sakaiya, a retired bureaucrat turned commentator on Japanese society, made an interesting observation when he wrote that Prince Shôtoku liberated the Japanese from religion. The last religious war ended during his regime. He established a seventeen-article constitution to promote interreligious harmony, including harmony between Shintôism and Buddhism, making it possible for the Japanese to believe in both faiths at the same time. He himself made contributions to both religions by such acts as the construction of the historic *Horyûji* (temple) in Nara (1994, p. 143).

5. We reversed the preference item for the Westerner. The percentages shown in Table 5.1 indicate those who chose the Western garden over the Japanese garden. We did so to achieve an equivalency in asking a common question across the four Western cultures.

6. Paternalism is used in the sense that the Japanese section head maintains personal relationships with his or her workers in such a manner that reciprocal relations prevail. The only difference between them is the hierarchical order observed by both sides. Such practices as gift exchange are reciprocal relation-ships in which the section head gives his or her workers just as much or even more than they give him or her. In other words, it is not a one-way system.

7. Our student surveys in Amman and Cairo suggest that this is not the case in the Arab world. The Arabs would not seek friendship in their workplace. They would say that they would go somewhere else to enjoy fellowship with others. They would not like to see any fraternization in the workplace. It is a place to work, not a place to enjoy friendship. They are very rational in this regard. In other words, the workplace is a secondary group, not a primary group. Our survey research was followed up by focused interviews in Arabic and English to find out why their responses are different from what we expected based on our past experience with Americans, Brazilians, Europeans, and Japanese.

8. Actually, there are more than nine items. However, we decided not to present them here since all those items dealt with such questions as whether or not one's family had to be careful in spending their money on vacation, food, beauty care, education, cigarettes, etc. We did not believe that these are significant items to be presented here in discussing the universality of culture since responses we receive probably depend more on particular economic conditions of each family and each nation at the time of survey than on their culture as such.

9. These figures are for the years around 1970 and are taken from Organization for Economic Cooperation and Development (OECD), as cited by McKean (1989), p. 202.

10. The reason for our fear of the Japanese misunderstanding the concept of individual freedom is based on our understanding of the Japanese self, as presented in Chapter 2. Likewise, we fear that the Western respondents failed to grasp the meaning of on used in the original Japanese questionnaire. The key here is what one includes in defining obligations in the West as opposed to what is customary in Japan.

11. A hypothesis is that Japan's efforts to Westernize the country since the Meiji period may have peaked after the energy crisis. On this point and other related hypotheses, see Kuroda, Hayashi, Suzuki, and Kuroda (1987).

12. The rate of natural children used to be one out of every ten babies in Meiji Japan. Today it is practically non-existent. Likewise, the rate of first-time offenders has decreased to about one-fifteenth of what it was at the turn of the century. The rate of divorce is one-third to one-half what it was at the turn of the century. On this and other related points, see Kuroda (1995).

13. Our concern is gender itself and not sexual orientation.

14. However, most cultures are male dominated, with more pressures to provide in general placed on men. Obviously, there may be other important factors operating to produce this difference between men and women. We need further studies to verify our hypothesis that the difference is a product of the physical make-up of men and women.

15. A set of questions has a common dimension along which a scalogram can be constructed successfully with 90 percent reproducibility (Young, 1956, p. 337 and the references therein).

16. See McKean (1989) and the references therein.

17. We realize that most revisionists as well as antirevisionists do not claim that Japanese culture is totally unique or completely the same as other cultures. Nevertheless, they often argue as if they deny the possibility of Japanese culture and other cultures being mixed types containing both common and unique characteristics.

CHAPTER 6

Unique Japanese Culture

Kozukatano oshironokusani nekorobite	Lying down on the grass by the Castle
Kozukata	
soranisuwareshi	My fifteen year-old mind is
jûgonokokoro	sucked into the sky

Takuboku Ishikawa

RASHOMONESQUE YAMAZAKURA: THE PAST AND THE PRESENT

The Japanese Self

Takuboku Ishikawa (1885–1912) died young. He was only twenty-six years of age, but he was one of the most sensitive Japanese poets ever to live. He left many poems that help us understand and appreciate the beauty and pathos of the world around us. Although he was born in 1885, his poems are strikingly similar to what our ancestors composed in the tradition of *yûrikon-kankaku*[1] (the concept/sense of the mind's separation from self/body) 1,100 years earlier. Earlier we cited Saigyô's poem about cherry blossoms. In that poem, his mind is absorbed, and he wonders if his mind will ever come back to his body after the cherry blossoms are blown away by the spring wind.

What an early American observer, Percival Lowell, discerningly calls the "Impersonality" in *The Soul of Far East* (1888), Hiroshi Minami (1983) talks about as the "uncertain Japanese self." Tetsuo Yamaori (1982) cites *yûrikon-kankaku* (separation of the mind from the body), Scott Matsumoto (1960) the "collective orientation,"[2] Yasumasa Kuroda (1974) the "absence of absolute ideology," Takie Sugiyama Lebra (1976) "social relativism," Bradley M. Richardson and Scott C. Flanagan (1984) "holism," Eishun Hamaguchi (1982) "contextualism," and Kinhide Mushakôji (1972) "adjusting culture." Taichi Sakaiya credits Prince Shôtoku as the first thinker in the world who liberated us from religion (1994, p. 143).[3] These authors are not the only ones to point out the lack of a well-developed autonomous self and absolute values in Japanese culture. All these concepts are related to one another in the sense that the Japanese do not have all-absorbing fixed beliefs of any sort and that the self is not really an independent salient unit. The self (the mind) can be floating in the air as the wind blows. If for any reason if it must go against the wind, it must do so as part of a group. Monotheism places a premium value on the belief in God, while Buddhism teaches the Japanese to free themselves of all worldly wishes.

Seeking nothing, one liberates oneself or himself from all concerns and finds peace. All these constitute an integral part of the Japanese mindscape, Rasho-monesque Yamazakura.

Our Yamazakura model posits that self is not the most salient and independent unit among the Japanese, while it is in American culture. Yamaori (1982, pp. 223–224) may be correct in his inference that the "underdeveloped self" in Japanese culture (in relation to American culture, that is) is traceable to the time of the *Kojiki* (712 A.D.), a legendary history of ancient Japan and the *Manyôshû* (759 A.D.), a collection of 4,500 ancient poems. Saigyô's poems, cited in Chapter 2 of this book, attest to his claim when one compares his poems with Takuboku's poems, one of which is cited at the outset of this chapter. The spirits of the Manyôshû were very much alive in the sensitive mind of Taku-boku. The only disagreement we have with Yamaori is that we do not consider the Japanese self as being underdeveloped as such; instead, it is well developed in its own diffuse form, as the American self (individualism) is well developed in its own format.

An implication is that the Japanese are less decisive in interpersonal relations and tend to shy away from making those choices likely to cause disagreements among people they know. This spirit of harmony and peace can be traced to Prince Shôtoku's seventeen-article Constitution, promulgated in 604.

In survey research, we sometimes include a neutral response or middle-response category, such as "depends on situation,"[4] "cannot say one way or another," and the like. We have decided to see if there is any difference between the Japanese and others in the frequency by which they choose a neutral response instead of a polar answer of "Yes" or "No." There are several studies cited here to make our point.

Ohajiki **survey**: A random sample of *Japan Times* readers was polled to answer this question in 1982. We provided them with five *ohajiki* (playing beads) and asked them to use the beads to indicate their answers on four questions that contained a neutral response.[5] They were asked to give zero or five for a polar answer and two, three, or four for the neutral response. The results as presented in Table 6.1 (see the Appendix for Chapter 6). Figure 6.1 in the Appendix for Chapter 6 indicates that the Japanese are more likely to choose the second or third beads than non-Japanese respondents. Obviously, non-Japanese respondents, mostly consisting of English-speaking Westerners, also use neutral responses but with much less frequency, no matter what a question might be, than the Japanese.

Cross-cultural survey: The first study was done in Japan. We decided to go further by analyzing eleven common questions that contained a neutral response category in questionnaires used for cross-national surveys conducted in Japan, the United States (including a Honolulu study), England, West Germany, and France in 1987 and 1988. The results of the analysis are summarized in Figures 6.2 and 6.3 in the Appendix for Chapter 6. Entries in Figure 6.2 indicate that the Japanese are more likely to use neutral responses when compared with Westerners. The Japanese on average chose neutral responses four to five times out of eleven questions, while Westerners did so only two to three times out of the eleven. The Americans, who have often been considered the most individualistic people in the world, are most decisive in choosing one or other polar response category rather than a neutral response. Americans were followed by the French, the British, and the Germans in order of frequency. Both Americans and the French are known for their strong sense of individualism.

The Study of Japanese Americans and Japanese Brazilians: How do Japanese Americans and Japanese Brazilians fare on this question in relation to the people of their ancestors and the people of their own country? Figure 6.3 presents an answer to this question. The figure shows that Japanese Americans are found between the Americans and the Japanese. Perhaps because of the heavy influence of Japanese and other Asian and Pacific cultures in Hawaii, non-Japanese Americans as a whole are located between the Americans at large and the Japanese Americans in Hawaii. Likewise, when we add the Japanese Brazilians to this discussion, we find that they are somewhere between the Americans and the Japanese, as expected. However, their percentage of not choosing any neutral response (approximately 25 percent) is about the same as the Americans. The only difference is that more of the Japanese Brazilians used neutral responses three, four, and five times than the Americans.[6] Japanese emigrants and their descendants seem to maintain the Japanese cultural heritage to the extent of preferring neutral responses over polar answer categories. Our finding that their preferences are between the people of their origin and those of the adopted countries precisely parallels the way we expanded the study of Japanese culture from the study of the Japanese in Japan to emigrants and their descendants in Honolulu and Brazil, followed by non-Japanese Americans in Honolulu and then eventually Americans at large in the United States as a whole. This resembles a chain reaction of a series of events triggered by the desire to know more about the Japanese themselves in relation to those with some cultural affinity and those with little cultural affinity.[7]

The Study of Japanese by Age and by Year: If this is indeed one of the basic dimensions of the Japanese culture, is it found less often among younger Japanese? Did it decline as Japan became industrialized and urbanized in the past half century? Answers to both of these questions are negative, as shown in Tables 6.2 and 6.3. The 1988 data was used to construct Table 6.2.

Entries in Table 6.2 suggest that age is not significantly related to the Japanese choosing middle-response categories. If there is any age-related trend, it is that younger Japanese avoid polar responses more than older Japanese people. Let us consider responses to three questions over the past forty years to see if there is any change (Table 6.3).

Table 6.2

Neutral Response by Age Group among Japanese

Age	0	1	2	3	4	5	6
20s	1%	3	8	15	16	16	17
30s	2%	3	9	16	17	18	17
40s	2%	3	10	15	18	19	13
50s	3%	8	10	17	18	12	14
60+	5%	10	13	16	16	15	12
Age	7	8	9	10	11	Total	#
20s	13	8	3	0	0	100	360
30s	8	6	3	1	0	100	438
40s	7	7	4	2	0	100	492
50s	8	6	2	1	1	100	453
60+	7	5	1	0	0	100	522

Table 6.3

Neutral Response by Year, 1953–1993

Item	1953	1958	1963	1968	1973	1978	1983	1988	1993
#2	19%	19	25	20	29	24	29	35	42
#4.10	7%	8	12	9	17	12	15	15	16
#7.1	17%	17	22	16	21	21	20	24	26

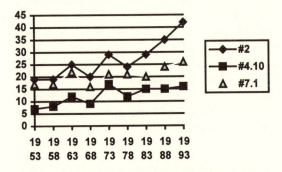

Answers to all three questions indicate a gradual increase in the use of the middle-response category, as entries in Table 6.3 demonstrate, in the range of 8 percent to about 15 percent in forty years. Although not shown, all eleven items examined indicate varying degrees of increases in the number of the respondents who selected middle-response categories over the forty years. Hence, if any-thing this proclivity of the Japanese for avoiding polar responses is not declining; in fact it is increasing. Furthermore, the Japanese as a whole tend to take less extreme positions on issues.[8]

Probability Preferred over Certainty: There are two comments on the safety of two airlines. The Japanese response to this question strongly suggests their preference for human ninjô over the promise of absolute safety.

> Please choose one of the two airline's statements with which you feel more agreeable. A: We have never had any serious accidents. As our records indicate, our planes are absolutely safe. B: We are well aware of the serious nature of air accidents whenever they occur. For this reason, we are doing our utmost to pay attention to even minute details so that there will never be any accident.

A high 93 percent chose Airline B, while only 6 percent selected Airline A. Approximately 90 percent of the Japanese, regardless of age and gender, prefers Airline B. They do not feel comfortable with anyone who makes a definitive statement. They apparently feel more comfortable with people who say they are doing what is humanly possible. This clearly suggests again the Japanese avoidance of extremes and their strong penchant for ambiguity. It is the world of probability they feel most comfortable with, for they know that there is nothing certain in human affairs. They feel more human warmth, ninjô, in the Airline B statement.

The Study of Japanese Culture, 1953–1993: Upon the development of our Rashomonesque Yamazakura model in 1994, we wanted to attempt to deny the validity of the model. We decided to subject responses to all opinion items asked in every survey from 1953 to 1993 to Hayashi's quantification method III to see if the results of analysis would invalidate the model.[9]

Thirty-two items met the criteria.[10] The results of the analysis are as follows: The first axis clearly separates modern from traditional and conservative responses, while the second axis isolates ambiguous responses found among the "modern" variables located in the lower right quadrant from decisive and rational answers in the upper right quadrant (Figure 6.4 in the Appendix for Chapter 6). Furthermore, an additional interpretation of the configuration is that diffuse-self and human-relations-oriented responses (ninjô [emotion]) are found in the lower left quadrant, and ambiguous and human-relations-oriented response of giri or obligation are in the lower right quadrant. As reported later in this chapter, the modern-traditional orientation has been breaking down. However, those items that are in disarray are items not related to human relations-oriented (giri-ninjô) questions. Those giri-ninjô-oriented responses and those responses not so oriented are clearly separated, and the basic configuration continues to appear in the data analysis. When all the longitudinal data are put into a group to be analyzed, apparently the modern-traditional attitudinal structure remains somewhat among the Japanese, despite its diminishing trend. This attitudinal structure developed in the past 100 years of modernization obviously is salient, but it cannot overshadow the importance of the giri-ninjô attitudinal structure and ambiguity pattern of the core of the Japanese culture, as proposed. Ambiguity and giri-oriented items are found among the "modern" variables, and the ninjô-oriented items are found in the upper left quadrant among the traditional items. In other words, modern-traditional orientation and items representing the Rashomonesque Yamazakura intermingle as a result of both being salient. More clearly discernible patterns of giri-ninjô and ambiguity constituting the Rashomonesque Yamazakura model appear in the third and fourth axes, decisively invalidating our null hypothesis that the core of Japanese culture is not related to the Rashomonesque Yamazakura. In short, the results of the data analysis using the thirty-two items repeatedly asked in the past forty years point to the validity of our model, the Rashomonesque Yamazakura.

Unless these six survey reports are incorrect, there must be something in the Japanese that makes them the way they are. Is it the Japanese "blood" or gene, as the Japanese chauvinists would answer?

THE CORE OF THE YAMAZAKURA: THE JAPANESE LANGUAGE

What is it about the Japanese that makes them appear ambiguous and nebulous? We already stated that this characteristic may have been a very important part of being a Japanese ever since the written language was developed in Japanese history. We knew from an earlier study of the Japanese Americans that the ability to use the Japanese language actively is the core of the Japanese American culture in Honolulu (The Research Committee on the Study of Honolulu Residents, 1980, pp. 53–63).

We have conducted a series of bilingual student surveys in Japan, the United States, and the Arab world (Cairo and Amman) to test our hypothesis that the language in use is what makes its speakers to respond the way they do as far as the predisposition to choose neutral response is concerned.[11] Our study revealed that indeed the Japanese students thinking in English behave almost as decisively as the Americans, and Americans reasoning in Japanese become not quite indecisive but much more ambiguous than when they are pondering how to answer questions in Japanese.[12] We found a similar trend among the Arab students. The nationality of students is not as consequential as the language they are using as far as this aspect of answering the survey questionnaire is concerned.[13]

Table 6.4 presents a summary result of the series of student surveys we conducted from 1985 through 1988 in Japan, the United States, Egypt, and Jordan with respect to the middle-response category by nationality and language.[14] Percentage entries in the table indicate the mean percentage of middle responses for five questions containing a middle-response category in the questionnaire.

Table 6.4

Neutral Response by Nationality and Language in Use

Nationality/ Language	Japanese in Japanese	Americans in Japanese	Japanese in English
Mid-response	57.8%	46.7%	34.3%
N	253	24	243
Nationality/ Language	Americans in English	Arabs in English	Arabs in Arabic
Mid-response	32.3%	31.9%	26.0%
N	335	539	552

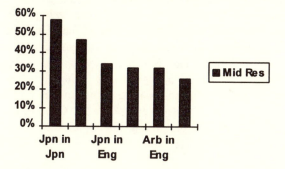

The Japanese students thinking in Japanese use the neutral response category at the rate of 58 percent, and Americans responding in Japanese 47 percent, Japanese in English 34 percent, Americans in English 32 percent, Arabs in English 32 percent, and Arabs in Arabic only 26 percent. The distance between English and Japanese languages appears to be greater than that of English and Arabic languages, whose written forms, share common origins and whose religious tradition is monotheistic.[15] As pointed out earlier, the partial correlation analysis of American and Japanese students indicated the highest correlation coefficients on three of the five items included in this analysis, with the language and the research site controlled (Kuroda, Hayashi, and Suzuki, 1986).

As exemplified in the old cliché "inscrutable Oriental," the Japanese are often said to be ambiguous in their communication with Americans. In contrast to this proclivity of the Japanese, a perceptive Palestinian scholar, Hisham Sharabi (1988, p. 86), characterizes the Arabic language as a decisive language. Classical Arabic language is decisive not only because of its religious background, but because it also imposes its own structures in all expressions.[16]

Hence we are unable to offer any alternative hypothesis other than to attribute the difference originally found between the Japanese respondents and the *Japan Times* readers, consisting of English-speaking non-Japanese, to the language in use. It is the language in use, not the Japanese blood as such, that makes the Japanese behave as they do, at least as far as their way of dealing with a choice of alternatives is concerned.

Our discovery of the Japanese language as the cause of the Japanese thinking did not stop at the middle-response category. We found very gratifying results in a three-way comparative quantification method III analysis (correspondence analysis) of American, Arab, and Japanese students in Arabic, English, and Japanese languages (Kuroda and Suzuki, 1991b). The first pattern separated traditional and rationalistic orientation from holistic and nondichotomous thinking orientation along the X axis. The Arabs thinking in Arabic were found in the logical/rationalistic orientation cluster, and Americans and Japanese responding to our questions in Japanese in the cluster of nondichotomous thinking (neutral responses). The second pattern separated contextualism or collective orientation and pessimism from individualism and optimism along the Y axis. All three nationalities thinking in English are found in the cluster of individualism and optimism, and Arabic and Japanese language groups are on the other side of the Y axis. We found three distinctive clusters elegantly separated by the three languages: Arabic language groups in the logical collective or binary contextualism cluster, English-speaking groups in the optimistic individualism cluster, and Japanese language groups in the ambiguous contextualism cluster. The nationality plays a part, but it is negligible in relation to the magnitude of the impact of the language on these respondents (specifically in the way they respond to our questions).[17]

The Japanese are thus non-linear-contextualism-oriented. The Americans are individualistic and somewhat logical/binary in thinking process, although not as much as Arabs. Arabs, too, are not as individualistic as the Americans. They place a premium value on their family and on religious groups to which they belong. However, they differ from the Japanese in not perceiving the workplace to be a secondary group situation, while the Japanese consider their place of work to be a very important primary group site (Kuroda and Suzuki, 1989a, 1991a). What Arabs and Americans share is their rationalistic thinking; that probably is attributable to Westerners learning two basic foundations of their civilization from the Arabs and Jews: monotheism and the written language. Japanese nonlinear contextualism may be traced back to Prince Shôtoku's contribution to the development of Japanese culture through such scholars as Saigyô, Norinaga Motoori, and Takuboku cited earlier. One way of viewing this Japanese characteristic is that the Japanese have developed a willingness to live with ambiguity from the point of view of the Western logical/rational paradigm. What the Japanese developed is a flexible system of employing an appropriate solution to problem solving depending on a particular situation, in accordance with the authority or otherwise prevailing opinions of a particular time in history. In this regard, we are in basic agreement with Ruth Benedict's *Chrysanthemum and the Sword* (1944) model of Japanese culture.

These two major findings from the three-language study are, therefore, in perfect agreement with our Rashomonesque Yamazakura model. First, the Japanese self is not a separate unit, as it is in American society, but it is an integral and inseparable part of a group. Second, the Japanese tend to shy away from dialectic or dichotomous ways of thinking. Thus, they believe that many questions defy a clear-cut binary answer of "Yes" or "No."

Will this generalization hold if we add European data to our comparison? We found ten common questions with a response category of "undecided" or "it depends on" in nationwide sample surveys conducted in 1987 and 1988 in France, the Federal Republic of Germany, Japan, the U.K., and the United States. We summarize our findings in Table 6.5.

Table 6.5

Ambiguity by Nation/Language

Item #/Nation	US (2265)	France (1013)	UK (1043)	FRG (1000)	Jpn (2265)
4.10: Adopt a child*	8.2%	9.6	11.9	24.0	30.5
7.1: Science & humanity	5.6%	7.0	6.6	13.2	39.3
4.5: Teach about money	4.1%	2.9	3.7	15.1	30.7
8.1b: Leave to politicians	3.0%	12.1	5.3	16.2	19.0
2.1: Custom *vs.* my way	9.5%	5.9	8.3	27.1	52.0
7.2: Mechanized society	3.5%	14.6	5.6	19.1	32.4
8.2e: Democracy	11.2%	17.2	22.1	11.0	37.7
8.2f: Capitalism	30.9%	36.9	37.5	43.2	48.3
8.2h: Socialism	32.2%	41.6	39.1	38.3	54.3
8.2g: Liberalism	43.6%	34.1	47.2	46.9	47.1
Range in percent	3–44%	3–42	4–47	11–47	19–54
Total percent	151.8%	181.9	187.3	254.1	391.3
Mean percent	15%	18	19	25	39

We found several interesting findings from entries in Table 6.5. First and most important, Europeans fall somewhere between the most binary-oriented Americans and ambiguous Japanese, with the French and British very close to Americans. The Japanese (39 percent) are more than twice likely to choose "undecided" and "it depends on" response categories than Americans (15 percent).

Second, the range of percentage differences among the ten questions within a nation varies around 40 percent among Americans, British, and the French, with Germans and Japanese differing within a 35 percent range.

Third, questions that attract relatively large "undecided" responses are the last two questions on socialism (Item 8.2h) and liberalism (Item 8.2g) among all nations. Although Americans and Japanese are far apart on the proclivity to choose an ambiguous response category, they both found it easiest to choose one or the other binary answer category for a question on politicians and democracy (Item 8.1b).

Thus far we have compared the Japanese with Americans, Arabs, and Europeans, who obviously have developed their civilizations apart from Japan. These civilizations have had little contacts with each other until recent centuries.[18] Let us add another point of comparison. China has had a continuous impact on Japan. The Japanese owe the Chinese for the development of their written language. Do Chinese and Japanese have similar concepts of work-place human relations? Our hypothesis is that the two countries are a world apart. The Chinese are rational, individualistic, and rational (logical), while the Japanese are not.

A comparative study of the Chinese and the Japanese conducted by Gordon Chu, Chikio Hayashi, and others at the East West Center in Honolulu found the responses shown in Table 6.6 when the researchers asked respondents in China and Japan to choose three most important criteria they would seek in their leaders (Hayashi, 1993, pp. 83–84).

Table 6.6

Chinese and Japanese Leadership Qualities

Chinese Leadership Criteria		Japanese Leadership Criteria	
Young and talented	82%	Experienced, senior, & respected	50%
Technically competent, superior	71%	Respected and liked by followers	46%
Decisive and firm	39%	Fair to all followers	41%
Beneficial (profitable) to followers	39%	Superior in judgment	36%
Fair to all followers	37%	Deals sincerely with co-workers	34%
Work seriously	33%	Sincere about work	32%
Sincere about work	33%	Known & excel in human relations	15%

The leadership quality sought by the Japanese centers around human relations values. A young and talented person whose leadership proved to be financially rewarding is not a very important criterion for the Japanese, but that is considered the most important single criterion among the Chinese. A Japanese leader is one who has technical skill and blends nicely among followers, who feel they are treated with dignity and sincerity.

Our 1993 longitudinal survey of the Japanese culture included a question derived from this cross-cultural study. The question asked was as follows:

What kind of qualities should a leader have in the workplace? Please choose the three most important qualities from the following:

1) Beneficial (profitable) to followers	(21%)
2) Respected and liked by followers	(77%)
3) Excel in technical skills	(47%)
4) Treat co-workers with sincerity	(69%)

5) Young and talented	(7%)
6) Adept in human relations and widely known	(49%)
7) Other (specify):_____	(8%)
DK (Don't Know)	(3%)
N	(1,905)

The Japanese define the workplace to be within the confines of primary group relations,[19] while the Chinese perceive and define the workplace as a rationally structured place to receive maximum profit for their labor, where the secondary group relations rules apply (Table 6.6). Arabs and Chinese seem to have something in common in this regard.[20] The application of the Hayashi's quantification method III analysis clearly separated the two peoples on this set of questions. The difference between the two peoples is exceptionally striking.[21] In fact, the difference is so clear that by knowing the respondents' answers to these questions, we could tell whether a respondent was a Chinese or a Japanese 88 percent of the time.

The Taiwanese respondents are found between the Chinese and Japanese when Hayashi's quantification method III is used. Perhaps half a century of Japanese colonization had some impacts on them. An alternative hypothesis is that the Taiwanese, many of whom came from Fuchian province, already possessed the characteristics different from those who reside in the Shanghai area.

The Chinese today are direct, logical and rational—"dry" from the Japanese perspective. The Chinese, at least in this regard, are very much like the Arabs and the Westerners. The self is a separate unit apart from a group.[22] The leader should stand above the group and be decisive and able. It is clear that the Chinese concept of self is closer to that of the Americans than to the Japanese. The Japanese are indirect and emotional by placing premium values on human relations. It is their belief that having good human relations in the workplace results in beneficial effects, not only for employees but also for the employer in the long run. This is precisely what the Rashomonesque Yamazakura model is all about. The objective of high productivity in a modern workplace is vague and diffuse as a consequence of the Japanese preoccupation with human relations or contextualism. Furthermore, Japanese workers are not specialized in any particular work. They move from one kind of work to another within a company as industries go through restructuring, thereby maintaining the life-time employment practice that became an established pattern of employment for large American corporations in the 1960s. When looking at the Japanese criteria for leaders, one gets a slight sense of their hope to increase productivity by working together harmoniously, as in Norinaga Motoori's response to the question of what is the Japanese mind.[23] What one gets from the Japanese is a fuzzy hint, not the clear, whole picture.

A new set of questions on self versus others was included in the 1993 survey to explore the question of self among the Japanese. The question asked was as follows:

Please rate the importance of each of the following, using 1 for the least
important and 7 for the most important issue in your life:
a) First, how do you rate the importance of your "family and children"?
b) How about "job and work"?
c) What do you think about "free time and relaxation"?
d) What do you think about your "friends and acquaintances"?

The results reported in Table 6.7 suggest that the Japanese self (26 percent)
is lower in priority to the family and children (75 percent), job and work (37
percent), and finally friends and acquaintances (34 percent). An assumption here
is that the desire for free time and relaxation represents a self-gratification value,
while others represent a series of human relation networks within which a self is
located. The Japanese self exists, but its importance in relation to others is much
less, to the point that it sets the Japanese apart from the Americans or Chinese.

Table 6.7

Important Values

Item #	1	2	3	4	5	6	7	8 Other	9 DK	Total
a)	1	1	1	4	8	10	75	0	0	100%
b)	1	1	4	14	18	21	37	0	2	98%
c)	0	2	6	21	24	20	26	0	1	100%
d)	0	1	3	13	22	26	34	0	0	99%

We present one last finding based on a question we could not ask in other
countries. There was an item Hayashi and his colleagues wanted to have
translated and included in the survey to be conducted in Hawaii in the 1970s.
The reason Kuroda advised that the question was inappropriate should be clear
to readers, as the following English translation of the question will show:

Suppose there was an air crash. Which of the following two responses would
be a better action for the airline president to take?
1) To visit all the families of the crash victims to apologize[24]
2) To devote his efforts to investigating the causes of the crash and other things

We found that a majority or at least a plurality of the Japanese, irrespective
of gender, age, and level of formal education, would recommend that the airline
president go apologize (Hayashi, 1993, p. 85). In the 1973 survey, 50 percent of
the respondents chose the former (apologize) and the latter 40 percent; in 1978
the figures were 51 percent and 41 percent, respectively. A larger percentage of
the Japanese would prefer to have the airline president apologize first, no matter
what. In other words, the maintenance of human relations has the highest
priority.[25] The question of guilt or responsibility is not as paramount a concern
as the necessity of maintaining good relationships with Japanese clients.

As pointed out in our cross-national surveys of three language groups, the Japanese are different from Americans and Arabs, although they become almost identical in their thinking when they are responding in English. Arabs are less individualistic than the Japanese are, but Arabs are diametrically opposed to the Japanese in their decisive, definitive, and less ambiguous thinking. We found in the survey of France, Japan, the U.K., the United States, and West Germany that Europeans by and large lie somewhere between Americans and Japanese on the question of ambiguity. Furthermore, the leadership study of Chinese and Japanese people suggests strongly that the Japanese are not as rational and individualistic as the Chinese are. Being fuzzy, ambiguous, indirect, and nondialectic or nonbinary by not taking any polar position, refusing to accept an independent and separate self, espousing a self diffuse with others in a group to the point that it cannot be separated from others (contextualism over individualism), and emphasizing the importance of human relations are what constitute the core of the Japanese culture, the Rashomonesque Yamazakura model.

OTHER JAPANESE CHARACTERISTICS

Each culture has a unique core of its implicit and explicit design for living. We have been discussing what we consider basic features of Japanese culture. We now go beyond them to see how Japan might be different from other cultures on less important dimensions. The first study discussed deals with a comparative analysis of American, French, and Japanese respondents.[26]

Comparison of Americans, French, and Japanese on the Quality of Life Issues

The study is divided into two levels of analysis. First, it represents our efforts to present several findings graphically by using a number of items in the questionnaires that relate to the quality of life in order to capture a general picture of what these three nationalities are like in relation to each other. We used Hayashi's minimum dimension analysis, specially designed nonparametric data to analyze the three-nation study data (1976). We present our findings in a summary format in Figure 6.5 in the Appendix for Chapter 6.

First, the French, the Japanese, the local Honoluluans, and Honoluluans who hail from the mainland are markedly different from one another. Although all Honoluluans live in a relatively small geographic urban section of the island of Oahu, it is amazing how different the local people are from the mainlanders who settled in the paradise. The Japanese Americans and other ethnic Honoluluans are very much alike and located in the middle between the Japanese and the mainland Americans. In fact, they are closer to the Japanese than to the mainland Americans as far as this data analysis is concerned.

Second, each nationality is characterized by a set of factors. The French (especially Parisians) are sensitive to noise pollution and are liberal in their attitudes toward divorce, which is diametrically opposite the traits of the local Honolulu population. The Japanese are home oriented and worry a lot about traffic and job-related accidents. The Tokyoites are closer to the French in relation to the Japanese in general. The local Honoluluans worry too, but what they worry about is different from the Japanese in that they were concerned with street crime, the high cost of living,[27] and the possibility of nuclear war breaking out.[28] They are also traditional when it comes to their concept of marriage, and they do not take divorce lightly. Their neighbors from the U.S. mainland are more concerned with values that are often associated with a postindustrial era, such as energy saving, the environment, and women's roles, to values the Japanese are not terribly sensitive to, such as housework being the task of both men and women. The Japanese are found to be exactly opposite from the mainland Honolulu voters, who are concerned with environment, development, and individual welfare.

Further analysis of the same data set by using Hayashi's quantification method III analysis revealed that the Japanese are positive in general toward their economic outlook and maintain a traditional family orientation. The French are negative in their economic outlook but very modern in their outlook on family. Americans (Honoluluans) are most positive on all accounts and are modern, but not as much in their views on family life (The Research Committee on the Study of Honolulu Residents, 1986, pp. 123–128).

Comparison of the French and Japanese on the Quality of Life Issues

By using the same set of the items included in the American, French, and Japanese comparative analysis cited previously, Hayashi (1992b) reports the results of his quantification method III analysis on Japanese and French respondents. Hayashi et al. found that the first pattern for the Japanese data was the middle-response dimension and the second pattern the positive-negative dimension, while the French data was reversed in the order of importance (i.e., the positive-negative first and then the middle-response pattern). This reconfirms the validity of our Rashomonesque Yamazakura model of the Japanese culture. Furthermore, when we examined the third pattern, we found that positive patterns on health, for example, were isolated from positive patterns on science among the French. Each area of concern was clearly either positive or negative and varied from one area to another regarding its positive or negative responses. The Japanese, on the other hand, are found to be positive in general but are not clearly divided into positive and negative responses. Again what we see is that the Japanese tend to remain unclear from the Western perspective.

Table 6.8

Frequency Distribution of Responses on Life and Work Items by Nation

Item #	Question Item	Response Category	Jpn %	US %
#2.2B	2 personality types	1 Principle first	44	48
		2 Interpersonal harmony	50	46
#2.4	Way of life	1 Get rich	14	07
		2 Become famous	02	06
		3 Suit one's own taste	39	36
		4 Cheerful and worry free	22	36
		5 Pure and just life	11	10
		6 Serve society	07	02
#2.8	Continue or	1 Continue to work	69	67
	stop working	2 Stop working	25	27
#5.1	Benefactor versus	1 Go back home	51	64
	Business meeting	2 Go to the meeting	42	29
#5.1C-1	Employment	1 The highest grade	71	72
		2 Your relative	23	22
#5.6H	Friendly vs.	1 Friendly but inefficient	72	65
	Efficient co-worker	2 Efficient but aloof	11	23
#8.10	Job objectives	1 A good pay	07	15
		2 No risk of unemployment	23	18
		3 Work with people you like	30	14
		4 Feel of accomplishment	38	52
Response		Number	2,032	1,322

Comparison of Japanese and Americans on the Preferred Way of Life and Work

Suzuki's analysis of the 1978 American and Japanese survey data sets at the Institute of Statistical Mathematics in Tokyo on the attitudes toward work and the preferred way of life consisted of eleven items and revealed considerable similarities between the two industrial powers in the world as far as the frequency distribution of responses to the eleven questions are concerned (1984).[29] However, there are differences revealed in the results of his data analysis (quantification method III). These items deal with the preferred way of life and the attitude toward work, two things each person experiences in the industrialized world today.

As percentages in Table 6.8 demonstrates, Americans and Japanese are remarkably similar in their choice of the preferred way of life and work attitudes. There are no real large percentage differences in responses between them. The differences are moderate to nonexistent. The largest percentage difference is found on Item #8.10 regarding job objective. A high 30 percent of the Japanese chose the third response of working with people they like, while only 14 percent of the Americans did so. A 12 to 14 percent difference between the two nationalities is observed on additional questions as well, (#2.4-4, #5.1-1, #5.1-2, #5.6H-1, #5.6H-2, and #8.10-4). The last three items have to do with human relations. Responses to #5.1 relates to the Japanese concept of giri we discussed earlier.[30] These differences are probably caused by the American preoccupation with individualism and the Japanese obsession with contextualism or human relationism, both of which we claim to be the core of American and Japanese cultural values, respectively—the monotheistic individualist model and the Rashomonesque Yamazakura model. On the whole, however, we must conclude that the differences found are minimal and that Americans and Japanese on the surface appear to share many values. Most public opinion survey reports published in newspapers and magazines in the United States do not go beyond the reporting of percentage differences and, at most, some demographic attributes for the differences found.[31] Suzuki's report went beyond superficial analysis by using Hayashi's quantification method III analysis.

The horizontal axis for the Japanese data set clearly separates what Suzuki calls the "old" values in the upper right quadrant from "new" values in the lower left quadrant in the configuration.[32] The tightly grouped upper right cluster consists of those who selected the following response categories: living cheerfully without worrying (2.4-4), no risk of unemployment (#8.10-4), working with people you like (#8.10-3), maintaining interpersonal harmony (#2.2B-2), and leave everything and go back home to see the benefactor rather than to attend the company meeting (#5.1).

The less tightly linked lower left quadrant cluster is made up of the following response categories: act according to principle (#2.2B-1), living a life that suits your own taste (#2.4-3), a job which gives a feeling of accomplishment (#8.10-4), and go to the company meeting even if the benefactor is gravely ill (#5.1-2). By examining these two sets of clusters, we would prefer to call these two clusters contextualism or human-relations-oriented individualism, respectively, in accordance with our Rashomonesque Yamazakura model. The former cluster essentially consists of items that place primary importance on interpersonal relations, while the latter cluster places priority on the feeling of one's achievement, living in accordance with one's own taste—individualism.

Suzuki found that the X axis clearly separates the two types of values, while it does not do so for the American data set. However, the X or the horizontal axis for the American data does not discriminate against the same set of answers. Suzuki discovered the human relations cluster not in the upper right quadrant, but in the upper left quadrant, and the individualism cluster in the lower right quadrant. In other words, the American configuration is tilted clockwise by about 60 degrees in relation to the Japanese configuration, but the extent of interrelation among the variables is remarkably similar to the Japanese data set (i.e., both Americans and Japanese, who prefer a person emphasizing the importance of "interpersonal harmony," also stress the value of "working with people you like").

Suzuki's further analysis revealed that those who are "human relations oriented" tend to be both Americans and Japanese with less education and women over men. However, the difference is that age is as important a factor as education in making younger Japanese believe more in individualism. This is not so for the Americans, among whom the level of education and gender, not age, is a discriminating factor. These two findings may represent the success of the American occupational goal of educating the Japanese to emulate the American model of democracy based on individualism. The two findings certainly suggest a curriculum resemblance between the two nations among younger Japanese, but not older generations. However, these changes are constrained by the continuing use of the Japanese language and the existing social institutions.

We learn from Suzuki's analysis that the human relations cluster of values and the individualism cluster of values constitute two analytically separate and competing systems of values for the Japanese. These two clusters in the American configuration are not separate but interdependent. They constitute the majority view of the Americans since their response categories are found tightly clustered close to the point of origin.

The second part of Suzuki's analysis deals with six additional items designed to depict the "traditional" and "modern" Japanese cultural values selected from the longitudinal Japanese culture study series (*Nihon kokuminsei chôsa*). Unlike the last eleven items, for which we found so much similarity in frequency distribution of responses between the two nations, what Suzuki reports is a set of items to which Americans and Japanese responded differently, as Table 6.9 indicates.

Second (#2.5), the question on man and nature is designed to separate the Industrial Age person from the postindustrial age person. The first response category of following nature is in a sense a pre industrial era values that could also be interpreted as post industrial values. The second answer category of using nature represents either the late industrial or the early post industrial value. The third one definitely represents early industrial era values. There is no majority opinion among the Japanese, while the second response is the majority view of the Americans (65 percent). The second answer of using nature is the plurality opinion among the Japanese, with 44 percent. The Japanese are more divided in their views, while there is a consensus in American that nature should be used, but is certainly no longer to be conquered. Our impression of Americans and Japanese people is that Japanese are more consumed by nature than the Americans as a whole. For example, an American viewing Japanese television programs would be shocked by the amount of attention the Japanese pay to nature—mountains, the weather, birds, insects, flowers, trees, and rivers. We are certain that any content analysis of Japanese television programs will find that the Japanese are more nature sensitive than the Americans. In other words, nature occupies a more important part of Japanese life than it does for Americans.

Table 6.9

Frequency Distribution of Responses to Traditional-Modern Items by Nation

Item #	Questionnaire Item	Response Category	Jpn %	US %
2.1	Custom vs. Right thing to do	1 Go ahead and do right	30	76
		2 Depends on. . . .	24	5
2.5	Man and nature	1 Man must follow nature	33	25
		2 Man must use nature	44	65
		3 Man must conquer nature	16	5
4.4	Rumor about teacher	1 Deny the rumor	27	3
		2 Tell the truth	57	85
4.5	Teaching children that money is the most important thing	1 Agree	45	5
		2 Undecided	13	1
		3 Disagree	40	94
5.6	Preferred type of supervisor	1 Impersonal but rule abiding	10	47
		2 Personal but demanding	87	50
8.1	Leave everything to good political leaders	1 Leave everything to them	32	8
		2 Discuss among the people	58	89
	No. of respondents		2,032	1,322

Third (#4.4), the question is on the teacher who gets in trouble. As a part of the Japanese giri or respect (in this instance for the teacher), one should deny the story as a rumor to children even if the story was true. However, just as any child in the United States sooner or later learns that there is no Santa Claus who literally comes down the chimney on Christmas, so the same would be for Japanese children. Honesty is another value Japanese parents must teach their children. Historically, the percentage of the Japanese who say one should tell the truth has been increasing from 42 percent in 1953 to 62 percent in 1988 and 59 percent in 1993. It used to be a plurality who favored telling the truth, but today it has become a majority viewpoint. In other words, the Japanese are shifting toward the direction of the American value system in this regard. The old giri toward the teacher seems to be on its way out, gradually.

Fourth (#4.5), is a question that is not a question in the United States, where a consensus exists that one should not teach a child that money is the most important thing in life (94 percent). Only 5 percent of the Americans would teach their children that money is the most important thing, as opposed to a plurality of the Japanese consisting of 45 percent. This too is an item that has changed over time. A large 65 percent of the Japanese in 1953 thought they would teach their children the supreme value of money. Since then the percentage has plummeted to 35 percent by 1993. Obviously, the reason for this change is related closely to the economic well-being of the Japanese today in relation to what the situation was like in 1953 after the disastrous war. Life was tough. When people do not have enough money to live, money becomes important since it enables a person to survive. As people become rich enough to eat and clothe themselves, money becomes less significant. The Japanese are fast moving toward the American value system in this regard.

The fifth item (#5.6) asks the respondent to choose a supervisor from two distinctively different types of supervisors: a rational supervisor, who goes by the book and never makes any unreasonable demands but at the same time never shows any interest in the personal affairs of his worker, and a paternalistic supervisor, who makes unreasonable demands at times but also takes good care of his workers beyond the call of his duty. The question essentially is if we should consider the workplace to be governed by the rule of what sociologists call primary group relations or secondary group relations.

Opinion in the United States is divided almost evenly, while the Japanese favor including the workplace to be under the rule of primary group relations. An extremely high 87 percent of them preferred the paternalistic supervisor over the rational supervisor. Unlike the items discussed so far, the Japanese have not changed at all on this question for the past forty years. They are not getting any closer to the way the American value system in this regard. Why? Our answer is the Rashomonesque Yamazakura model. The Japanese consider the workplace as an extension of family. The Japanese have managed to keep the sense of alienation low despite Japan's rapid industrialization and urbanization by developing this strong sense of identity with the workplace. Indeed, the Japanese replaced their national anthem, which they used to sing during World War II at the start of each workday, with the company song.

Sixth (#81), one of the key concepts the United States attempted to instill in the mind of the Japanese was American democracy following demilitarization, the idea that the government must be by the people and not just for the people. The item states "If we get good political leaders, the best way to improve the country is for the people to leave everything to them, rather than for the people to discuss things among themselves." The percentage of the people who agree with the proposition has been declining, while the percentage of those who disagree with the proposition has been rising. Unfortunately, the original response categories have been altered in 1978, which makes it difficult to compare the results of the question before and after 1978. The original item had four answer categories: (1) Agree, (2) It depends on circumstances, (3) Disagree, and (4) Cannot imagine such an outstanding politician would ever surface. The second and fourth response categories have been eliminated since 1978. However, the data between 1953 and 1973 show that those who agree with the proposition has declined from 43 percent in 1953 to 23 percent in 1973. At the same, time there was a corresponding rise in the percentage of respondents who disagreed with the proposition, from 38 percent in 1953 to 51 percent in 1973.

Despite the changes noted prior to 1978, the Japanese have not reached the enthusiasm for the government-by-the-people theory of the Americans. A majority or 58 percent of the Japanese support the idea, but a vast 89 percent of the Americans espouse the concept, with only 8 percent dissenting. About one-third of the Japanese still disagree with the proposition.

What we see here is that on those items for which changes over time are noted, all of the Japanese views are becoming similar to those of the Americans, suggesting the validity of convergence theory. All industrial nations sooner or later will develop a similar set of values and institutions.[33] Of the six questions examined here, five favor the notion of convergence as far as frequency distribution analysis is concerned. The only item that is going the way of divergence is the one on supervisor personality types. These superficial examinations give us the impression that Americans and Japanese are eventually going to be very much alike. As Suzuki has done, we need to go deeper into the attitudinal structure of the Americans and Japanese to see how they organize these values even if the Japanese views may be growing closer to the American views.

Suzuki combined the first eleven variables with six additional items we just described to perform Hayashi's quantification method III analysis. The analysis yielded the following results: First, the first horizontal axis successfully separated the traditional values from the modern values among the Japanese, but not the Americans. However, a 60 degree rotation of the American configuration clockwise indicates a similarity in the extent of interrelation among all the variables. Second, Suzuki found that the traditional values are more likely held by women, older persons, and those with less formal schooling among the Japanese. In the United States, however, the single most discriminating variable was the level of education. These findings suggest that (1) Americans are no longer changing, while the Japanese are still changing or being modernized. Hence, age is an important variable affecting their attitudes with respect to the traditional versus modern values. (2) Women's rights are far more advanced in the United States than in Japan, even if women in the United States believe their position leaves much to be desired. (3) Education certainly is a vehicle through which modernization proceeds in both countries.

Third, there is a definite competing set of values between the traditional and modern among the Japanese, while there is none among the Americans. Even from the frequency distribution table (Table 6.9), we can infer that all but one question yielded the results in which a large majority opinion exists; 76 percent would go ahead with their own idea, 65 percent chose to utilize nature, 85 percent would tell the truth about the teacher in trouble, 94 percent would not teach children that money is most important, and 89 percent would not leave everything for good politicians to decide. On all these items, with the notable exception of the fifth item (on the supervisor), a strong sense of consensus exists among the Americans. There is a consensus because the Americans are no longer modernizing but going beyond modernization. Fourth, another point of difference is that the Japanese configuration suggests the existence of a third cluster independently from the traditional and modern clusters—that is, response categories consisting of work-related items (#2.8, #5.1C-1, #4.6, and #5.6H). In the words of Suzuki, "in the individual's attitude toward work in Japan there are no specifically 'new' or 'old' outlooks" (Suzuki, 1984, p. 94). In our view, these items are independent of being either traditional or modern because they touch on human relations, the core of the Japanese cultural values, the Rashomon-esque Yamazakura model, which has not changed much in essence over a thousand years even if its manifestations or forms may have changed.

We agree with Suzuki's conclusion that there is not much evidence for the validity of convergence theory even if there are some areas of convergence between Americans and Japanese in values at the level of frequency distribution and some clustering of variables.

Comparison of the Americans, British, French, Germans, and Japanese on Science

Table 6.10

Positive Attitudes toward Science

Item	American %	British %	French %	German %	Japanese %
Improve daily life	61	50	33	37	48
Computer	34	16	32	15	31
Modern medicine	72	76	62	77	72
Understand mind	58	50	65	34	14
Solve problems	47	43	49	44	15
Dispose nuclear waste	32	34	28	17	33
Discover cancer cure	62	64	68	37	65
Cure senility	25	12	23	17	29
Life in space	41	33	23	36	19
Total %	432	378	383	314	326
Mean %	48	42	43	35	36

We used nine questions concerning various aspects of science (See the Appendix for Chapter 1) to see if Japanese are any different from Westerners on their views on science and its impact on our lives. Table 6.10 summarizes our findings.

Entries in Table 6.10 represent percentages of the respondents who answered positively to the nine questions on science (i.e., science is useful in improving daily life, the computer age is desirable, some illnesses can be cured through the use of modern medicine, science can eventually read the minds of people, social and economic problems can be solved by the development of science, and the following will be possible in the next twenty-five years: (1) the safe disposal of nuclear wastes, (2) a cure for cancer, (3) cure for senility, and (4) life in space.

American optimism is unmatched even in the field of science. The most enthusiastic supporters of scientific civilization are Americans, followed closely by the British and the French, as indicated by the mean percentages for positive responses to science. Germans and Japanese respondents are not as optimistic and positive about the benefit of science to them as the other three nationalities.

The Japanese by and large are positive in the field of progress in physical science toward medical science (72 percent) and a cure for cancer (65 percent) and senility (29 percent). However, they are least optimistic about the successful application of scientific discovery to analyze the mind of people (14 percent) and the society (15 percent), and to live in space (19 percent). The last three items deal with human relations, considered crucial in understanding the core of Japanese culture.

Comparison of German and Japanese on Nature

This is derived from several studies on the attitudes toward nature conducted in German and Japanese cities: Freiburg, Neunburg, Tokyo, and Miyasaki (Japan-Germany Collaborative Study, 1977, and Shidei and Hayashi, 1984). The studies revealed that the Japanese are divided. Those who do not believe in the sacredness of mountains and forests and the need for humans to maintain and take care of forests through various conservation programs are found within one cluster, and those who like and believe in the sacred nature of forests and non-intervention in forests by humans in another cluster. The Germans, on the other hand, are found to combine their love for forests, the sacred nature of forests, and the need for humans to take care of the forests in one cluster. The Germans appear to be more realistic since no forests can be maintained without some degree of human care in this day and age. Another bit of interesting information is that when the Japanese are shown pictures of well-managed forests and virgin forests without human care, they like the forests well taken care of by humans over others. However, the same people insist that humans should not interfere with nature, an apparent contradiction from the logical or rational viewpoints.

Comparison of the American, British, French, German, and Japanese on Nine Items

Responses to nine items were divided into three categories of positive, middle, and negative responses: (1) orientation toward money, (2) trust-distrust orientation, (3) ideological orientation (capitalism, democracy, socialism and liberalism), (4) future economic outlook, (5) anxiety level, (6) family orientation (modern-traditional), (7) respect for ancestor, (8) health, and (9) science (Hayashi, 1993, pp. 88–90). A series of quantification III analyses performed on these eleven items among all five nationalities brought to light the following:

1. The Americans are respectful of ancestors, positive toward the development of science and technology, not money oriented, and are found to be in the middle as far as their family orientation is concerned.
2. The British are money oriented and found in the middle of all other four nationalities and on all other items are almost equal distance from all four.
3. The French are distrustful of other people, favor a socialist economy, are pessimistic in their economic outlook, are high on their anxiety level, and are dim in their attitude toward health.
4. The Germans are modern in their family orientation, do not respect their ancestors much, and are negative on the outlook for the development of science and technology.
5. The Japanese are trustful of others, preferring neither capitalistic democracy nor socialist economy, not are religious but think religion is important, take a middle position on economic outlook, and are low in their levels of anxiety.

Here again, we are struck by the Japanese penchant for the middle position in general and the priority placed on human relations in comparison to four Western nationalities.

SUMMARY

First, we learned that the Japanese tend to avoid polar answers and choose an ambiguous or a middle-response category, while the Westerners were decisive and were less likely to select a nonpolar neutral response.

Second, the results of the analysis of the thirty-two items repeatedly asked from 1953 through 1993 invalidated our null hypothesis. The items associated with the Rashomonesque Yamazakura model did merge as salient patterns, attesting to the validity of the model.

Third, we discovered that it was not so much the nationality but the language in use that affects our respondents' penchant for an ambiguous response. Of course, the extent of influence varied by items in question as well as by nationality to some extent, but it was far more of a determining factor than nationality. When the Westerners were asked in English to use ohajiki (playing beads) to indicate their opinions, it was obvious that they were thinking in their mother tongue, English and other European languages.

Fourth, the Arabs are most constrained by their mother culture by not changing their response pattern when they switch from thinking in Arabic to English; the Americans are next and the Japanese last. The Japanese switch their mindscape almost totally, from a Japanese cap to the American baseball cap, as if they are totally different persons. Indeed, as Mushakôji (1972) puts it so fittingly, the Japanese culture is the culture that adjusts, *awase no bunka*."

Fifth, our quantification method III analysis results indicate that the choice for the middle (ambiguous)-response category does not mean that the Japanese take a middle-of-the-road position on an issue at hand, but suggest that the Japanese are approaching the choice of alternatives from a nonlinear, nondialectic paradigm that constitutes its own cluster in relation to both those who said Yes and No in the configuration. In this sense, none of the middle-response categories represent a neutral or a middle-response category answer, but rather they denote a paradigm that says that the nature of a question defies a dichotomous response.

Sixth, in addition to the Japanese difference, with the Americans and the Japanese thinking in English regarding the middle-response category, we found that the Japanese and the Arabs are pessimistic and not individualism oriented. The American and the Japanese thinking in English, in particular, and to some extent the Arabs thinking in English are both individualistic and optimistic. In short, we found the second difference between the Japanese and the Americans—namely, the Americans are individualist oriented. We realize that this is hardly a new discovery. However, what is different from many who made a similar generalization is that it is American English that performs the trick. The Japanese are just as individualistic and optimistic as Americans if they are thinking about a question in English. China, both Koreas, India, and many other countries after World War II have produced charismatic leaders that stood out from the crowd, from Sigman Lee and Mao Tse-Tung in East Asia to Gamal Abdul Nasser in Egypt. Japan, which places less emphasis on any particular individual, has not produced anyone close to Mao in stature. Japan, thus, must be different from China in this regard.

Seventh, a comparative analysis of the Chinese and the Japanese normative concept of leadership strongly suggests again that the Japanese self is considerably different from the Chinese self. The Chinese are very individualistic and rationally oriented, while the Japanese are human relations oriented in contextualism par excellence. The study of the airline accident question reconfirms the leadership study conclusion.

Eighth, these basic characteristics of the Japanese culture are preserved by Japanese emigrants and their descendants to some extent and constitute a midposition between the American culture or Brazilian culture at large and the Japanese culture.

Ninth, on several sets of value orientation items, we found that the Japanese find themselves in a diametrically opposite position in relation to the mainlanders living in Honolulu on such values as spouses sharing household work, concern for the environment, and postindustrial values. The Americans who settled in Honolulu are most likely to better educated and enjoy higher incomes than Americans at large, which may account for this difference and not a difference between Japan and the United States. The Japanese, on the one hand, are most home-bound in that they can relax best at home, but their views on divorce are not as traditional as the local population, including Japanese Americans in Honolulu, who are found in a diametrically opposite position in relation to Parisians (who are most liberal on the divorce issue). The Japanese and the local population in Honolulu are concerned more with mundane problems of crime, traffic, and accidents. The French are most sensitive toward noise pollution.

Tenth, American optimism and Japanese pessimism extend to their views on science and its beneficial effects on people. The Japanese view of nature in relation to the German is unrealistic. The Japanese simply love nature as it is without trying to find out how to keep nature the way we all idealize it—lush, green, filled with healthy-looking trees (an impossible scene without the intervention of humans to maintain the forest). The Japanese are trustful of other people and neutral on ideological questions and economic outlook in relation to Americans and Europeans. The Japanese are money oriented, but not as much the British, while Americans are least money sensitive, at least normatively speaking.

Eleventh, even where an apparent similarity exists in frequency distribution between American and Japanese respondents, further analysis by quantification method III revealed structural differences between the two nationalities. The Japanese, for example, used to view traditional values as a competing set of values with modern values, while Americans do not. In a way, the Americans are not traditional at all from the Japanese perspective. Another difference that lies beyond the frequency distribution analysis is that attributes for modern values are different between Americans and Japanese respondents. In other words, causes of their beliefs are not the same in the United States and Japan. Gender, for example, may be a possible causal factor in one country but not necessarily in the other country.

There are considerable similarities between Americans and Japanese in their preferred way of life and work attitudes, a difference that appears when a question concerns the place of an individual in a society in the two countries, suggesting the basic difference between Americans and Japanese with respect to their concept of self and society. Suzuki's study (1984) concludes by saying that the two nations have not converged in values and their structures to any significant extent as they approach the end of the twentieth century.

Significance and Implications

What do all these findings mean? First, we conclude that empirical evidence presented in a clean manner confirm the validity of our Rashomonesque Yama-zakura model of the Japanese culture. The core of the Japanese culture consists of ambiguity (Rashomonesque) or, at least, nonbinary thinking in relation to the American way of thinking and diffuse self (Yamazakura). Perhaps the Kuroda-Suzuki study of Arab, American, and Japanese students most elegantly and graphically presents this point (Kuroda and Suzuki, 1991a).

Second, the Japanese cultural core is deeply ingrained in its language, which influences its speakers to perceive and structure reality from a different perspective than English language does. The Japanese do not view things from the perspective of should one believe or not, accept or reject, good or bad, and the like. Rather, they structure their reality from the perspective of how and where one can place what one sees into their system of the total world, a radically different means of thinking from the individual-centered and rational mode of reality-grasping processes.

In addition to the language in use, which appears to affect the basic way in which the Japanese structure their reality, their religious beliefs are entrenched in the language they use on a daily basis. For example, such a frequently used expression as *arigatô* (thank you) is derived from Buddhism.

We are drafting this chapter as the Japanese annual obon season begins in August. The obon is the biggest annual event for nearly all Japanese, the time to remember their deceased relatives and loved ones. Obon is derived from *ullambana*, the Sanskrit. The original meaning of the word is "hanging upside down." It is the time to reverse the order of priority from self-centered "me-firstism" to being an integral part of all things in the world. The teaching of the Buddhist sutras is certainly in keeping with the Japanese self we have been describing.

Another way of describing the Japanese culture is that it is liberated from all forms of absolute beliefs of a religious and political nature including monotheism. Unlike Confucian Chinese or the Islamic Judeo Christian paradigm, it lacks a systematic thought system. The Japanese adopted only portions of Confucianism, rejecting the concept of mandate of heaven, an absolute belief. The Japanese culture is nebulous, unsystematic, chaotic, and contradictory without the center of one's own world since the concept of individual as the salient unit is absent. However, the Japanese way of doing things makes perfect sense if one learns to think and view the world the way they do (i.e., learn to think, write, and speak in Japanese). For a Westerner to do that would require liberation from all forms of absolute beliefs and the willingness to take a relativistic position in viewing the world and forgetting about the Western self.

The Japanese self is ambiguous, floating, diffuse with surroundings—be they other humans, sparrow, sky, river, ocean, or mountain forests. Collectively the Japanese are often very self-assertive and unyielding; individually, however, they may act differently. The Japanese often unconsciously seek a way out rather than to make a rational choice if they are forced to make a decision from a set of alternatives. One might characterize the Japanese self as the dynamic, centerless entity without gravity. This is not to deny the existence of the Japanese self. It is there in every Japanese. There are many Japanese with a sense of self, including one of the few Japanese political leaders with an explicit set of his own ideas, Ichirô Ozawa (1993, pp. 251–257), who is urging the Japanese to have more *shutaisei* (positive and independent self) and to educate children to develop a strong sense of independent self. His major political rival, Masayoshi Takemura, has his own ideas and a very strong sense of self-assertiveness. Yet, Takemura (1994, pp. 213–215) talks about an alternative to his current active political life. His aspiration is to become a Buddhist priest, manage a temple, and find his place in the universal order of things before his demise from this world. Meanwhile he wants to make Japan not another "normal country" like what Ozawa wants Japan to be, but rather a small country with a bit of brilliant color emanating from within (*chiisakutomo kirari to hikarukuni*).

Takemura (1994) has a very assertive and independent self, and yet he remains very Japanese in his heart at the same time, as Ozawa (1993) is to a lesser extent. Ozawa's strategy of running a government without becoming prime minister himself certainly is very Japanese, for example, even if what he advocates appears as if untraditional. We see in Takemura's mindscape a core element of the Japanese culture unchanged from waka poets who composed poems that appear in the Manyôshû (759 A.D.). Mountains, fields, sky, forests, and rivers are very much an inseparable part of the Japanese self and are something from which the Japanese find it impossible to escape.

Suzuki's study of the 1978 data suggests the existence of a competing cluster of values operating among the Japanese.[34] However, Hayashi's study (1991, 1993, 1995b, pp. 88–90), using more recent data presented in Chapter 4, revealed that the traditional-modern clusters started breaking down in 1978 and continue to this date.[35] In a limited sense, Japan is becoming closer to the United States in that the demarcation of two competing values (traditional versus modern) that existed probably since the Meiji Restoration (1868) is disappearing as the twenty-first century draws near. However, this does not mean that traditional values are being replaced by modern values. Instead, a combination of what makes up the traditional and modern value sets is getting mixed up. Neither one is disappearing. They are no longer organized or "hang together" as they used to. In a sense, the Japanese mindscape shaped by the Meiji government policy of modernization is going through a transformation toward internationalization as we approach the end of the turbulent century, while the Japanese continue to maintain their ambiguity and giri-ninjô (at least in its attitudinal structure). The point is, however, that the traditional-modern dimension of the Japanese attitudinal structure is not a part of the Rashomonesque Yamazakura model.

Our model of the core of Japanese culture, Rashomonesque Yamazakura, remains intact despite upheavals of the twentieth century. It is a probability model, not a certainty model, and as such it does not apply to every trend or attitudinal pattern found in Japan. However, it is the best model we can find and is applicable to the Japanese culture of the past as well as the foreseeable future as long as the Japanese continue to speak the same language and maintain their religious beliefs or nonbeliefs, depending on the reader's perspective.

NOTES

1. The concept assumes that our mind is an entity that can go in and out of our body either temporarily or permanently. When one is attracted to something one is watching, it is assumed that one is moving away from one's body toward that object. However, the Japanese of the Manyôshû era (759 A.D.) assumed that only at death does the spirit leave our body forever to the mountains or sky, returning to nature.

2. Kuroda found the collective orientation dimension as the most important pattern in a component factor analysis of over 100 items for both a random sample of the voters and the leaders (selected through the use of a variant of Hunter's reputational technique) in a Japanese community (Kuroda, 1974, p. 59).

3. His reason for calling the brilliant Prince Shôtoku the first thinker freeing us from religion is that Shôtoku was responsible for not only proclaiming the coexistence of indigenous Shintoism and imported Buddhism side by side, but for practicing what he preached by building the Shitennô temple in Osaka when he was only twenty years old. He also earned the respect of naturalized citizens from China and Korea, who brought Buddhism to Japan, by building *Hôryûji* (temple) in Nara while at the same time allowing his maiden princess to serve in the Ise national shrine (Shintô). In other words, he officially espoused Buddhism without abandoning Shintoism, thereby placing an end to the religious war that existed between the Soga and the Mononobe clans—the only religious war in Japanese history. However, he paid a price for it. His sons and grandchildren were killed by the Soga clan, who opposed Buddhism.

Prince Shôtoku's contribution to the development of the Japanese culture is significant in establishing the concept of *wa* (harmony) by allowing Shintoism, Buddhism, and Confucianism to coexist side by side. This meant that imported religions must be modified to eliminate the absolutist notion from their system, as exemplified by the rejection of the mandate of heaven concept in Confucian philosophy. In a way, the Japanese reluctance to adopt logical thinking of the Western and Semitic civilizations can be attributed to Prince Shôtoku, who freed the Japanese from absolutist ideologies of any sort even if they were to accept parts of absolutist doctrine, as in the case of Confucianism.

4. Whether or not Japanese people concern themselves with either Buddhism or Shintoism or some other religion depends on a particular situation. They celebrate the birth of children and new year through the Shintô tradition and bury the corpses and observe the mid-August *bon* (mid-summer Buddhist ancestral dance ceremony) season in accordance with the traditional Buddhist rituals (For more details on bon or obon, see p. 120 of this book). Meanwhile, they do not show much concern for either one. They may marry in accordance with the Shintô rituals or Christian church wedding, especially in Hawaii, by combining their wedding ceremony with their honeymoon. It depends on a situation, but that situation may be clearly defined. There is practically no one who would marry by calling on Buddhist priests to help a couple celebrate and certify their wedding.

5. For the four questions used for this survey, see the Appendix for Chapter 6.

6. Some of the reasons for this discrepancy between the two groups are the fact that the first-generation Brazilians, who originally hailed from Japan, used neutral response more often than younger Japanese Brazilians (women especially are least likely to use any neutral responses). For more details, see Tôkeisûrikenkyûjo. 1993 (pp. 75–77).

7. See Figure 1.1.

8. Less educated Americans are reluctant to take extreme positions, probably reflecting the fact that they are less informed on matters. Americans with higher education tend to take definitive positions on many questions.

9. The results of the data analysis proposed by Kuroda are reported by Hayashi (1995a, pp. 8–10).

10. The Appendix for Chapter 6 lists all the items included in the analysis.

11. The study by Yasumasa Kuroda of the University of Hawaii and Tatsuzô Suzuki of the Institute of Statistical Mathematics in Tokyo was financially supported by the Toyota Foundation from 1984 to 1990. Two methods were used to secure our respondents: (1) We visited classrooms, where we divided each class into two by separating those who were sitting on the right and left. (2) We used a list of Japanese students who were officially enrolled at the University of Hawaii, for example, to mail out questionnaires. In so doing, we mailed an English questionnaire to an even-numbered student and a Japanese one to an odd-numbered student on the list. Then we compared the two groups' social attributes to make sure that there were no statistical differences between them.

12. These studies were carried out from 1985 through 1988 in Japan, the United States, Egypt, and Jordan. Unfortunately, there were not many American students with enough proficiency in Japanese to answer questions. Students from the Arab world and Japan studying in the United States were included in the survey. Ideally, we also should have included Arab students who are proficient in Japanese and Japanese students who are familiar with Arabic. We were unable to do so for both financial as well as practical constraints.

13. The results of our partial correlation analysis revealed that the language in use and the neutral response had the highest correlation coefficients with the student nationality (American and Japanese) and research site kept constant. For more details, see Kuroda, Hayashi and Suzuki (1986).

14. We regret that we were unable to find more Americans with sufficient proficiency to respond to our questions in Japanese. Ideally, we should also have Arab students respond in Japanese and Japanese students in Arabic. We should also point out that we only had three out of the five questions for 227 Japanese students at the Tsukuba University. The five questions used were 2.1, on going one's own way, 4.4, on teacher in trouble, 4.5, on the teaching of money, 7.1, on science and the lost feelings, and 7.2, on the richness of human feelings. All of them had a neutral response category, such as "it depends." The exact wording of the questions will be found in the Japanese culture study survey questionnaire in the Appendix for Chapter 1.

15. Kuroda's Israeli friend, who speaks Arabic, Hebrew, English, and Japanese, informs him that Hebrew is quite similar to Arabic in this regard. Semitic language speakers seem to be very definitive in their belief of what is right and what is wrong in accordance with their absolutist beliefs, while the Japanese define things in terms of a particular situation at a particular time in history. This professor of Japanese history at the Hebrew University reports that his experience of living in Japan and the United States fits with our findings.

16. Written Arabic is based on classical Arabic language, the writing in the Quoran. The Arabs, like the Chinese, have many dialects, but their written language is essentially the same throughout the Arab world.

17. Readers interested in details should see Kuroda and Suzuki (1991b). Arabs and Japanese share in their orientation that they are not as individualistic and optimistic as Americans. However, the Arabs are separated from the Japanese in their acceptance of rationalistic, logical thinking. The Semites, after all, originated the three monotheistic religions in the world that have had so much impact on the rest of the world.

18. There is evidence that the Japanese had some contact with Arabs, Egyptians, and Iranians as early as the sixth century. First, artifacts preserved in the Hôryûji (temple) built by the Prince Shôtoku came to Japan probably by way of the silk road from West Asia. Second, there were Buddhist temples in Alexandria around the sixth century. However, the extent of contact appears to have been sporadic and remained very limited until the modern period. For more details, see (Kuroda, 1986).

19. Primary group relations are characterized by intimate association, cooperation, and sustained person-centered interaction in which mutual personal satisfaction plays the primary role. Secondary group relations are characterized by narrowly circumscribed scope and easily transferable relationships, such as purchasing an item at a department store.

20. We found that students at the American University in Cairo as well as at the University of Jordan in Amman consider the workplace to be the domain for secondary group rules, as do the Chinese. When Kuroda, in his focused group discussions, asked Arab students why they do not seek friendship with co-workers and managers, their response was that they would find friendship elsewhere. They do not wish to be treated any different from others just because they are friends with their manager. They do not want favoritism to prevail in their workplace. The Kuroda-Suzuki study was a two-stage study of the survey research based on their questionnaire and focused interviews in Arabic and English.

21. Interestingly enough, this remarkable difference is reflected in their word for work. The Chinese character for work means "man moving," while the Japanese word for work is *hataraku* (which means "to make things easy or comfortable for others"). The Chinese are analytical, rational, and individualistic, whereas the Japanese are human-relations centered. Language is intricately related to the core of a culture.

22. Although one finds some Japanese business leaders with these characteristics who run their company without much consultation with their workers, this is not typical, particularly in the field of politics, despite Ichirô Ozawa's call (Ozawa, 1993, pp. 16–32) for a strong leader to surface in Japanese politics to the contrary. See Kuroda's point on this (Kuroda, 1988).

23. As you may recall, Motoori would respond to the question by saying it is a mountain cherry blossom barely visible under the morning sun. The Japanese tend to communicate through fuzzy expressions that often make logical Westerners respond, "Why don't they come out and say so in the first place?"

24 An implication here is that he will visit the families with an envelop containing some money and/or some gift, signaling admission of guilt on the part of the airline.

25. By smoothing its relationship with the victims' families, the airline may cause them to demand less financial compensation than they would other-wise. Obviously, however, there is no such guarantee.

26. This is derived from Chapter 5 of our monograph, The Research Committee on the Study of Honolulu Residents, 1986. For more details of the study, consult the original monograph, distributed by the University of Hawaii Press.

27. The Honoluluans' cost of living is estimated to be over 130 percent of that of the average city in the United States. A medium-priced single-dwelling unit there costs about twice as much as in the rest of the United States. In other words, they have more reasons to worry about their standard of living.

28. First, the survey was conducted before the end of the Cold War. Second, Honolulu has military bases filled with nuclear arsenals ready to be mobilized even today. Hence, there was a good reason for the people to be fearful. For more detail on this survey, see The Research Committee of Honolulu Residents, 1986, Chapter 5, pp. 100–130.

29. Our presentation herein is primarily based on Suzuki's article, but our interpretation of the results of his analysis is not always the same as his. Also, we have included some data and their interpretations that are not found in his article. We are using the same data set and same technique of analysis, but our interpretations are not always in agreement.

30. The company president has an obligation to the company employees just as he or she has an emotional attachment (ninjô) as well as an on (obligation) to his or her benefactor. The president is faced with a dilemma here of choosing between the two alternatives. He or she has the giri to both the benefactor and the company that must be fulfilled to live as a good member of a community.

31. Japanese newspapers often carry reports that go beyond simple comparison of percentages to show multivariate analysis of public opinion data. The most popularly used method is Hayashi's quantification method III (correspondence analysis).

32. Suzuki (1984), Figure 1, p. 82.

33. As Suzuki notes, Inkeles and Smith (1974), among others, advance the theory that a person will be "modernized" as the nation is industrialized and urbanized, while Moore (1979) would emphasize the growth of rationalism as a consequence of modernization.

34. Responses to some items historically indicate a trend toward "individualism" and "democracy," while there is a decreasing trend toward those who believe in "going ahead with one's own belief" (41 percent in 1953 and 30 percent in 1978 to 26 percent in 1993).

35. On a similar point made earlier, see Kuroda, Kuroda, Hayashi, and Suzuki (1987).

CHAPTER 7

The Vitality of Japanese Culture

諸 行 無 常

All phenomena are transitory. Buddhist teaching

Change alone is eternal, perpetual, immortal. Arthur Schopenhauer

THE DYNAMIC NATURE OF CULTURE

We are all aware, and scholars agree, that culture is not static, but dynamic. However, just how dynamic a given culture is, and in which direction a culture is heading, has been the subject of study for centuries without any scholarly consensus. Theories and facts abound. The Japanese are taught that "all phenomena are transitory," the first sentence of the *Heike monogatari* (*The Tale of the Heike*), which was originally written in the thirteenth century. This quotation is initially derived from the teaching of Buddhism (*Nehan [nirvana] kyō*)[1] but was popularized through the story of the Heike clan's rise and fall. The objective of this chapter is to generate what we consider the most probable scenario of twenty-first-century Japanese culture concerning its viability in particular.

Many have written about the rise and fall of empires or civilizations. For example, Paul Kennedy (1989) published his acclaimed book entitled *The Rise and Fall of the Great Powers*. As its subtitle indicates, its focus is on economic change and military conflict from 1500 to 2000. Its focus is not on culture as such.[2] While the subtitle is not synonymous with culture, Japanese culture is the same as a state or even the civilization. This is so because of its geographic and political position.[3] Japan is sometimes grouped together with China and Korea under East Asian or Confucian culture. Nevertheless, Japan as an island nation developed a culture distinct from its continental neighbors. Confucian ethics constitute only part of the Japanese culture. Paul Kennedy (1989, p. 444), among many others, points out the rise of the Pacific Basin economy in recent decades. He also correctly notes that development is not even in the Pacific Basin. The world system dominated by the Euro-American-centric system in the modern period appears to be tilting toward Asia as we approach the twenty-first century.

If change is an inevitable fact of life, then the question becomes what kinds of changes will come about and how will they come about in the years ahead. In discussing the vitality of culture, we must address the direction of change, the process of change, and the relationship of culture to political economy. How will our culture adapt itself to ever-changing conditions? The future is an extension of neither the past nor the present. However, knowledge is cumulative. We must review how social scientists have thought about the past changes. Let us begin with the direction of change.

The Direction of Change: Cyclical, Linear, Other Developments and Demise

The Buddhist views the world in a cyclical perspective that has no end. Many scholars, including Ibn Khaldun (1332–1406 A.D.), Giambattista Vico (1968), Oswald Spengler (1932), Arnold J. Toynbee (1947–1957), Vilfredo Pareto (1935), Pitirim A. Sorokin (1937–1941), and others, have all proposed a view the world from an essentially cyclical paradigm. Although cyclical views of the world existed in ancient Babylon, China, India, Persia, and other parts of the world, Khaldun was probably the first social scientist who generated a cyclical theory of history. His model explains history as cyclical in nature by pointing out that powerful barbarians conquer amenity-loving urbanites, but in time aggressive barbarians themselves become accustomed to their newly acquired luxuriant life in cities. Eventually they, too, become targets of attack and conquest by other vigorous warriors.

Such theories as the circulation of the elite of lions and foxes by Pareto, Michels, and Mosca are bluntly cyclical, while others are not. For example, Sorokin's three types of culture, consisting of the "sensate, ideational and idealistic," or Toynbee's acceptance of the "Great Man" theory of history and his views on Christianity suggest that they are not purely cyclical thinkers. Toynbee, however, is a cyclical thinker in the sense that he also proposes an organic cycle of birth, growth, decay, and death while rejecting Spengler's determinism.

Some of these theorists were seldom purely cyclical in their thoughts. Largely, however, all these theorists, from the thirteenth-century Arab historian-philosopher-social scientist Ibn Khaldun to Russian-born American sociologist Pitirim Sorokin, believe in looking at reality from one kind of circle or another.

Linear theorists, on the other hand, assume that history is on a noncyclical path, be it decline, status quo, or progress. The dominant nineteenth-century paradigm in the West was basically evolutionary thinking, from Auguste Comte (1875, 1876, 1877), Karl Marx (1936), Max Weber (1930), to Talcott Parsons

(1960). Comte views human evolutionary process in three stages of develop-ment: the "theological" state, followed by the "metaphysical" and last, the "scientific."

Herbert Spencer (1924), William Graham Sumner (Keller and Davie, 1969, p. 56; p. 95), and others follow social Darwinism. Spencer sees the world mov-ing from simple homogeneous societies to an increasingly heterogeneous one according to natural law. Social Darwinists perceive in this process of progress the survival of the fittest. Any interference in this natural process would be contrary to progress. This reasoning gave laissez-faire thinkers a rationale for their theory of market-oriented capitalism.

Karl Marx likewise sees the world in stages of progress from feudalism, capitalism, revolution, and then socialism, leading to the utopian stage of devel-opment. The last stage is where people will acquire total freedom, allowing them to be fisher in the morning and scholar in the evening. To Marx, the strug-gle was not for survival of the fittest but for the promotion of equality and free-dom for all, especially those who do not own the means to make their living (the workers). Engels and Marx claimed that the state will disappear in the end.

Opposed to Marxian utopia are many laissez-fair theorists, from Adam Smith (1937) and Adam Ferguson, to Milton Freidman and others. Many of them observe how humanity has evolved from hunting, fishing, shepherding, and farming to industry and commerce. Others, such as Emile Durkheim, be-lieve that society moves from the mechanical to the organic. Similarly, many have argued that society and culture move from rural to urban, primary to secondary, prelogical to logical, sacred to secular, *Gemeinschaft* to *Gesellschaft*, status to contract, traditional to modern, industrial to postindustrial, manufactur-ing to information, and Robert Redfield's folk to urban (1953).

Some linear theorists are not strictly linear. Let us focus on the residual category of scholars who do not fit into the linear paradigm. Lewis Henry Morgan (1877) presents an argument that the history of progress coincides with successive advancements in technology. William F. Ogburn sees that culture lags behind material progress (1922). Alfred L. Kroeber observes a more com-plex pattern of cultural dynamics, as seen in his *Configurations of Cultural Growth* (1944). He contends that significant achievements in human endeavor appear in clusters or patterns. Such patterns, however, reach "saturation" at some point. A culture then may cease to grow or improve, reproducing or re-peatedly re-creating the same thing. Then it is ready for transformation again, whatever that may be. He is too cautious to suggest any direction of change, however.

There is a host of literature on the modernization process characterized by the proliferation of the division of labor and industrialization. Futurists, too, view this process with humans going through a series of revolutionary changes starting with agricultural revolution, then an industrial revolution, and then on to the postindustrial or the Information Age revolution. On the whole, these scholars treat all human cultures as though they go through the same stages of development at different periods in history. However, some scholars believe that there is more than one way to modernize.

Culture cannot survive without language. A recent Associated Press report based on a warning by Michael Krauss of the University of Alaska predicts that half of the world's 6,000 languages will disappear in the next century if nothing is done to prevent their extinction. The viability of a culture depends on the continuing existence of its language. Many languages in the world today are in danger of demise. Culture in its full capacity cannot survive without its language.[4] Some languages, such as those of indigenous people conquered by colonial powers, are no longer spoken in many parts of Asia, Africa, America, and the Pacific. Such peoples as Hawaiians are today making efforts not only to restore their dignity and sovereignty but their language as well.

In summary, we found that the direction of change can be roughly divided into three categories: (1) cyclical, (2) linear development, and (3) demise. Theorists differ not only on the direction of changes but also on how these changes come about.

The Process of Change

If change is continuous, will it be evolutionary, discontinuous, or revolutionary? Is this process of change inevitable or just probable? Schneider contends that adaptation and transition from "homogeneity to heterogeneity" constitute the concept of evolution (1976, p. 1).

Charles Tilly's theory of radical change in Western Europe totally ignores cultural elements and focuses on the development of modern states in Europe (1975 and 1992). Theda Skocpol (1979) approaches her study of revolutionary process from cross-national historic perspectives. She treats ideas as motivating factors to bring changes. Goldstone (1991) considers multiple factors in viewing revolutionary changes in the early modern world. He posits that the role of ideology or culture is to surge at a certain juncture in history and then lose its drive into oblivion in the fabric of life. In other words, culture is started at a certain revolutionary corner but becomes dormant after passing the corner.

Modernization theorists are divided on the issue of the number of paths to modernization. Will all countries become alike as they go through modernization and/or industrialization? Japan, especially since 1945, presents a case for arguing that the industrialization process can take a different path and end up at a different destination than the Western pattern. Not only was Japan's economic development miraculously rapid, especially in the 1960s, but it resulted in the strengthening of the social fabric. In other words, the Marxian prediction that industrialization leads workers to a heightened sense of alienation turned out to be false for postwar Japan.

Cultural Change and Related Factors

The rise or decline of a culture does not occur in a vacuum. Both are results of change in some aspects of a society. The development of spoken language and the subsequent construction of written language greatly facilitated the development of culture. The evolution of spoken language seems to have taken place early in many parts of the world, as evidenced in the existence of so many languages.[5] However, only a limited number of ethnic groups invented a written language (i.e., the Chinese, Hamites, Indians, and Semites). The Europeans and Japanese generated their written languages by borrowing from the Syro-Palestinians and the Chinese. Most people on earth today have written languages that were the result of borrowing or transmission from others. Hence, the development of culture based on written language was a product of either adapting from others or innovation.

Adaptation is the process of meeting the challenge of changes in conditions. The changes could be either technological or material or ideological/teleological in nature. They could be a result of the diffusion of new technology or an innovation within a society. Following this line of theory is a theory of historical development from magic to religion and then to science. Max Weber (Schroeder, 1992) and Frazer (1958), for example, assume that magic preceded religion in their analysis of modern society.

The development of science led the West in acquiring technological innovation unmatched by others as the Industrial Revolution started in Britain and spread to the rest of the world in a matter of only a few hundred years since its inception. China, Ancient Greece, and Rome and Western Europe in the twelfth century experienced rapid technological development, but it did not result in an industrial revolution. The Industrial Revolution in the West contributed to the spread of Eurocentric culture in much of the world today. It also contributed to the decline and sometimes even the demise of indigenous cultures in Asia, Africa, and America because of the Western colonization of less technologically developed parts of the world.

Some nations, such as Japan, successfully avoided Western colonization and adopted the Eurocentric culture of the West.[6] The way Japan achieved its industrialization and independence was to adapt to the new world order by becoming another colonial power.

Two new thoughts appeared in recent years: Francis Fukuyama's end of history (1989) and Huntington's clash of civilizations (1993a and b). The former claims that the fall of Soviet communism resulted in the "universalization of Western liberal democracy." Thus, he claims that the end of history is here. We see neither the end of history nor a victory for liberal democracy for humanity. Fukuyama oversimplifies anti-Communist forces in the world. Chalmers Johnson opines that the Cold War has ended and Japan won (1995, p. 8). Japan has modern liberal state institutions, but they operate differently when compared with the West. The United States and Japan both run under the general principles of capitalism and democracy. However, Japan does not practice the market-centered American system. The U.S. liberal democracy is based on individualism, while Japan, in the words of Beer (1989), practices a "communitarian feudal democracy" (1989, p. 85).

Robert Putnam (1995) has been speaking out and spreading the idea that America must build up "social capital" if it is to be revitalized. Michael Lerner of *Tikkun* (1994) wants President Clinton to promote communitarianism in America. Amitai Etzioni (1988 and 1983) also has been advocating social communitarianism in America. What these perceptive American social scientists and social engineers are saying is that America should be more like Japan to reduce detrimental effects of industrialization and urbanization. If so, Johnson is right when he said Japan won. Our interpretation of his words is that he was not only referring to the economic success of Japan, but to its success in strengthening the social fabric, as demonstrated in the drastically reduced rate of violent crime, divorce, babies born out of wedlock, poverty, and other forms of social disorganization.[7] If these authors are on the right track, American individualism has reached its height. Putnam and others are urging their compatriots to promote the sense of community over individualism. The task in America is made more challenging because of the mutlicultural and ethnic nature of America and its belief in monotheism.

Huntington's thesis (1993a) is that the clash of civilizations will replace the ideological war of the Cold War era. We agree with him on points such as that language is "central to culture" and that Japan achieved its modern status without becoming another Western country by keeping its traditional values. However, we remain skeptical of his assertion that no longer will ideology or economic concerns be the primary cause of clash, but civilization.

To those who challenge him, Huntington responds by entitling his defense of his thesis, "If Not Civilization, What?" (Huntington, 1993b). We would respond to his challenge by claiming that the source of conflict will be not civilization or culture, but absolutist beliefs—be they monotheism, Communism, or nationalism—which claim that they possess the exclusive truth. In other words, we fail to see any reason to believe that causes of war in years to come will be radically different from the past. Wars and conflicts that erupted in the Gulf, the former Yugoslavia, and Africa are derived from one or another absolute belief.[8] For a culture to remain viable, it must be either like Japan (ambiguous, thereby thwarting potential conflicts), or economically and militarily strong enough to resist any challenge from opposing absolutist forces. We concur with Huntington that we all must "learn to coexist with others." We would add that economic interdependence among nations has made learning to coexist imperative. One way of learning to live side by side in peace is to liberate ourselves from the belief that we alone possess the truth.

In summary, when faced with changing technological, military, and social conditions, a culture reacts by either innovating, adapting, or succumbing to the technologically superior culture. Having briefly reviewed the literature, we are now ready to assess the vitality of Japanese culture.

THE VITALITY OF JAPANESE CULTURE

和と以て貴しとしと為す。

Let harmony be the guiding principle.

神仏儒習合

Learning to harmonize Shintoism, Buddhism, and Confucianism

History: Challenges from Abroad

We have attributed the nature of Japanese culture to the Japanese language, which structures thought patterns reflecting an ambiguous view of reality and self. We have alluded that these basic tenets were set at the time the Japanese developed their written language over several centuries, from the fifth to ninth centuries.

Japanese culture faced a number of challenges from abroad before and after the formation of Japan as a nation. Japan faced the technologically superior and culturally richer cultures of China, Korea, and India in its nascent state of formation as a nation.[9] The first written record of the cultural crisis came about the time of Prince Régent Shôtoku's reign (592–622).

The so-called seventeen article Constitution represents a normalization of the cardinal norm Prince Régent Shôtoku is said to have promulgated in 604.[10] It begins with wa (harmony) as the principal rule of Japan, as cited previously. It goes on to describe the society as it existed then. In the early seventh century, during Shôtoku's tenure as the Régent, for thirty years Japan was a society filled with conflicts among superiors and inferiors, among neighbors, and among rival political groups. Government officials were corrupt. People formed groups that refused to obey the emperor. The constitution called to an end to corrupt officials abusing their positions to acquire personal wealth. In short, Shôtoku wanted an end to all these conflicts and corruption domestically and internationally by establishing the imperial authority. The constitution also urged public officials to heed the public. It was in this period in Japanese history when Japan started to develop a constructive relationship with China and stopped attempting to invade divided Koreas. The religious war between the Soga and Mononobe clans had lasted over fifty years when Prince Régent Shôtoku offered his "administrative guidance" by supporting both Buddhism and Shintôism.[11]

Although Prince Régent Shôtoku's "administrative guidance," called the seventeen-article constitution, especially the concept of Shinbutsujyushûgô (Learn to harmonize Shintoism, Buddhism and Confucianism) was not observed by such powerful clans as the Soga clan,[12] Prince Régent Shôtoku's administrative guidance became the foundation of Japanese culture, denying the existence of any absolute idea, one of the two key elements of the core of Japanese culture according to our Rashomonesque Yamazakura model. Moreover, his promotion of Buddhism contributed to the formation of the Japanese concept of self in Japan, which was filled with selfish, clannish, and religious conflicts then. Hence, Prince Régent Shôtoku is not just the liberator of the Japanese from religion, as Sakaiya (1994, p. 143) would characterize him, but is the father of Japanese culture. If he was not the only father, he at least was one of the creators of what was to become the core of Japanese culture, along with the authors and the editor of *Manyôshû*,[13] Fumimaro Ôno, the editor of *Kokinwakashû*, Tsura-yuki Kino, and others.

Our comparative survey of the Chinese and the Japanese reveals an interesting insight into their concept of law. A high 92 percent of the Chinese thought law was designed to bring about fairness and justice. Only 50 percent of the Japanese thought so. A 42 percent plurality in Japan said law was designed to enable people to get along in society. A small minority (8 percent) of the Chinese chose the second interpretation of law. A large minority of the Japanese believe law exists to bring about social harmony, or wa.

Prince Régent Shôtoku's achievement was not an innovation as much as a successful adaptation for Japan to the new spiritual and old social conflicts that existed in the seventh century. The arrival of Buddhism coincided with the coming of Chinese characters and the Chinese written language. Again the Japanese adopted the Chinese written language to express themselves. The first document ever written in Japan was the *Kojiki*. Motoori studied it for thirty years to give it a modern rendition. Again the Japanese did not invent a writing system but adapted the Chinese system to devise their own phonetic systems to supplement the Chinese characters, as the Koreans did. The Chinese and Indians have invented a number of things, from gun powder to the concept of zero. The Japanese have not.

This is not to say that the Japanese are incapable of developing a new idea or theory. There are exceptions. An example is a random sampling theory developed in 1920 by a statistician. Although the Japanese learned survey sampling methodology, which was developed in the United States after World War II, a pioneering work on the development of random sampling methodology was done by Toyojirô Kameda in 1920. He devised a random sampling procedure from a limited universe for the 1920 census survey. His method is essentially the same as what the Americans later developed.[14]

A casual review of Japanese history reveals a definite pattern of Japan adjusting to challenges by adopting, not by inventing a radical new way of dealing with the challenges. Confucianism was adopted after Japan took out absolutist doctrines, such as the concept of the mandate of heaven.[15] The Japanese predisposition is "how do I adjust" to new situations and "what can I invent to deal with this challenge." It is also not acceptance or rejection. The Japanese do not perceive challenges as things to respond to in a binary fashion—either reject or adopt. Their predisposition is to find a good way to adjust.[16] This is a different aspect of the Japanese when compared with people of the Judeo Christian Islamic culture.

The Japanese steadfastly refused to accept any absolutist idea throughout history, at least since the written history began in the seventh century. Prince Régent Shôtoku's principle is very much alive today. The principle applies to even contemporary political parties ostensibly established to give the appearance of democracy in the Diet. The very existence of *Kokkaitaisaku iinkai* (The Diet Countermeasure Committee) established by all parties is an embodiment of Prince Régent Shôtoku's administrative guidance announced in 604.[17] The committee's principal task is to adjust to each party's stands in such a way as to minimize open conflicts among the different groups the Prince spoke of in 604.[18]

A survey report prepared by the *Shakai shisutemu kenkyûjo* (The Social System Research Institute) in the Kansai area contains a question on policy statement of two airlines. The respondents were asked to choose a statement with which they felt more agreeable. The first statement claims that the airline has never been involved in any accident, leading it claim that it is absolutely safe to fly. The second statement claims that the company is doing all it can to prevent accidents from happening. A very high 93 percent chose the latter statement as their choice, while only 7 percent selected the first airline, which claimed to be absolutely safe. The Japanese do not believe in anything absolute.

Our hypothesis is that another aspect of Japanese history that separates Japan from its neighboring countries and the Judeo Christian Islamic cultures is the absence of revolution. The Taika Reform (645–650) took place shortly after the death of Prince Régent Shôtoku and was followed by the Meiji Restoration in 1868 and the postwar reform. There have also been lesser reforms and changes, but they were not revolutions as experienced by China, France, Russia, and the United States. There have been bloody regime changes, but not a change in systems as such. Instead what prevailed has been the spirit of kaizen, or improvement, over the past. What could have been a revolutionary bloody war was successfully avoided by the negotiation represented by Kaishû Katsu (1823–1899), a nonviolent warrior-negotiator who happened to be a Zen Buddhist on the side of the Tokugawa regime, and the rebels represented by Takamori Saigô.[19]

The fate of the last shogunate of the Tokugawa era, Yoshinobu Tokugawa (1837–1913) points to the unique nature of Japanese change. Following the fall of the shogunate system in 1868, Yoshinobu Tokugawa went on to become the President of the House of Peers and received the title of *kôshaku*, the highest title of nobility. He was, however, briefly under house arrest immediately following the Meiji Restoration in 1868. The Meiji Restoration was far from qualifying as a revolution, but it was indeed an evolution of the shift in de facto power from that of the Tokugawa family to the *genrô* (elder statesmen of the Meiji era), who were responsible for the toppling of the Tokugawa government.

There has been some rise and fall of Japan as a nation and as a culture in Japanese history. However, the extent of the vicissitudes has been much less when compared with other cultures, such as the Arab and Chinese cultures. Likewise, one may characterize the history of Japanese culture as cyclical if one looks at the past fifty years of Japanese history. We would contend that it is not cyclical as much as a spiral development in that it was enriched by the infusion of American culture, especially ideas promoted by New Dealers. The evidence for this generalization is best manifested in the Japanese constitution, which was initially drafted in English. However, Japan did not become an America. It successfully avoided the escalation of alienation, and its social fabric strengthened instead of weakened as Japan industrialized and urbanized (Kuroda, 1995).

These observations of Japanese history lead us to conclude that there is no existing theory that can adequately explain the past dynamics of Japanese culture. Parts of the existing theories, such as those that claim that cultural change comes as a result of technological development and the diffusion of new ideas, are applicable to Japan. We posit that our language theory of Rashomonesque Yamazakura is applicable in examining the vitality of Japanese culture.

The Source of Vitality: Rashomonesque Yamazakura

Our inference from the generalization of Japan being nonrevolutionary is that the Japanese are incapable of totally denying the past and creating a radical new system that characterizes other cultures used to select this or that system. The Japanese are prone to adjust to new needs and social conditions that precipitate changes. The Japanese prefer to think of everything in terms of this and that, not this or that. We posit that this is a consequence of the Rashomonesque Yamazakura nature of Japanese culture operating to diffuse conflicts by making everything ambiguous. By so doing, the extent of cognitive dissonance that Theodore Newcomb (1953, pp. 393–404) spoke of is successfully minimized and consonance is maximized to maintain harmony.[20]

Just as Prince Régent Shôtoku did not totally reject the old religion and espouse a new religion of Buddhism, the Japanese today are trying to preserve good parts of their culture by adopting whatever new things grow well in Japanese soil. So it was with Meiji Japan, when the government adopted the slogan of *wakon yôsai* (Japanese spirit and Western knowledge and technology).[21]

The arrival of a new religion, Buddhism, and the written language of Chinese constituted a challenge to leaders of the Prince Régent Shôtoku era. The crisis that nineteenth-century Japanese leaders faced involved not only the military but was the cultural product of industrial revolution. What faces us as we approach the dawn of the twenty-first century is the development of the information superhighway, which is ready to revolutionize the culture of many countries, including such culturally isolated nations as Saudi Arabia (*Business*

Week, August 21, 1996, p. 40). The Japanese culture is likely to change as the people come into direct contact with people outside of Japan through the Internet and other electronic media. The diffusion of ideas is made continuously easier with the development of printing technology. The third stage of human revolution following agricultural and industrial revolution centers around information technology. This latest wave is likely to alter culture ubiquitously. Prime Minister Nakasone made "internationalization" a priority policy in the early 1980s. Japan's bent on Westernization and industrialization has been replaced by a new slogan of "internationalization" following Japan becoming on par with the West in its economic and technological achievement. The new slogan to internationalize Japan was initiated by a conservative politician known for his nationalistic leanings among the ruling Liberal Democrats.

The Japanese, historically speaking, seem willing to adopt new ideas even though those ideas appear to contradict with their values once they perceive a new idea as inevitable. However, in so doing they will try to accommodate it within their traditional paradigm of ambiguity and relativism set in the seventh century. They will never totally reject or accept a new idea. We posit that this willingness to accommodate new ideas without totally accepting them and flexible relativism, which are built into the Japanese culture, are what made the Japanese culture viable thus far. As the results of our data analysis reveal, the Japanese have not changed one iota on these key aspects of their culture from 1953 to 1993. Our hypothesis is that they have not changed much in this regard since the seventh century.

As we view empires that rose and fell and that went through violent revolutionary changes, we are struck by the fact that they all firmly believed in their absolute righteousness. The Japanese lack such determination. When they attempt to deviate from the traditional relativism position, they fail as the wartime army leaders did. Japan did not totally disintegrate at the end of war as Germany did.[22]

Of course, we have no idea what the future holds as far as challenge from abroad or outer space are concerned. First, we maintain that if culture is to survive, it must maintain its language. Second, a culture most likely to survive the challenges of an unknown future is the type of culture characterized by ambiguous and flexible Rashomonesque Yamazakura. Third, Japanese culture has been known to adjust to the outside world by adapting—be it Buddhism, Confucianism, industrialization, or Westernization—without losing its basic traditional values. Fourth, our culture constrains us from making the two aforementioned points absolute and definitive. Hence, the Japanese sun will not likely set, even though clouds may form over Japan at times, typhoons may threaten, and earthquakes may shake people up from time to time to remind them of the frail existence of humanity (which is subject to constant change and challenge, as Buddhism teaches).

SUMMARY

Theories suggest several models of change. The ways they describe directions as well as the process of change differ. Most theorists find applicable cases in history, but no one theory is applicable in all cases. The task then is to look for a model that best fits Japanese culture as characterized by our model.

Some cultures have disappeared from earth, as some species have. At least one scholar believes that half of the existing 6,000 languages will vanish in the next century. Will Japanese culture be one of them? Our answer is probably negative. Moreover, even if there are some declines and upsurges in the future, the magnitude will remain relatively narrow. Our reasoning is as follows.

First, most cultures that rose and fell or experienced revolutionary changes are based on absolutist doctrines. The Japanese culture is not. Some cultures, such as those of the Arabs and Chinese, have experienced tremendously wide magnitudes of vicissitude. One moment they were the most advanced and the next they were found on the bottom, although they did not fade away as the ancient Egyptian culture did. Egyptians became almost totally Arabized, along with other North Africans, by adopting Arabic and Islam (except for Coptics and Jews in Egypt, who at least remained faithful to their religion).

Second, our optimistic inference is derived from the Japanese proclivity to avoid extreme positions of either for or against. Some Japanese may be obsessed with such a religion as the religious cult *Aum Shinrikyô* (Religion of the Truth), but never it will be followed by a majority. We do not mean to equate Aum Shinrikyô with the three greatest monotheistic religions in the world today. However, the fact is that all followers of monotheism absolutely believe in the existence of God.

Third, the Japanese so far have been successful in meeting the challenges of external powers if they have something to learn from technologically and intellectually superior outside forces. They initially chose to avoid outside forces, but once they are convinced that they cannot continue to do so they are willing to accommodate. They do not either accept or reject new ideas and institutions. They assume their task to be to adjust to the challenge.[23] By attempting to adjust, they never totally fail even if they could not accomplish as much as they had wanted, and thereby they avoid catastrophic disasters.

Fourth, since our theory of Japanese culture is based on the language theory presented in Chapter 2, unless the Japanese language is eliminated, for whatever reason, our position is likely to be upheld. Such a probability is rather low.

This reasoning leads us to infer the relative well-being of Japanese culture for years to come. The Japanese sun may be eclipsed from time to time and the people will change, but the core of the Japanese culture is likely to remain intact, as it has for the past 1,400 years.

NOTES

1. *Shogyô* refers to all things that are made or created, while *mujô* means subject to change. All things are subject to change: Nothing is permanent or absolute. This is one of the four basic tenets in Buddhism (Kajimura, 1988, pp. 62–65).

2. We cannot deny, however, how culture is affected by the rise and fall of a state or society. Culture cannot grow without having an economic basis to support the development of ideas and technology or tools of developing human capacity. For example, the invention of written language and the printing machine facilitated the development of cultures. They significantly helped to expand our knowledge.

3. This is not true of many other countries, such as India, Iran, Spain, and Switzerland. The Swiss have little identification with their nation since four distinct language groups make up the nation state (Bendix, 1992, p. 784).

4. We realize that some elements of culture will survive even if a language dies. We found in our study of Honolulu that the Japanese Americans, regardless of their generation and age, like Japanese food. Younger Japanese who cannot speak a word of Japanese love Japanese food, an important part of the Japanese culture.

5. Itzkoff (1985, p. 52) says that it does not take more than an IQ of 40 to speak. Early hominids used language to facilitate their survival.

6. Of course, Japan did not stop by just resisting Western colonialism but became a colonial power by conquering its neighboring countries, an action that culminated in its military defeat in 1945.

7. The percentage of babies born to single parents used to be 9 to 10 percent at the turn of the century. Today it is under 1 percent, while the rate for the United States is nearly one-third. The rate of divorce in Japan at the turn of the century was almost three times what it is today. The rate of murder is about one-fifteenth of what it used to be. The number of homeless has also been radically reduced to an insignificant number in Japan. For these figures in more detail, see Kuroda (1995).

8. For the basic causes of the Gulf War and U.S. involvement in it, see Kuroda (1994).

9. Buddhism officially came to Japan in 538 (A.D.) from Korea. However, there is evidence that it came earlier through nonofficial routes (Yuasa, 1990, p. 156).

10. The seventeen-article constitution is generally attributed to the work of Prince Régent Shôtoku, but there are some who do not accept his authorship, as Wakamori (1974, pp. 87–92) points out. As Varley (1983, p. 20) says, Prince Régent Shôtoku "has been greatly idealized in history." There seems, however, little doubt about his contribution to expand the relations with China to advance Japanese culture (Varley 1983, pp. 20–21; Wakamori, 1974, p. 92).

11. Despite his efforts to resolve the conflict, his offspring met with their demise at the hands of the Soga clan.

12. The Soga's rule was overthrown by a coup d'état in 645. Imperial rule was restored, which led to the Taika Reform in 645–650.

13. This and *Kokinwakashû* were compiled in the seventh century. The former includes poems composed by members of society, from beggars to the Imperial Family, while the latter contains only aristocratic poetry.

14. For more detail and other Japanese pioneers in survey research, see Hayashi, Ikeuchi, Morita, and Terada (1974).

15. Some might argue that the Japanese emperor system is absolute. Our answer is that this has not been so in reality, even if the emperor system has an appearance of an absolutist rule of Japan, as seen in the Meiji Constitution (1890). The appearance remained just that. The emperor had been the de jure ruler of Japan. The emperor barely ruled the country in its long history. Someone else ruled Japan in his name, be they feudal rulers, elder statesmen during the Meiji era, or military rulers during World War II. Hence, Japan had a dual system of ruling for centuries and was not ruled by an absolute monarch as such.

16. Kinhide Mushakôji (1972) and Johan Galtung (1983) make a similar observation when the former calls the Japanese culture a culture that adjusts and the West a culture that selects. The latter says that Japanese culture is an addition, not a selection.

17. There is already a Diet standing committee called giin unei iinkai (The Diet Steering Committee). It acts like the U.S. House Rules Committee. The so-called *Kokutai iinkai* is not a Diet committee; it is organized by each party to work out differences informally among parties. The former is a committee designed as a formal tatemae organization, while the latter is a place where honne is exchanged to avoid serious conflicts. The word tatemae refers to the formal principles people say they live by, while the latter honne is their real view or opinion.

18. A large sum of money is exchanged between parties to minimize open conflict. Even when open conflicts are staged in the Diet through heated debates or questioning of the Cabinet members by opposition parties, they are usually devoid of critical questions, suggesting prior agreements among the parties, and thus assuring no real conflicts. The current coalition of Socialists and conservative Liberal Democrats is not an unlikely event when one considers that they have been working together as a team behind closed doors. They have known each other personally and maintained what the Japanese call *mochitsu motaretsutsu* (mutually dependent relationship) for years. Viewed in this perspective of Shôtokuism, the current coalition is not an accident at all but a culmination of years of "friendship" that existed between the Socialists and Liberal Democrats. Our position is that regardless of the forms it took for them to govern Japan, they have brought about a great deal of benefits to postwar Japan. Our intent here is to explain why things happen the way they do in Japan, not to criticize the principle by which they operated and continue to operate.

19. This is not to deny that there was blood shed by many, especially by those who refused to give into rebels, but large-scale bloodshed was avoided and Tokyo was saved from fire as a result of the successful negotiation between the rebels and the feudal regime.

20. His theory is that one maintains a balance among one's own position, one's friend or any closely associated person's position, and one's view of that person. For example, a citizen who admires President Eisenhower may like his position on an issue that he shares. However, if he discovers that the President's position differs from his own views on the issue, there is a cognitive dissonance between him and the President, causing him to attempt to reduce the extent of dissonance. Newcomb's weak-link hypothesis states that the weakest link breaks down when such a dissonance is generated. For example, the person might start disliking the President if he did not think him to be as important as his stand on the issue. There are other similar theories that are based on the principle that we, as humans, tend to avoid conflicts and move toward the reduction of tensions.

21. Note that the word *wa* (harmony) was used to refer to Japan. They are synonymous.

22. Japanese leaders have been criticized bitterly by many of Japan's former enemies and the people who were colonized by Japan at the fiftieth anniversary marking the end of World War II in 1995. The reason is largely due to the failure of the Japanese to admit to their aggressive war behavior and unambiguously apologize. One of the sources of their reluctance may be derived from cultural constraints. The Japanese do not view right and wrong in absolutist terms, as do the people of Asian and Judeo-Christian-Muslim traditions. They feel that everyone involved in the conflict is somewhat guilty, even if some are more so than others. On the other hand, Americans would feel that either a person is guilty or not guilty.

23. Professor Haruo Shimada of Keiô University proposed to Prime Minister Murayama to establish a permanent body to deal with the trade friction with the United States. He calls it the "Trans-Pacific Economic Adjustment Mechanism." He and seventy other scholars, lawmakers, and bureaucrats think of dealing with the trade friction problem in terms of adjustment, not an invention of totally new mechanisms. After all, the existing system did not work for the past fifteen years since the serious trade friction threatened an otherwise friendly bilateral relationship. What appears to be needed from the Western paradigm is not to adjust to each other's needs as much as to create a new way of dealing with what appears to be a chronic problem.

CHAPTER 8

Conclusion

Many scholars have sought the essence of Japanese culture in order to define who they are in relation to other cultures in the world. Many non-Japanese have followed suit. We, too, set forth the task of identifying the core of Japanese culture, but our efforts differ somewhat from others. Our approach was to develop a theory of Japanese culture and to examine its validity from both historical and comparative perspectives by using survey data. Though neither of one of us specializes in literature, we found ourselves in agreement with literary figures. They range from the foremost Japanologist Norinaga Motoori to a recent Nobel laureate, Kenzaburô Ôe, in search for the core of Japanese culture. The results of our comparative data analysis bore out the reliability and validity of our model, Rashomonesque Yamazakura.

We outlined our objective, approach, data set, and methodology in Chapter 1. Our approach to the study of Japanese culture was to infer the enduring-core values of Japanese adults from a sustained theoretical perspective. Our research design called for using a longitudinal and comparative sample survey data set gathered every five years from 1953 through 1993. Its aim was identifying enduring, unique Japanese values as well as values that the Japanese share with Americans and Europeans. The design required us to obtain these objectives from a sustained theoretical perspective. It also called for identifying Japanese values that had changed over the forty years, from the time Japan became independent until the fall of the 1955 system in 1993.

We proposed our theory of Japanese culture in Chapter 2. We offered language as the key factor, among other factors, in shaping the nature of Japanese culture. We based the theory on our findings of Japanese American voters in Honolulu and a cross-language survey of Americans, Arabs, and Japanese students.

Our theory focused on the idea of Japanese self and their worldview. Our objective was to isolate the persistent salient-core values and thought patterns held by a majority of the people from other fewer enduring and prominent values and thinking patterns. Many authors on Japanese culture have pointed out the ambiguity of the Japanese as well as the diffuse nature of the Japanese self in a variety of ways, from amae, collectivity, and social relativity to Zen. Our language theory of Rashomonesque Yamazakura is new in the sense that no one has combined these two salient features as the core Japanese value and thought patterns. Furthermore, no one has proposed that these Japanese characteristics are derived largely from the Japanese language. However, numerous observers of the Japanese language have noted the ambiguous nature of the language. They include a nineteenth-century American diplomat in Japan, Percival Lowell (1888), and the Japanese "father of simultaneous translation," Masumi Muramatsu (*Japan Economic Survey*, 1989). We explicitly specified how the language causes its speakers to think on certain limited matters in certain prescribed ways inherent in the language.

In more than one way, our approach to the study of Japanese culture resembles the way Norinaga Motoori went about his thirty-five-year study of the *Kojiki* (Record of Ancient Matters). Our data set was collected over forty years. He used the oldest written document to look for *Yamato gokoro* (Japanese spirits/mind). We looked for the salient pattern of Japanese culture by using the longitudinal comparative data set. He used his knowledge of Chinese and Japanese classics to render a modern interpretation of the Kojiki. We used multivariate statistics to search the salient pattern in Japanese thought. He expressed his findings in the form of waka (Japanese poem).[1] We report our findings in the tradition of survey research by setting up a theory and testing it with our data. Yet our conclusion of what constitutes the enduring core of the Japanese values is very similar to his thirty-one-syllable response.

In Chapter 3, we reported on what we called the "five enduring predominant" values held by a two-thirds majority of Japanese without any regard to age, education, and gender over the four decades. The Japanese have often been said to be homogenous people, but we found that there are not too many values they hold in common among all strata of the Japanese population. They believe in fairness on the employment question. They prefer Japanese gardens. They prefer workplaces to be governed by the rule of primary group relations. They do not have personal religious faith, but they think religion is important. These values separately are values shared to a varying degree by Americans and Europeans as well, with the notable exception of religious faith.[2]

The majority of Japanese consider religion important, but they do not consider themselves to have religious faith. Many have pointed to many differences in religious belief between the Japanese and Westerners. A couple of our findings not discussed in the literature deserve some attention here. Japanese Americans probably constitute the only immigrant ethnic group that has had many of its members adapt the dominant religion of the host country in the United States. Our findings from sample surveys in Honolulu from 1971 to 1988 indicate that Buddhists, Christians, and others were about evenly divided, with each constituting one-third of the population. Most other immigrants keep their religions even if they adopt a new language.

Our second finding of interest refers to people who do not have religious faith but who consider religious minds to be important. The percentages of each group who consider religious minds important but do not personally have religious faith are as follows: Japanese Americans in Honolulu (1988)—67 percent; Japanese Brazilians (1991)—67 percent; Japanese (1988)—64 percent; Americans (1988)—56 percent; Italians (1992)—44 percent; French (1989)—31 percent; British (1987)—30 percent; Dutch (1993)—22 percent; and West Germans (1989)—14 percent.

The mindset that incorporates two attitudes that seemingly contain a cognitive dissonance is found most frequently among Japanese (64 percent) and Japanese emigrants who settled in Brazil and the United States (67 percent). Europeans, and particularly the Germans, in this regard are most internally and cognitively consistent. We believe that this mindset relates closely to Japanese ambiguity and the denial of absolute value. One reason for the Americans to be similar to Japanese in this regard may be derived from their multiethnic and religious nature, which sets them apart from Europeans.

A story published in 1774 by Nan-a alludes to this type of mindset in discussing *gengenkai*.[3] It is the Japanese tradition not to take any one idea seriously, for doing so works against the wa that Prince Régent Shôtoku preached in 604. In the tradition of Murasaki Shikibu, it is learning that is of utmost important in acquiring the Yamatogokoro (the Japanese mindset). Thus Japanese emigrants continue to maintain one of their core values even after several generations have passed since their ancestors settled in Brazil and the United States.

Since the time of Prince Régent Shôtoku, the Japanese have learned not to take religion too seriously, as in the words of Sakaiya the Prince liberated the Japanese from religion. Prince Régent Shôtoku ended the Japanese history of religious war. The Japanese have learned to accept the Rashomonesque world-view by rejecting any absolutist doctrine and by learning to espouse the imported religions of Buddhism, indigenous Shintôism, and other religious beliefs all at the same time. Wa is impossible if anyone claims his or her ideas to be explicitly absolute and exclusive. The Japanese, in response to the first "administrative guidance" in history promulgated by the Prince Régent Shôtoku, seem to have developed a way of putting his words into practice. Their means of achieving wa was to diffuse the role of individual or self and to define an object ambiguously or make things barely visible, as Motoori would put it.

The concept of wa is a key norm in Japan, but it is still a norm, not always an empirical fact. The wa as the key norm in Japan has a very influential role to play in shaping the nature of Japanese culture. A similar norm also exists in the United States, but its strength has been modified by the existence of a strong sense of individualism. Theories of balance and congruity have been developed in social psychology since 1953 to explain why people who experience cognitive dissonance are likely to change some part of their attitude. Theodore Newcomb (1953) is considered to have pioneered his theory of cognitive dissonance. It points to the tendency for people to seek balance among different people with whom they come into close contact. The limitation of this proclivity is the omnipresence of the clearly defined and salient sense of self that characterizes American culture.

Prince Régent Shôtoku urged bureaucrats, through his administrative guidance of the seventeen-article constitution, to learn from the teachings of Buddhism, Confucianism, Shintôism, and Taoism. It is not clear exactly when what is referred to as the theory of *honjisuijyaku* (combining Buddhism and Shintoism) came into being. But both sides started to respect each other's religion by the end of the seventh century as the imperial system firmly established itself. The theory of honjisuijyaku says that the home base of god is Buddha, who descended to Japan to save the Japanese (Nakamura, Fukunaga, Tamura, and Konno, 1989, p. 749). This theory became the basis for learning to accept both religions.

If Max Weber is correct that Judaism first gave rise to rationalism in the line of progress from magic and religion to science or rationalism, then the Japanese never fully developed rationalism. The five values found to be salient are to a varying degree related to the Rashomonesque Yamazakura model. Wa in society would be difficult to realize if unfair practices prevail. The Japanese love for the Katsura Detached Palace indicates a diffuse view of self. The idea is that a person is an integral part of nature, of the environment. One should be in harmony with the nature that surrounds one.

A culture and its language are alive and subject to change over time. The Japanese culture has changed over the years, as we studied from 1953 to 1993. We concentrated on looking at a dynamic dimension of the Japanese culture in Chapter 4.

First, the major structural change we found was the disintegration of traditional-modern paradigm. The Japanese learned to view the world from the perspective of traditional versus modern values after the Meiji Restoration in 1868 following the opening of Japan's doors to the world. This attitudinal structure started to fall apart in 1978, and its disintegration became definite by 1988. For example, the "conquering" nature was an important value during the era of Japan's modernization process, but it has since been replaced by the "following" nature. The traditional perspective of catching up with the West and categorizing what is Western and Japanese has become meaningless.

Second, the majority of Japanese are finally accepting democracy as an ideal in the 1990s, over forty years after democracy was imposed on Japan.

There are limited signs of growing individualism as well. There are, however, other findings that contradict with the trend, such as a decrease in the number of people who are willing to go their own way against traditional customs.

These dynamic aspects of the Japanese culture may be a product of economic changes that took place in the last half of the twentieth century in Japan. Japan also became more integrated into the rest of the world, particularly in the area of trade with other nations. The Japanese regained their self-confidence as they recovered from the war-torn economy and built an industrial society characterized by relatively equal distribution of income and the paucity of alienation.

Every culture has its own unique qualities not found in other cultures. Japan is no exception. Our efforts in Chapter 5 centered on the core of Japanese culture, which we found in contrast to American and other Western cultures. First, we discovered that what leads us to have different ways of looking at the world may be derived largely from differences in language and religion. We found that the Japanese thinking in English comes closer to the way Americans view the world in choosing their position among alternate positions. Americans too become more like the Japanese when they are thinking in Japanese.

Second, a series of findings pointed to the validity of our Rashomonesque Yamazakura model. For example, the Japanese are strongly inclined to avoid extreme positions and prefer an ambiguous position; resist a view of the world in rational, linear, and binary terms; and focus their attention on human relations.

Perhaps the most severe effort to invalidate our model was to analyze all thirty-two items in the questionnaire included in every survey from 1953 to 1993 by using Hayashi's quantification method III. If our theory is invalid, indicators for Rashomonesque Yamazakura should not appear as salient patterns. Findings in Chapter 3 (Appendix for Chapter 3, Figures 3.7 and 3.8) indicate that the first and second axes separate modern rational response values from traditional and ambiguous responses, strongly validating our Rashomonesque Yamazakura model. It is a gratifying feeling for researchers to find that their theory bears out in an empirical test. The original intent of the research team in 1953 was to collect items that can best describe Japanese culture. Since then we added some items and discontinued others. The remaining item that made up the body of data from which we thought should emerge the salient pattern of the Japanese culture was Rashomonesque Yamazakura. Even a more clear delineation of the pattern of Rashomonesque Yamazakura appeared in the third and fourth dimensions.

Third, the Japanese are pessimistic in their views of science, especially social science and its beneficial effects on people, in contrast to optimistic Americans. Germans in relation to the Japanese are more realistic in their love of nature. The Japanese blindly love an idealized view of nature. The Japanese tend to trust other people more than Westerners do. They are not attached to a particular ideology or economic doctrine, as are Americans and Europeans.

These generalizations lead us to conclude that industrialization alone does not constitute a sufficient condition to result in a common culture among industrialized nations of the world today. The Japanese are different in some basic ways even after their economy has reached the same level of development as America and Europe. Continuing trade issues largely derived from cultural differences that plagued Japan-U.S. relations particularly in the past fifteen years are not going away anytime soon.

The key difference between American and Japanese culture centers on two dimensions: the definition of self and the definition of the world. This difference emanates largely from the difference in language.

While the industrialization process produced divergent values for Japan and the West, it also is responsible for the development of some homogeneous cultural values. We looked for commonly shared values in the five industrialized nations in Chapter 6. We found three levels of similarities: (1) frequency distribution of single variables, (2) similar impacts of age and gender on attitudes, and (3) similar structures in the way people categorize their experience.

First, the majority of respondents in all five industrial nations compared thought they were members of the middle class.[4] This is an example of the validity of conversion theory, while other beliefs such as the importance of family and children may be something the five nations all shared to begin with before the industrial era. There are relative emphases on human relations in the workplace, employment exams, the importance of religion in life, and the sense of beauty.[5]

The importance of religion does not relate to the question of whether one is religious or not in Japan. We discussed this point in detail in Chapter 5. We shall not labor any further here.

Second, two demographic factors, consisting of age and gender, often have similar or the same impacts on the attitudes of the respondents. The younger the respondents, the more they are optimistic about the future of their standard of living everywhere. Women in all five nations experienced more common illnesses of headaches, depression, insomnia, and others than men do. The impacts of the demographic factors on all five nations may be a consequence of the industrialization process.

Third, we classify our life experience in similar fashions, but we do not always share the same set of values. The Japanese are often found in the middle of two extremes, while American and English cultures are often found close to each other in the configuration.

Our concern for Japanese culture did not stop at examining its current status. We wanted to probe its future viability, as we did so in Chapter 7. All theorists seem to agree that culture is not static; the Buddhists taught generations of Japanese that "all phenomena are transitory." Hence the question is how and what parts of Japanese culture will change as we look into the twenty-first century. Our study of the past and present suggests that some aspects of Japanese culture may have survived from the time of the Prince Régent Shôtoku in the seventh century. Even if Japanese culture and its language survive, will its character be changed if what we found to be the core of Japanese culture, Rashomonesque Yamazakura, is no more? Or will it survive? Many great cultures have risen and fallen. We present the argument that the Rashomonesque Yamazakura model of Japanese culture will survive even in the twenty-first century, for several reasons.

First, when one examines the history of Japan, one finds that factors affecting cultural changes occurred as a result of challenges from abroad. Written records date back to the time of the Prince Régent Shôtoku onward through the Meiji Restoration and the Allied occupation of Japan. The history of Japanese culture reveals a pattern of adjustments through adopting and inventing. Its tradition, set forth in the Prince Régent's first actions of "administrative guidance," is to develop a way of incorporating foreign elements that fit its basic Rashomonesque beliefs—relativism. It is the spirit of Shinbutsujyushûgô (Learning to harmonize Shintoism, Buddhism, and Confucianism) that characterizes the Japanese way of meeting challenges from abroad. It is not total acceptance of an absolute value, such as the way the Chinese or North Koreans espouse Marxism or South Koreans accept Christianity. As Galtung (1983) and Mushakôji (1972) claim, the Japanese "adjust" to rather than "select" a new idea in its totality. This certainly was the case with Confucianism, with the Japanese rejecting the idea of the mandate of heaven while accepting many other Confucian teachings.

The same posture is observed even today by Japanese officials and scholars, who are struggling with trade issues with the United States. Their basic attitude is how Japan can adjust to U.S. demands to open its markets. They are not looking for the development of a new way of trading with Japan's largest trading partner, which operates different from the Japanese system. The United States, on the other hand, is interested in imposing its market-centered capitalism on Japan. Both have been too culturally blinded to achieve a successful relative trade balance, especially since 1980. Obviously, Japan's ability to adjust has its limitations as does the U.S. ability to impose its system on Japan in an increasingly interdependent global economy. Nevertheless, the Japanese way has survived for centuries. The Japanese are likely to succeed in resolving their trade conflicts with the Untied States in the long run.

Second, the Japanese way of adjusting rather than accepting or rejecting a challenge has resulted in reform rather than revolutions. This has been true throughout history since the Prince Régent's time—from the Taika Reform (645–650), to the Meiji Restoration (1868), to the Allied occupational reform (1945–51). This separates Japan from other nations, such as China, Egypt, France, Russia, and the United States, which experienced revolutions. It is the practical spirit of kaizen (improvement) and not invention that characterizes Japanese industry. In other words, we do not expect the Japanese culture to go through revolutionary change, but only gradual changes from time to time to adjust to new realities.

Third, ambiguity is a weapon the Japanese use in dealing with new ideas. Their ideas are not written in stone in the tradition of Judeo-Christian-Islamic beliefs. It is difficult for outsiders to grasp what the Japanese are looking for since their idea of self is so diffuse. These conditions make it difficult for foreign ideas to come into open confrontation with the Japanese. They create much confusion but never a complete loser in the end.

Fourth, if Japanese culture is to survive, it must maintain its language. Although there were some efforts made by a limited number of Meiji leaders to romanize the language, they failed. We do not see any future possibility of an end to the use of the Japanese language.

Fifth, many cultures that died in the past and will likely have their demise in the next century have been consequences of conquest in much of Asia, Africa, and the Pacific. Many of them possessed absolutist doctrines. Japan survived the unprecedented colonization efforts by the West in recent centuries by first isolating itself from the rest of the world. Then it quickly built up its modern state apparatus to be equal with the colonizing forces of the West in a relatively short time. Today's era, characterized by an increasingly interdependent global economy, makes it difficult for us to visualize Japan being conquered by other countries.

For these reasons, we concluded in Chapter 7 that although the Japanese sun may be eclipsed from time to time, it is not likely to set for at least decades to come or even centuries to come.

IMPLICATIONS

Our position is that the root of Japanese culture is in the Japanese language, which, in turn is affected by Japanese religious beliefs. Our assumption here is the Western culture is basically shaped by the Semitic root of written language, and Western monotheism is shaped by the Western civilization adopted from the Arabs and Jews. The essence of Japanese culture derived from the Japanese language is twofold: the Japanese self and the Japanese view of reality, which we call Rashomonesque Yamazakura.

The validity and reliability of the Rashomonesque Yamazakura model are upheld against the data we collected in the past forty years both in and out of Japan. We have hypothesized that the Rashomonesque Yamazakura nature of Japanese culture has not changed much since seventh century and is not likely to change for years to come.

Japanologists have argued over the question of whether Japanese culture is unique in the world, particularly in relation to the West. Our basic position is that there is no simple answer. The Japanese culture, like many other world cultures, does have some unique elements, as symbolized by the Rashomon-esque Yamazakura model. However, the Japanese culture in some fundamental ways shares its ways of thinking with at least six other industrial nations of the West. We would contend that the question defies a Yes or No answer. Both camps are correct in insisting that they are right. Both of them are, however, wrong if they insist that their generalizations are true of all aspects of Japanese culture. We should learn to refrain from simplifying excessively and to make serious efforts to understand the world for what it is—a complex human creation.[6]

For those who claim there is nothing new offered in this book, we would respond as follows: If one looks at part of our findings, it is true that one will find many things that have been said before about Japanese culture, from amae to Zen. However, there are several important contributions we have made in expanding the horizon of the *Nihonjinron*[7] and *Nihonron*[8] literature.

1. The evidence for our inferences and generalizations is derived from the most extensive longitudinal sample survey data of the Japanese people we know, spanning forty years from shortly after Japan's independence to 1993. The data set was enriched by comparative studies conducted in six other industrial nations of the world, in addition to other limited survey results from Brazil, China, Egypt, Hawaii, and Jordan.

2. No author before us has combined two essential ingredients of Japanese culture, the Japanese view of reality and self, as the core of Japanese culture. Many authors, however, pointed out the relativistic nature of the Japanese culture and its paucity of autonomous self. We agree with many authors of Japanese culture in this regard.

3. We have not been able to find any author on Japanese culture attribute its basic characters to its language. We contend that the language affected by religious beliefs is the single most important factor in shaping the essential base of Japanese culture.

4. No author of Japanese culture has traced the probable beginning of Japanese culture to the first administrative guidance issued by the Prince Régent Shôtoku in the seventh century. We would, in this sense, go beyond Sakaiya in claiming that the Prince Régent Shôtoku was not only the liberator of the Japanese from exclusive religious beliefs but is at least a father of Japanese culture.

5. Unlike other studies, we went beyond the frequency comparison of values or attitudes by examining the way we configure our life experience through Hayashi's quantification method III or correspondence analysis. Most of the studies of Japanese culture did not go beyond the comparison of the "this and that" character of the Japanese people. Our studies demonstrated how the Japanese categorize what they see and how they structure what they see into what they consider reality.

6. Most authors of Japanese culture stopped at characterizing the nature of Japanese culture. We made efforts to probe the viability of Japanese culture into the twenty-first century. The pattern of adaptation in Japan is often characterized by the development of a dual structure. For example, the Japanese Diet, as directed by the New Deal reformers, erected the Diet structure along the American standing committee system while keeping the parliamentary system. The Steering Committee in each House directs parliamentary operations. However, there is a party committee called the Diet Countermeasure Committee. Unlike the Diet Steering Committee, this committee is organized by each

party to adjust to policy differences on important issues among different political parties. This is the place where dangô (informal consultation) takes place to ensure the smooth operation of the Diet. A large sum of money (the amount of spending by the Liberal Democratic Party was reduced to $14 million in 1994 from over $70 million spent before 1993) changes hands, especially from the ruling Liberal Democratic Party to the Social Democratic Party members. Informal exchange of ideas and deals are made between opposing forces to ensure the appearance of political stability, which is needed for economic growth. Viewed in this perspective, the coalition formation of conservative Liberal Democrats and Socialists in 1994 is well within the realm of possibility. They enjoyed friendship behind the scenes for many years. This is a manifestation of the way the Japanese adjust to the need to accommodate the demand for democracy where policy differences are openly debated and to achieve harmonious relationships among the Diet members.

Having said that, we must admit that we have not gone much beyond what Norinaga Motoori said over a century ago when he composed his ode. He elegantly alluded to the essence of Japanese culture as being "barely visible cherry blossoms." Japanese culture is the world of ambiguous self and multiple realities. Motoori said it all in thirty-one syllables. It took us almost 200 pages. The qualitative nature of empirical data he used from his reading of the Kojiki and other ancient writings was different from our scientific data. Yet our conclusions are remarkably similar to his findings summarized in his ode, which provides us with evidence for the reliability of our sample survey instruments.

Our frequent citing of Norinaga Motoori in describing the essence of Japanese culture should not be interpreted to mean that we endorse the wartime interpretation of Motoori's works. The military and chauvinists during the Japanese colonial era abused him to promote what they wanted to do, especially to promote absolute loyalty to the emperor. While it is true that he strongly supported the imperial system, what we interpret as the meaning of Yamato (Japanese) spirit is strictly limited to his poem on the subject. To the best of our information, our interpretation is new and different from the traditional interpretation. Furthermore, we would side with Kenzaburô Ôe (1995, pp. 18–20) in that our interpretation of Yamato spirit is the way Murasaki Shikibu understood it to be as described in The Tale of Genji (1007). She emphasized the importance of learning in understanding the significance of Yamato spirit, not the blind obedience the wartime nationalists demanded of the Japanese people.

An important implication of our findings is that it is of utmost importance for the Japanese to preserve the Japanese language as is. We realize that expressions of many words change over time, and we have no objections to this. What we contend for Japan to preserve is the Japanese configuration of thinking that is often manifested in the language. In the language of the streets, we would like to see the omakase-ryôri (leave-it-to-us-dish) stay on Japanese restaurant menus.

We have presented here the best way we know how to demonstrate to a Western audience in general and American readers in particular what Japanese culture is. We made the "barely visible" nature of the Japanese cultural essence "clearly visible." We are confident that the Rashomonesque Yamazakura model provides Americans with a 20-20 vision of Japanese culture. If readers want to learn about Japanese culture beyond what we presented here, they must experience the language by learning it as Percival Lowell, a pioneering American diplomat-scholar, did in 1877 through 1893.[9] Lowell (1888) was the first American author to point out the paucity of individualism in the Japanese language. He loved the Japanese language because of its contrast with his mother tongue, American English.

We began our theory chapter with Norinaga Motoori's poem. We end this book by citing Rikyû Sen, who, like Socrates, remained true to himself by committing suicide. In Sen's case, it was *seppuku* ("hara-kiri"), suicide ordered by the ruler of his era, Hideyoshi.[10] Rikyû, the master of the tea ceremony, was often considered the father of tea ceremony. He meant in the poem cited below that exercise or learning is to figure out everything about an item by learning the foundation or step one.[11] The task then is to return to the original basics. You digest thoroughly what you learned and then create your own by returning to the basics of the way of tea. We believe that we have just gone through the process Rikyû taught us in the sixteenth century in the tradition of *Yamato gokoro* (Japanese mind) as described by Murasaki Shikubu, even if we used Western scientific methodology, a contemporary equivalent of then *kara gokoro* (Chinese mind).[12]

稽古とは一より習い十を知り十より帰るもとのその一。

Learning is how to get from one to ten by being taught one first, then returning to the one.

NOTES

1. *Waka* literally means harmonious or Japanese poem. Since the word *wa* could mean either Japan or harmony, the Prince Régent Shôtoku proposed it as the first principle in his "constitution" or "administrative guidance."

2. The question on gardens was not included in the questionnaire used in the comparative survey series. Our hypothesis is, however, that Westerners are likely to prefer Western gardens.

3. We are uncertain about the way the author's name is pronounced. Nan-a is most likely the author's pen name. The word *gengenkai* literally appearing in the book's preface refers to a deep-deep world. The author writes about how everything— Confucianism, Buddhism, etc.—has wastes or noise. The world is filled with competing ideas, some which confuse while others enlighten. Do not take any one of them seriously, the author seems to warn.

4. The five nations are Japan, France, West Germany, Great Britain, and the United States.

5. We are assuming that the traditional sense, of beauty in Japan and the West are different, but they are similar in that both cultures believe that their garden is most

beautiful. We are saying that the Japanese are similar to the Westerners in thinking that they like the Japanese garden and the Westerners, the Versailles garden.

6. Of course, one might successfully accuse us of being very Japanese in answering the question. We avoided taking sides in the controversy in the tradition of Rashomonesque Yamazakura. We plead guilty to that, for that is the way we construct the world.

7. *Nihonjinron* refers to a new genre of the study of Japanese culture developed since the 1970s, particularly after the publication of Shichihei Yamamoto's *The Japanese and Jews* under the name of Isaiah BenDasan (1971).

8. Nihonron includes the literature on Japanese culture written prior to the rise of the Nihonjinron literature.

9. His sister (Amy Lowell), a well-known poet and the leader of imagism, incorporated *ukiyoe* (A traditional Japanese painting style developed during the Tokugawa era) and *haiku* poems (consisting of 17 syllables) in her poems (Waggoner, 1984, p. 348).

10. He probably expected Rikyû to beg for his life. To this date, we do not know why he was ordered to commit suicide. He was regarded highly by Hideyoshi until he was so ordered in 1591. Sen Rikyû chose death over his life on earth to perpetuate the art of tea ceremony. The spirits of Rikyû lived and continue to flourish even today many centuries after his death. He won over Hideyoshi, just as the spirit of Socrates lives after many centuries.

11. Sen Rikyû (1522–1591) is said to be the third generation of tea ceremony master following his predecessors of Murata Shunkô (1423–1502) and Musashino Jyôô (1502–1555) (Kuwata, 1958, pp. 63–78).

12. We believe that the Japanese tradition is to be creative, not just to maintain the tradition as we inherit it from our ancestors. What separates us from the West is that we value harmony by respecting all others' competing values. Harmony, as Prince Shôtoku preached, cannot exist without respecting others. The Japanese education system has been criticized for not being creative enough. Critics may be correct in saying that we are not being radical enough, but they are wrong if they say that we are not creative at all. Our way of doing things is more often incremental than path breaking. Nevertheless, Japanese culture fosters its creativity in its own way. It does tolerate individualism and dissidents.

Murasaki Shikibu emphasized the learning aspect of the Japanese mind and not what one learned from the Chinese (kara gokoro) then. An implication of her definition of the Japanese mind is that the Japanese continue to learn by examining ideas from abroad. The Japanese mind is not static but dynamic. No one can deny Shikibu's literary creativity, so different from the Chinese culture (which despised love affairs as not worthy of high literary treatment), which was demonstrated so early in the Japanese history.

Appendix to Chapter 1

QUESTIONNAIRE ITEMS

The original questionnaire used in 1953 has been revised and expanded over the forty years. We have included here items that were introduced in the preceding chapters. Some are added for the purpose of conducting surveys in Hawaii. A common numbering is used throughout this Appendix. Most items mentioned in the book are included. Response categories for "Other" and "DK" (don't know) are used in many items but not reproduced here. All items, except items used in Honolulu among Japanese Americans, have a number beginning with the sign #.

#1.1 Gender
1) Male   2) Female

#1.2 Age
1) 20–24   4) 35–39   7) 50–54   10) 65–69
2) 25–29   5) 40–44   8) 55–59   11) 70+
3) 30–34   6) 45–49   9) 60–64

#1.3 Education
1) Elementary   2) Middle   3) High   4) University

#1.4 Occupation
1) Professional   4) Small proprietor   7) Unskilled
2) Managerial   5)Farming/fishing/forestry 8) Not employed
3) Clerical and sales 6) Skilled

#1.5 Area of Residence
1) Six metropolitan areas   3) 200,000–500,000   5) 50,000–100,000
2) 500,000+   4) 100,000–200,000   6) Under 50,000

#1.6   Region
        1) Hokkaidô   3) Kantô   5) Kinki   7) Shikoku
        2) Tôhoku   4) Chûbu   6) Chûgoku   8) Kyûshû

#1.8   (Card shown) Suppose one were to divide present Japanese society into
        the five strata on this list. Into which stratum would you place yourself?
        1) Upper   2) Upper middle   3) Middle   4) Lower middle   5) Lower

#2.1   If you think a thing is right, do you think you should go ahead and do it
        even if it is contrary to usual custom, or do you think you are less apt to
        make a mistake if you follow custom?
        1) Go ahead   2) Follow custom   3) Depends on . . . .

#2.2   Suppose someone wants to do something which he thinks is right and he
        gives a complete explanation to others about it, but they refuse to listen to
        him. Which of these two persons do you think has the better attitude?
        (Answer sheet shown)
        1) Somebody who ignores the opposition and goes ahead
        2) Somebody who give up the idea if it is opposed
        3) Other: Specify_____

#2.2b   (Card shown) Which sort of person do you prefer: somebody who always
        sticks to his principles, or somebody who's prepared to compromise to
        avoid ill feeling?
        1) Somebody who's most concerned about sticking to principles
        2) Somebody who's most concerned about preparing to compromise to
        avoid ill feeling

#2.3c   (Card shown) Are you satisfied with your family life? Or are you
        dissatisfied?
        1) Satisfied   2) Rather satisfied   3) Rather dissatisfied   4) Dissatisfied

#2.3d   (Card shown) How do you feel about society?
        1) Satisfied   2) Rather satisfied   3) Rather dissatisfied   4) Dissatisfied

#2.3h   (Card shown) Are you satisfied with your living conditions or
        dissatisfied?
        1) Satisfied   3) Somewhat dissatisfied
        2) Somewhat satisfied   4) Dissatisfied

#2.4   There are all sorts of attitudes toward life. Which one of the following
        statements would you say comes closest to your way of life?

1) Work hard and get rich
2) Study earnestly and make a name for yourself
3) Don't think about money or fame; just live a life that suits your own taste
4) Live each day as it comes, cheerfully and without worrying
5) Resist all evils in the world and live a pure and just life
6) Never think of yourself, give everything in service of society

#2.4* There are all sorts of things to live for. Of the things listed here, which would you say is closest to your own ideas?
1) To get rich   3) To live just as one wants to live
2) To become famous   4) To devote to one's efforts to serve society
*Used in the 1973 survey

#2.5 Here are three opinions about man and nature. Which one of these do you think is closest to the truth?
1) In order to be happy, man must follow nature
2) In order to be happy, man must use nature
3) In order to be happy, man must conquer nature

#2.6 Do you think more about the past or about the future? Please choose one of the following answers: (Answer sheet shown)
1) I think more about future than about my past
2) I think about equally of the past and of the future
3) I think more about my past than about my future
4) Other: Specify_____

#2.7 What single thing do you think is the most important in life?
(Do not give an example; anything is fine)
1) Health   2) Child   3) Family   4) Happiness   5) Wealth

#2.8 Suppose you had acquired enough money to live the rest of your life in comfort. Would you go on working, or would give up work?
1) Go on working   2) Give up work

#2.11 (Card shown) Which of these two approaches to life do you agree with?
1) Do what you want to do, even if it doesn't benefit other people
2) Do what is of benefit to other people, whether or not it is what you want to do yourself

#2.12 Would you say that most of the time people try to be helpful, or that they are mostly just looking out for themselves?
1) Try to be helpful   2) Just look out for themselves

#2.12b Do you think most people would try to take advantage of you if they
       got the chance, or would they try to be fair?
       1) Would take advantage   2) Would try to be fair

#2.13 (Card shown) Youth is a time both for storing up for the future and also
       for enjoying the present. Which of the two do you think young people
       ought to put the emphasis on?
       1) Storing up for the future   2) Enjoying the present

#2.30 (Card shown) From time to time, people worry about themselves or their
       families. How much do you worry about the following kinds of
       problems?
       First of all, how much do you worry about serious illness?
       1) Extremely worried   3) Slightly worried
       2) Fairly worried   4) Not at all worried

#2.30b (Card shown) How much do you worry about being injured on the job?
       1) Extremely worried   3) Slightly worried
       2) Fairly worried   4) Not at all worried

#2.30c (Card shown) How much do you worry about violence around town?
       1) Extremely worried   3) Slightly worried
       2) Fairly worried   4) Not at all worried

#2.30d (Card shown) How about traffic accidents?
       1) Extremely worried   3) Slightly worried
       2) Fairly worried   4) Not at all worried

#2.30e (Card shown) How about unemployment?
       1) Extremely worried   3) Slightly worried
       2) Fairly worried   4) Not at all worried

#2.30f (Card shown) How about war?
       1) Extremely worried   3) Slightly worried
       2) Fairly worried   4) Not at all worried

#2.30g (Card shown) How about accidents at nuclear power plants?
       1) Extremely worried   3) Slightly worried
       2) Fairly worried   4) Not at all worried

#3.1 I'd like to ask you a question about religion next. Do you, for example, have any personal religious faith?
  1) Yes   2) No

#3.2 Without reference to any of the established religions, do you think that a religious attitude is important or not?
  1) Important   2) Not important

#3.2b Without reference to any of the established religions, do you think that a "religious attitude" is important or not?
  1) Important   2) Not important

#3.9 Some Prime Ministers, when they take office, pay a visit to the Imperial Shrine at Ise. What do you think about this practice?
  1) Should go   3) Can please himself   5) Should not go
  2) Better to go   4) Better not to go

#3.9b (Card shown) Some Prime Ministers, when they take office, pay a visit to the Imperial Shrine at Ise. What do you think about this practice?
  1) He should go as part of his official duties
  2) No objection to his going if he does so as a private individual
  3) Even as a private individual he should not go
  4) It is a matter of indifference whether he goes or not

#4.4 Suppose that a child comes home and says that he has heard a rumor that his teacher had done something to get himself into trouble, and suppose that the parent knows this is true. Do you think it is better for the parent to tell the child that it is true or to deny it?
  1) Tell the truth   2) Deny it

#4.5 In bringing up children of elementary school age, some people think they should be taught as early as possible that money is one of the most important things in life. Do you agree with this or not?
  1) Agree   2) Disagree   3) Undecided

#4.10 If you had no children, would you think it desirable to adopt a child in order to continue the family line, even if there is no blood relationship? Or do you not think this is important?
  1) Would adopt   2) Would not adopt   3) Depends on. . . .

#4.11 Would you say you are on the whole more or less inclined than the average to honor your ancestors?
  1) More than the average   2) Less than the average   3) Average

#4.30 (Card shown) Some people say that home is the only place that you can be comfortable and relax. Do you think so, or do you disagree?
    1) I think so   2) I do not think so

#4.32 (Card shown) Which of the following three opinions is closest to your own?
    1) One must not divorce
    2) In extreme circumstances, it is all right to divorce
    3) As long as both agree, divorce is all right at any time

#5.1   Imagine this situation. Mr. A was orphaned at an early age and was brought up by Mr. B, a kind neighbor. Mr. B gave him a good education and sent him to a university, and now Mr. A has become the president of a company. One day he gets a telegram saying that Mr. B, who brought him up, is seriously ill and asking if he would come at once. This telegram arrives as he is going to an important meeting that will decide whether his firm is to go bankrupt or to survive. Which of the following things do you think he should do?
    1) Leave everything and go back home
    2) However worried he might be about Mr. B, he should go to the meeting

#5.1b The last question supposed that Mr. B had taken him in as an orphan in his youth and brought him up. Suppose that was his real father who was on his deathbed. Which would have been your answer then?
    1) Leave everything and go back home
    2) However worried he might be about his father, he should go to the meeting

#5.1c-1 Suppose that you are the president of a company. The company decides to employ one person, and then carries out an employment examination. The supervisor in charge reports to you, saying, "Your relative who took the examination got the second highest grade. But I believe that either your relative or the candidate who got the highest grade would be satisfactory. What shall we do?" In such a case, which person would you employ?
    1) One with the highest grade   2) Your relative

#5.1c-2 In the last question we supposed that the one getting the second highest grade was your relative. Suppose that the second was the son of someone to whom you felt indebted. Which person would you employ?
    1) One with the highest grade   2) Son of your benefactor

#5.1d If you were asked to choose two out of the following, which two would they be?
DON'T FORGET TO GET TWO ANSWERS FOR THIS QUESTION
1) Love and respect for your parents
2) Repaying obligations to benefactor
3) Respecting rights of the individual
4) Respecting freedom of the individual

#5.6 Suppose you are working in a firm in which there are two types of department chiefs. Which of these two would you prefer to work under?
1) A: A man who always sticks to the work rules and never demands any unreasonable work, but who, on the other hand, never does any
2) B: A man who sometimes demands extra work in spite of rules against it, but who, on the other hand, looks after you personally in matters not connected with work

#5.6b (Card shown) Suppose there were two firms that differed in the way I am going to describe.
Which would you prefer to work for?
a) A firm that paid good wages, but that did nothing like organizing outings and sports days for the employees' recreation
b) A firm with a familylike atmosphere that organized outings and sports days, even if the wages were a little bit less

#6.2 If you could be born again, would you rather be a man or woman?
1) Man   2) Woman

#7.1 Some people say that with the development of science and technology, life becomes more convenient, but at the same time a lot of human feeling is lost. Do you agree with this opinion or do you disagree?
1) Agree   2) Disagree   3) Undecided

#7.2 Some people say that however mechanized the world gets, nothing can reduce the richness of human feelings. Do you agree with this opinion or do you disagree?
1) Agree   2) Disagree   3) Undecided

#7.20 (Card shown) Do you agree or disagree with the view that the things that happen to people, both the good things and the bad things, are their own responsibility?
1) Agree   3) Rather inclined to disagree
2) Rather inclined to agree   4) Disagree

#7.24 (Card shown) Here are the various things people most commonly talk about concerning jobs. Which are you most concerned about?
1) Getting a fairly good salary
2) Not having to fear bankruptcy and unemployment
3) Having co-workers you get along well with
4) A job that gives you a sense of achievement

#7.24b (Card shown) And which next?
1) Getting a fairly good salary
2) Not having to fear bankruptcy and unemployment
3) Having co-workers you get along well with
4) A job that gives you a sense of achievement

#7.25 (Card shown) Here are two opinions about work. Which is closest to your thinking?
1) No matter how much money one has, without work, life isn't very interesting
2) As long as one has money, I don't think that life is uninteresting just because one doesn't have work

#7.4 Please choose from among the following statements the one with which you agree most.
1) If individuals are made happy, then and only then will the country as a whole improve
2) If the country as a whole improves, then and only then can individuals be made happy
3) Improving the country and making individuals happy are the same thing

#7.30b Compared with ten years ago, do you think the standard of living of Americans as a whole is
| 1) Much better | 3) Same | 5) Much worse |
| 2) Slightly better | 4) Slightly worse | |

#7.31 Compared with ten years ago, do you think your standard of living is
| 1) Much better | 3) Same | 5) Much worse |
| 2) Slightly better | 4) Slightly worse | |

#8.1 Some people say that if we get good political leaders, the best way to improve the country is for the people to leave everything to them, rather than for the people to discuss things among themselves. Do you agree with this or disagree?
| 1) Agree | 2) Disagree | 3) It depends on the situation |

#8.1a   Some people say that if we get outstanding political leaders, the best way to improve the country is for the people to leave everything to them, rather than for the people to discuss things among themselves. Do you agree with this, or disagree?
1) Agree   2) Disagree

#8.1b   Some people say that if we get good political leaders, the best way to improve the country is for the people to leave everything to them, rather than for the people to discuss things among themselves. Do you agree with this or disagree?
1) Agree   2) Disagree

#8.2   What do you think about democracy, capitalism, socialism, liberalism, and conservatism? Are you favorably or unfavorably disposed to these ideas?
1) Favorable   2) Depends on   3) Unfavorable
a) Democracy   b) Capitalism   c) Liberalism   d) Socialism

#8.6   (Card shown) What do you do in general elections for the House of Representatives?
1) Let nothing stand in the way of voting
2) Try to vote as much as possible
3) Not much interested in voting
4) Hardly ever vote

#8.9   (Card shown) Suppose that you had some dissatisfaction with society. What attitude would you take?
a) Take it into account when you go to vote
b) Take other legal action like making a petition, collecting signatures
c) Possibly, in some circumstances, resort to illegal measures
d) Not anything, even if you did have some dissatisfaction

#9.6   Generally speaking, would you say that Japanese people are superior to or inferior to Western peoples?
1) Japanese superior   3) The same
2) Japanese inferior   4) Undecided

ITEMS USED IN HONOLULU SURVEYS

01   Compared with ten years ago, do you think he standard of living Americans as a whole is
1) Much better   3) Same   5) Much worse
2) Slightly better   4) Slightly worse

02 Compared with ten years ago, do you think your standard of living is
    1) Much better   3) Same   5) Much worse
    2) Slightly better   4) Slightly worse

03 Do you think that your living conditions will get better or get worse over the
    next five years?
    1) Much better   3) Same   5) Much worse
    2) Slightly better   4) Slightly worse

04 Do you think people will become more happy or more unhappy?
    1) More happy   2) More unhappy   3) No change

05 What do you think about people's peace of mind? Will it increase or
    decrease?
    1) Increase   2) Decrease   3) No change

07 Do you think that people's health will improve in the future, or do you think
    it will get worse?
    1) Improve   2) Get worse   3) Not change

08 There is a lot of talk these days about what the country's goals should be for
    the next ten or fifteen years. On card A are listed some of the goals that
    different people say should be given top priority. Would you please say
    which one of them you yourself consider most important in the long run.
    (Show Card A)
    1) Maintaining order in the nation
    2) Giving the people more say in important governmental decisions
    3) Fighting rising prices
    4) Protecting freedom of speech

09 From the answers on card B, to what extent do you worry, either for yourself
    or for your family, about each of the following?
    1) Very much   2) Somewhat   3) Slightly   4) Not at all

	1	2	3	5	6	7
A Serious sickness						
Mugging						
B Car accident						
C Unemployment						
D War						
E Nuclear power accident						

11   Same as #4.11

12   Same as #4.12

15   Compared with others of your age, how do you feel about your health?
     1) Very satisfied   2) Satisfied   3) Dissatisfied   4) Very dissatisfied

16   From the answers on this card, how would you classify your standard of
     living? (Show Card)
     1) Upper   2) Upper middle   3) Middle   4) Lower middle   5) Lower

17   If you had to choose between more money and free time, which would you
     choose?
     1) More money   2) More free time

18   If you were to get enough money to live as comfortably as you would like
     for the rest of your life, would you continue to work or would you stop
     working?
     1) Continue to work   2) Stop working

19   Which one of these opinions comes closest to your own?
     1) No matter how much money you have, life without work is wasted
     2) As long as you have money, life isn't wasted even if you don't have a job

20   Here are some of the things people usually take into account in relation to
     their work. Which one would you personally place first?
     1) A good salary so that you do not have any worries about money
     2) A safe job with no risk of closing down or unemployment
     3) Working with people you like
     4) Doing an important job that gives you a feeling of accomplishment

22   Same as #2.4

23   How do you feel about the quality of life in the area where you live?
     1) Very satisfied   2) Satisfied   3) Dissatisfied   4) Very dissatisfied

25   There is a story of an idle grasshopper and diligent ant in one of Aesop's
     fables. When winter came, the grasshopper, who spent the summer singing,
     came for help to the ant, who worked all through the summer. The ant
     could have given either of the following two replies. Which one of the two
     do you think suits you best as the conclusion of the story?

1) The ant sends the grasshopper away because it is only natural that the grasshopper should suffer now

2) The ant first admonishes the grasshopper, saying, "You are to blame for having been idle and you should work harder from now on," and then shares his food

26a What is the single most important thing in life for you? Please tell me one thing only.
Write in

_____

26b What other things are very important to you? You can mention as many things as you like.

_____

27 Using this scale, can you tell me how important each of the following is to you?
Not important at all = 1   Very important = 7
A Your immediate family and children, if you have any
B Career and work
C Free time and relaxation
D Friends and acquaintances
E Parents, brothers, sisters, and other relatives
F Religion and church
G Politics

28 All things considered, how satisfied are you with your family life—the time you spend and the things you do with members of your family? Please indicate your feelings on the five-point scale shown on your answer card.
1) Very satisfied   4) Dissatisfied
2) Satisfied   5) Very dissatisfied
3) Neither satisfied nor dissatisfied

29 Now I want to ask you about your life as a whole. How satisfied are you with your life as a whole these days? Which number on the five-point scale comes closest to how satisfied or dissatisfied you are with your life as a whole?
1) Very satisfied   3) Neither satisfied nor dissatisfied   5) Very satisfied
2) Satisfied   4) dissatisfied

32 Same as #7.1

33 Same as #4.5

34   Same as #8.1

35   Same as #2.1

36   Same as #7.2

37   Do you agree with the following statement: "Home is the only place where one feels good and can relax"?
     1) Yes   2) No

38   Among the following opinions, which one comes closest to your own opinion?
     1) Marriage is permanent
     2) Marriage may be broken under serious circumstances
     3) Marriage can be broken by simple agreement of the two partners

39   What do you think about housework and child care?
     1) That's women's work
     2) Some of the work is more suited for women
     3) All of the work should be divided without differentiation between men and women

40   Same as #4.4

41   Same as #5.1

43   Same as #5.1b

44   Same as #7.4

45   Same as #5.5

46   Whom do you consider more desirable as a person?
     1) A person who is friendly and can be counted on to help others but is not an efficient worker
     2) A person who is an efficient worker but is indifferent to the worries and affairs of others

47   Which one of the following personality type do you like best?
     1) A person who stresses rational decisions according to principle without regard to interpersonal harmony
     2) A person who stresses the value of maintaining interpersonal harmony even if it may go against his own principle

48   Same as #5.1c-1

51   Same as #5.1c-2

52   Do you think most people would try to take advantage of you if they got the
     chance, or would they try to be fair?
     1) Would take advantage   2) Would try to be fair

53   Generally speaking, would you say that most people can be trusted or that
     you can't be too careful in dealing with people?
     1) Can be trusted   2) Cannot be too careful

54   I am going to read some things that people have said about life today. As I
     mention each one, would you tell me from the answers on this card how
     much you agree or disagree?   (Agree strongly, somewhat, disagree some-
     what, disagree strongly, DK)
     A   Most people will go out of their way to help someone else
     B   I feel I am part of a close-knit local community
     C   Nowadays a person has to live pretty much for today and let tomorrow
          take are of itself
     D   The way you earn money is more important than how much you earn

55   To what extent do you think that science and its applications bring
     improvements in your everyday life?
     1) A lot   2) A little bit   3) Not at all

56   In the future, computers will change our lives. How do you feel about this
     development?
     1) A desirable thing
     2) An understandable but inevitable thing
     3) A regrettable and dangerous thing

59   One hears a lot about energy conservation today. Do you feel that saving
     energy is
     1) Very important   3) Not very important
     2) Important   4) Not important at all

60   How important is environmental preservation to you?
     1) Very important   3) Not very important
     2) Important   4) Not important at all

61   What comes first to your mind when you think of American culture? (If
     only one item is mentioned, ask, Is there anything else you can think of?)

62   Same as #3.1

63   Same as #3.2

64   There are some people who say about religion that there are many sects, all
     with their own different positions, but that their teachings all amount to the
     same thing. Would you agree with this or not?
     1) Yes   2) No

66   How interested are you in politics?
     1) Very much   2) Somewhat   3) Little   4) None

67   Same as #8.2

69   With what you know of our legal system, how do you feel it is working in
     our country today?
     1) Very well   2) Fairly well   3) Poorly   4) Very poorly

71   Which one of the three following views toward society comes closest to
     yours?
     1) The entire way our society is organized must be radically changed by
        revolutionary action
     2) Our society must be gradually improved by reforms
     3) Our present society must be valiantly defended against all subversive
        forces

73   How often do you attend political rallies, campaign fund-raising events, and
     the like?
     1) Very often   2) Sometimes   3) Rarely   4) Never

75   Which political party do you support?
     1) Democratic party   3) Other party
     2) Republican party   4) Independent

77   In what year were you born?   _____

78   Sex (Don't ask this question. Just identify.)
     1) Male   2) Female

79   Where were you born?
     1) Hawaii: specify town or city and island
     2) Elsewhere in the U.S.: specify state _____
     3) Elsewhere outside U.S.: specify country _____

80 If you were not born here, how many years have you been living in Hawaii?
    1) ___ Years   2) Born here

81 What is your educational background?
    1) Elementary school or less   4) Technical/Business school
    2) Junior high school   5) University or college
    3) Senior high school   6) Graduate work or professional school

82 What is your regular occupation? Please be specific. Specify the nature of
    the job.
    1) Professional: professor, physician, teacher, engineer, lawyer
    2) Managerial: high government official, manager/proprietor (large)
    3) Skilled worker: carpenter, electrician, machinist
    4) Farmer: agricultural worker
    5) Semiskilled or unskilled worker: bus driver, laborer
    6) Clerical worker: clerk, insurance salesperson, police officer
    7) Service worker: waiter, barber, cab driver
    8) Housewife/student/not gainfully employed/on welfare
    9) Small businessperson: small store owner/manager

83 Are you single, married, divorced, or widowed?
    1) Single living with parents
    2) Single living without anyone of the opposite sex
    3) Single living with someone of the opposite sex
    4) Married
    5) Widowed
    6) Married but separated
    7) Divorced

84 What ethnic group do you identify with?
    1) Caucasian (island born)   8) Portuguese
    2) Caucasian (mainland born)   9) Puerto Rican
    3) Caucasian (foreign born)   10) Mixed: specify
    4) Chinese   11) Other
    5) Hawaiian   12) DK
    6) Japanese   13) Filipino
    7) Korean

85 How often do you read newspapers?
    1) Never   2) Occasionally   3) Regularly/often

86 How often do you watch television?
    1) Very often   2) Often   3) Not very often   4) Never

87   How often do you watch Japanese television programs?
     1) Never   2) Occasionally   3) Regularly/often

88   Have you ever visited Japan?
     1) No   3) Yes, 2 to 5 times   5) Yes, 11 or more times
     2) Yes, once   4) Yes, 6 to 10 times

89   In general, do you approve or disapprove of Japanese investment?
     1) Approve   2) Disapprove

90   THOSE WHO APPROVE ONLY: In what areas of Japanese investment

92   Regarding the Middle East, are you sympathetic more with Israel or the
     Palestinians?
     1) Israel   2) Palestinians   3) Neither

93   Compared to before the Palestinian uprising, would you say you are more
     sympathetic or less sympathetic to the Israeli/Palestinian position?

     Israeli position
     1) More sympathetic   2) Same   3) Less sympathetic

     Palestinian position
     1) More sympathetic   2) Same   3) Less sympathetic

THANK YOU VERY MUCH FOR YOUR COOPERATION. MAY I HAVE
YOUR TELEPHONE NUMBER SO THAT THE DIRECTOR CAN CALL TO
THANK YOU PERSONALLY FOR YOUR KIND COOPERATION AND TO
VERIFY THIS INTERVIEW?

   Telephone #: _____

Interviewer Remarks

In general, what was the respondent's attitude toward the interviewer?
     1) Friendly and interested   3) Impatient and restless
     2) Cooperative but not particularly interested   4) Hostile
B. How was the respondent's understanding of the questions in general?
     1) Good   2) Fair   3) Poor

TO INTERVIEWERS: IF A RESPONDENT IS A JAPANESE AMERICAN,
     THE FOLLOWING ADDITIONAL QUESTIONS SHOULD BE ASKED:

ID #

Interviewed by: _____

J01 How often do you read Japanese-language newspapers?
　　1) Never　　　　　　　　2) Occasionally　　　　　　　3) Regularly/often

J02 How often do you listen to Japanese radio broadcasts?
　　1) Never　　　　　　　　2) Occasionally　　　　　　　3) Regularly/often

J04 Do you like Japanese music?
　　1) I like only Japanese music　　　　　　4) I do not like Japanese music
　　2) I like Japanese and non-Japanese music　5) I do not like any music
　　3) I like only non-Japanese music

J05 What does your family call you?
　　1) By Japanese name　　　　　　2) By American name　　　　　3) Both

J06 Which prefecture did your parents or grandparents come from?
　　1) Yamaguchi　　　　　　4) Okinawa　　　　　　7) Hokkaido
　　2) Fukuoka　　　　　　　5) Hiroshima　　　　　8) Elsewhere
　　3) Other part of Kyushu　　6) Other part of Honshu

J07 What generation are you?
　　1) Issei　　　　4) Yonsei　　　　　　7) Parents: nisei and sansei
　　2) Nisei　　　　5) Gosei　　　　　　8) Parents: sansei and yonsei
　　3) Sansei　　　6) Parents: issei and nisei　9) Kibei

J08 How many years of Japanese language school did you have either in Japan
　　or here?
　　1) None　　　　　　　3) 1 to 2 years　　　　　5) 6 to 10 years
　　2) Less than a year　　4) 3 to 5 years　　　　　6) 10 years or more

J09 How well do you use Japanese?
　　1) Fluently　　　　　　　　　　　4) Very poorly
　　2) Passably　　　　　　　　　　　5) Not at all
　　3) I can understand it, but I cannot speak it
J10 Do you have anyone in your immediate family, such as brother or sister,
　　son or daughter, who is married to a non-Japanese?
　　1) No　　　　2) Yes, one　　　3) Yes, two or three　　4) Yes, four or more

J11 Have you ever lived in Japan for any length of time?
　　1) Yes　　　　　　　　　　　2) No

J12 Which one of the following response choices best describes your preference?

Foods	1) Japanese
	2) American
Language	1) Japanese
	2) English
Television	1) American
	2) Japanese
Radio	1) Japanese
	2) English
Spouse	1) Japanese
	2) Non-Japanese
Close Friends	1) Non-Japanese
	2) Japanese
Needs	1) Family needs
	2) Individual needs

J13 Do you find it easier to write letters in English or in Japanese?
1) Japanese   2) English   3) Makes no difference

J14 Do you have any occasion to write in Japanese to someone?
1) Yes   2) No

J15 Do you do your mental arithmetic in English or Japanese?
1) English   2) Japanese   3) Both or mixed up

J16 Which of the following statements best describes your closest friends?
(Answer Card 1)
1) All of my closest friends are Japanese
2) Most of my closest friends are Japanese
3) Some of my closest friends are Japanese, but I have some who are not Japanese
4) Most of my closest friends are not Japanese
5) Most of my closest friends are Japanese

J17 What kinds of organizations (e.g., church, service groups, neighborhood association) do you belong to?
(Answer Card 2)
1) Most of the organizations I belong to are almost exclusively Japanese
2) Most of the organizations I belong to are ethnically mixed

J18 If you are employed, which one of the following statements best describes
   your co-workers or colleagues at the place where you work? (Answer Card
   3)
   1) All of my co-workers are Japanese
   2) Most of my co-workers are Japanese
   3) Some of my co-workers are Japanese, but some are not
   4) Most of my co-workers are not Japanese
   5) None of my co-workers are Japanese

ITEMS ON SCIENCE AND TECHNOLOGY USED IN CROSS CULTURAL SURVEYS

Q55 To what extent to do you think that science and its applications bring
   improvements to your every day life? Would say. . . . (READ)
   1) A lot   2) A little bit, or   3) Not at all

Q56 In the future, computers in general will continue to change our lives. Do
   think this is . . . . (READ)
   1) A desirable thing
   2) An understandable but inevitable thing, or
   3) A regrettable and dangerous thing

Q57 (HAND CARD 57) Using the answers on this card, would you tell me how
   much you agree or disagree with the following statements. (READ EACH
   IN TURN)
   Card 57:
   1) Strongly agree   3) Disagree somewhat
   2) Agree somewhat   4) Disagree strongly

A   There are some illnesses that are better treated by methods that modern
     medicine does not recognize
B   Some day science will permit the complete understanding of the
     functioning of the human mind
C   Most of the social and economic problems we face today will be resolved
     by the advancement of science and technology

Q58 (HAND CARD 58) How likely do you think it is that we will see each of
   the following things in the next 25 years?
   Card 58:
   1) Very likely   2) Possible but not too likely, or   3) not at all likely

A   A safe method for the long-term storage or disposal of waste products
     from nuclear plants

B   A cure for common forms of cancer
C   A cure for senility
D   People living in space stations

Appendix to Chapter 3

Figure 3.1

Giri-Ninjô Scale by Year

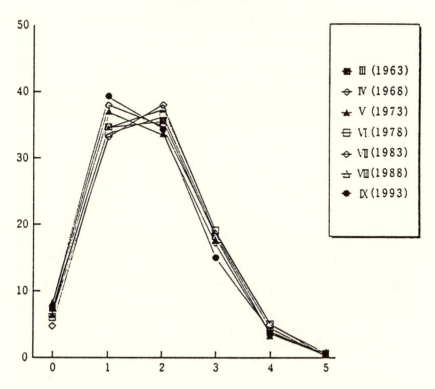

Figure 3.2 Giri-Ninjô Pattern by Year

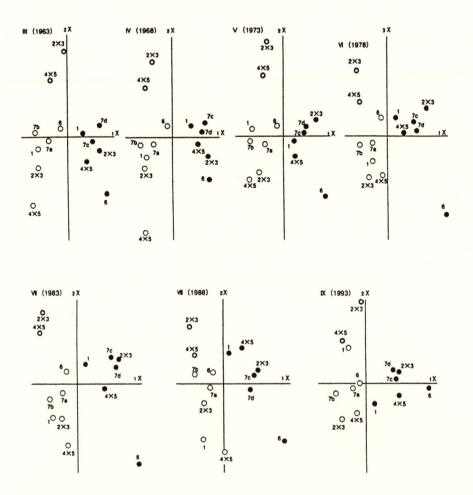

Giri-ninjô (Traditional) response
1   O (#4.4) To deny
2x3 O (#5.1) Attend the meeting + (#5.1b)
     O Go home
4x5 O(#5.1c-1) One with the highest grade
     O (#5.1c-2) Son of your benefactor
6   O (#5.6) Paternalistic department chief
7 a O (#5.1d) "On" (Moral indebtedness)
7 b O(#5.1d) Filial piety

Non-giri-ninjô (Modern) response
● To tell the truth
● Attend the meeting for both items
●One with the highest grade for both
   items
● Rational department chief
● Individual right
● Individual freedom

Figure 3.3   Giri-Ninjô Pattern by Age

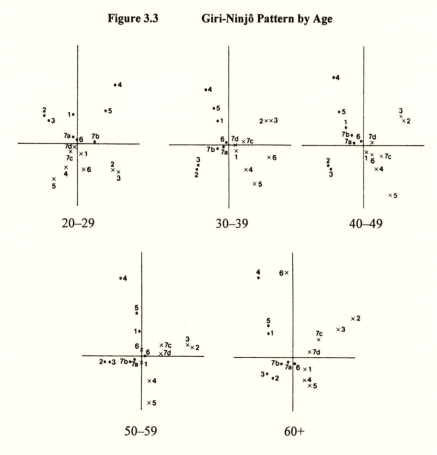

20–29   30–39   40–49

50–59   60+

Figure 3.4   Giri-Ninjô Pattern for 1988 Respondents in Their Twenties

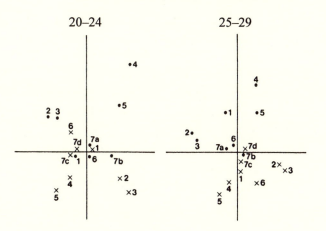

20–24   25–29

Figure 3.5

Giri-Ninjô Scale by Nationality

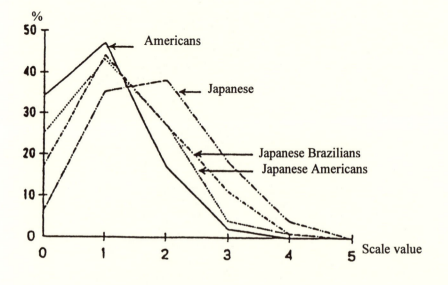

Appendix to Chapter 4

Figure 4.1

Traditional-Modern Orientation by Year

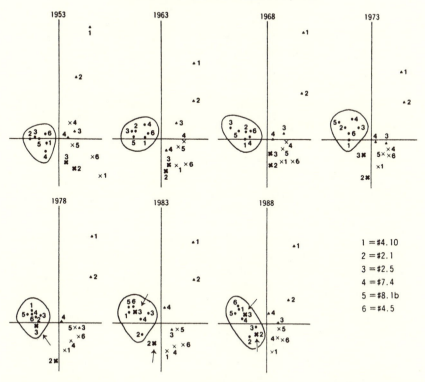

1 = #4.10
2 = #2.1
3 = #2.5
4 = #7.4
5 = #8.1b
6 = #4.5

• Traditional response   × Modern response   ▲ Middle response

Appendix to Chapter 6

FOUR QUESTIONS (TABLE 6.1 AND FIGURE 6.1) USED IN THE OHAJIKI SURVEY (1982)

We have listed four ways of governing the country. How important do you feel each way is? Please assign an appropriate number of beads to each pair depending on its importance to you, 5 being the most important and 0 being the least important.

1) a) The government does not have to keep the people informed of every detail, but it is important to cope with problems promptly.

   b) The government should inform the people of all details even if doing so may keep it from acting quickly.

2) a) The government should take action only after the majority of the people are persuaded to accept its position.

   b) The government should take action with strong leadership even if objections may be voiced by a minority.

Note: The English translation of the questionnaire has been edited to convey the meaning of original Japanese items to the reader. What follows is the original questionnaire used in 1982 in interviewing randomly selected *Japan Times* readers who live in Tokyo:

   Several pairs of choices are listed here as the ways a government should be run. We want to find out how important you think each choice is. Within each pair, please assign these five marbles to the two choices according to their importance. The more important one gets more marbles (five marbles maximum)

1) a) The government does not have to keep the people informed of minor details, but should cope with problems promptly.

   b) The government should inform the people of all details even if it may keep it from acting quickly.

2) a) The government should take actions only after the majority of the people have been convicted.

b)   The government should take actions with strong leadership even if objections
     may be voiced by a minority.

Table 6.1a

Ohajiki by Nationality

	0	1	2	3	4	5	NA	N
Japanese	6.5	10.5	22.5	37.2	16.3	6.5	.6	325
Westerner	4.5	1.5	3.0	28.8	40.9	18.2	3.0	66

Table 6.1b

Ohajiki by Nationality

	0	1	2	3	4	5	NA	N
Japanese	14.8%	24.9	35.1	17.5	4.9	1.8	0.3	325
Westerner	16.7%	21.2	19.7	25.8	9.1	3.0	4.5	66

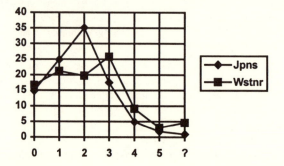

Eleven items used for the construction of the Neutral Response scale in Figures
6.2 and 6.3 are as follows: #12, #32, #33, #34, #35, #36, #67a, b, c, and d.

Figure 6.2

Middle-response Pattern by Nationality 1

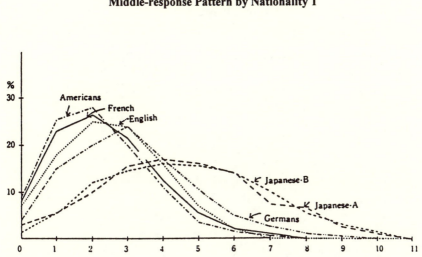

Figure 6.3

Middle-response Pattern by Nationality 2

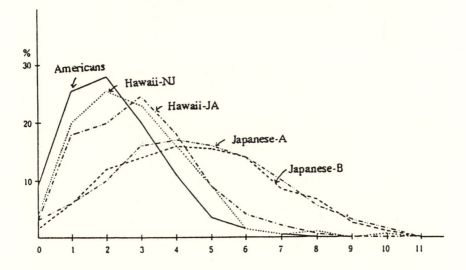

Figure 6.4

Common Items, 1953–1993

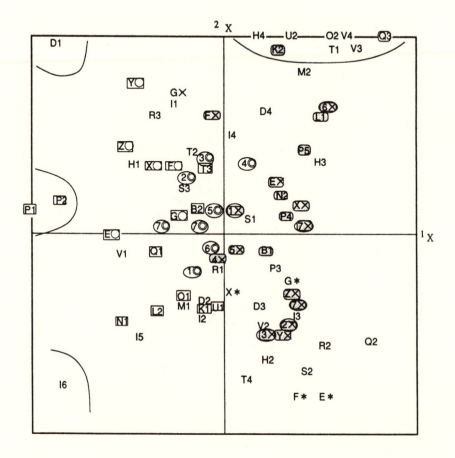

The following is a note on Hayashi's minimum dimension analysis used in Figure 6.5.

Table A

Rank Order by Frequency Distribution

Group by Rank Order

Response Category	1	2	3	4	5	N
Q1 Alpha	3	2	1	.	.	N
Q1 Beta	5	1	3	.	.	2
Q1 Gamma	.	.	.	.	.	.
Q2 Delta	.	.	.	.	.	.
. .	.	.	.	.	.	.
. .	.	.	.	.	.	.
QN Omega	.	.	.	.	.	.

Table B

Selected Response Categories

A	Relax at home	A	1.Yes
B	Marriage	B	3.Can be broken by simple agreement of the two partners
D	House work	D	3.To be done both men and women
E	Quality of life in your area	E	1.Very satisfied/2. Satisfied
Z	Bothered by noise	Z	1.A little/2. A lot
Y	Energy conservation	Y	1.Very important
F	Environmental protection	F	1.Very important
G	Health	G	1.Excellent/2. Good
H	Money & connection for health	H	1.Strongly agree/2. Agree
L	Your current standard of living	L	1.Much better/2. Slightly better
M	National standard of living	M	1.Much better/2. Slightly better
N	Your future standard of living	L	1. Much better/2. Slightly better
W	Science helps to improve life	W	2.A lot
R	Computer development	W	1.Desirable
a	Worry about serious illness	a	1.Very much/2. Somewhat
b	Worry about accident at work	b	1.Very much/2. Somewhat
c	Worry about street crime	c	1.Very much/2. Somewhat
d	Worry about car accident	d	1.Very much/2. Somewhat
e	Worry about unemployment	e	1.Very much/2. Somewhat
f	Worry about war	f	1.Very much/2. Somewhat
g	Worry about nuclear power accident	g	1.Very much/2. Somewhat

One of the common problems we face after gathering the survey data and analyzing them is how to present many findings by going through reams of computer outputs in a concise and succinct manner. A solution developed by Chikio Hayashi is used here to present our findings of what Honoluluans are like with Japanese and French respondents. Hayashi's minimum dimension analysis enables us to present many findings at once graphically (Hayashi, 1974b). Table A is constructed to describe this method.

Table C

Rank Ordering of Responses by Group

Category JA	Response HH	HM	TR	Group* JR	FR	PR	
A	4	5	7	1	1	3	6
B	7	6	4	4	4	2	1
D	4	5	1	7	6	3	2
E	1	1	3	7	6	4	5
Z	7	6	2	3	5	4	1
Y	2	3	1	6	7	4	4
F	5	4	2	7	6	2	5
G	2	3	1	6	7	5	4
H	5	6	7	4	3	2	1
L	1	2	3	5	4	6	7
M	1	2	4	5	3	6	7
N	2	2	1	4	5	6	6
W	3	2	1	7	4	6	6
R	4	3	2	7	6	5	1
a	2	3	7	4	5	1	5
b	2	3	7	4	1	4	6
c	1	2	3	5	4	6	6
d	2	4	7	4	1	4	6
e	1	3	6	7	5	2	4
f	2	1	3	7	4	4	6
g	1	2	3	5	4	6	7

*JA= Japanese Americans in Honolulu
HH = Honolulu-born Non-Japanese Americans in Honolulu
HM = Mainland-born Caucasians in Honolulu
TR = Tokyo respondents
JR = Japan nationwide survey respondents
FR = French nationwide survey respondents
PR = Parisian respondents

Response categories consist of answers (alpha, beta, gamma, delta, . . . omega), such as "Important" to "Not important," while groups in this analysis refer to groups, such as Japanese respondents, Japanese American respondents in Honolulu, Caucasian respondents in Honolulu, and Paris residents. Entries in Table A represent the rank order based on the magnitude of frequency distributions for each group. The smaller the numerical value of the rank order, the larger the percentage of respondents who chose that particular response over others in a given group. For example, the third group in Table A has the largest percentage of respondents choosing the "alpha" response category of Question 1. This is followed in descending order by the second group and then the first group.

Table B represents a summary of response categories selected to show how respondents in the three nations answered our questions regarding the quality of life in each respective country.

Having presented the list of response categories that are common in all surveys conducted in the three countries, Table C presents the results of rank ordering of the selected items included in the data analysis. Obviously, what is presented in the table is difficult to read, and the reader cannot begin to comprehend the whole picture we are interested in obtaining. To enable the results to be presented in a manner that is most succinct yet comprehensive and detailed, Figure 6.5 is constructed through a method called the "arrow and point method," or the APM. Each arrow line denotes the position of a response category (alpha, beta, gamma, delta, . . . omega), and each dot represents the position of each group on all twenty-one items. Accordingly, if one draws a straight line perpendicular to a line representing a particular response category from a given point representing the position of a group, the result will be a point at which the two lines intersect. The distance between the intersection point and the position of an arrow on the line represents the position ranking of a particular response category for a given group. The smaller the distance between the two points, the higher the ranking is. In other words, the closer the position of the intersection of the two lines to an arrow sign at the end of the line, the larger the percentage of that group choosing the particular response category with other groups. Spearman's rank correlation coefficient is used as the goodness-of-fit test to determine the responsibility of the results in Figure 6.5 (i.e., the results of rank ordering and those of intersection points). Two cases of low coefficients consist-ing of those items "a" (.52) and "e" (.46) are reported, while others yielded sufficiently high coefficient values. Consequently, our findings will focus on the remaining nineteen items.

Figure 6.5

Rank Ordering by Intersection Point

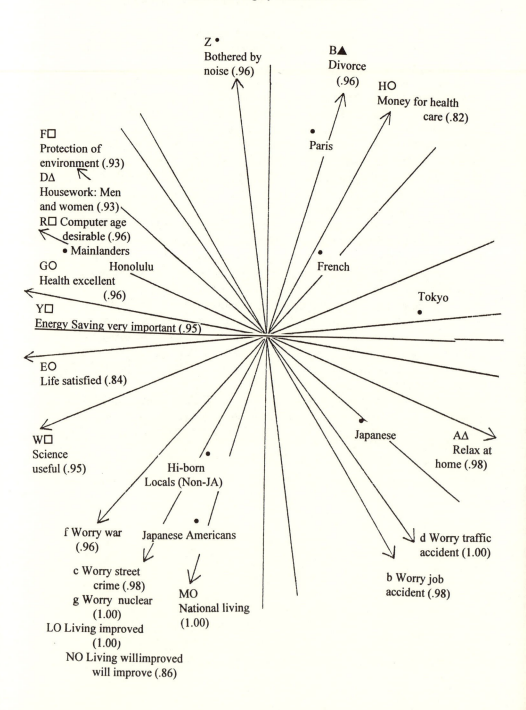

COMMON ITEMS FOR THE STUDY OF JAPANESE CULTURE, 1953–1993

The following thirty-two items were included in all surveys conducted from 1953 through 1993.

Table D

Common Survey Items, 1953–1993

		1	2	3	4	5	6
1	#4.4(2) Teacher	Deny	⊆ True				
2	#5.1(2) Benefactor	Home	⊆Meeting				
3	#5.1b(2)Parent	Home	⊆Meeting				
4	#5.1c1(2)Exam	⊆ Exam	Relative				
5	#5.1c2(2)Exam	⊆ Exam	Benefac*				
6	#5.6(2)Paternalist	⊆ Rational	Paternal				
7	#5/1d1(1) F Piety	Chosen					
7	#5.1d2(1)R Favor	Chosen					
7	#5.1d3(1) Right	⊆ Chosen					
7	#5.1d4(1)Freedom	⊆ Chosen					
E	#4.10(3) Adapted	Yes	⊆ No	⇐Depend			
F	#2.1(3) Custom	⊆ Push	Follow	⇐Depend			
G	#2.5l(3) Nature	Follow	⇐ Use	⊆Conquer			
X	#7.4(3)Individual	⊆ Ind*	Nation	⇐ Both			
Y	#8.1b(2) Politician	Yes	⊆ No				
Z	#4.5(2) Money	Yes	⊆ No				
B	#2.2b(2) Logical	Logical	Harmony				
D	#2.3d(4) Soc s*	Satisfied	Smwt s*	Smwt d*	Dis*		
H	#2.3h(4) Living	Satisfied	Smwt s*	Smwt d*	Dis*		
I	#2.4(6)Way of life	Rich	Name	Taste	No w*	Pure	Ss*
K	#2.8(2) Work?	Yes	No				
L	#2.11(2) Life	⊆ For me	For others				
M	#2.13(2) Life	Future	Now				
N	#3.1(2) Faith	Yes	No				
O	#3.2(2) Religion	Important	Unimpo*				
P	#3.9(5) Premier	Must go	Better go	Ind chc *	Betr*	No	
Q	#4.11(3) Ancestor	Honor	Average	No			
R	#7.1(3) Human feel	Lost	Cannot say	Preserved			
S	#7.2(3)Mechanized	Lost	Cannot say	Preserved			
T	#7.24(4) Criterion	Pay	Stable	Coworker	Acvt*		
U	#7.25(2) Work?	Yes	No				
V	#8.6(4) Election	Always	My best	No care	No vt*		

* Benefac = Benefactor; Ind = Individual; Soc s = Social satisfaction; Smwt S = Somewhat Satisfied; Smwt d = Somewhat dissatisfied; Dis = Dissatisfied; No w = No worry; Ss = Social service; Unimpo = Unimportant; chc = choice; Betr = Better not go; Acvt = Sense of achievement; No vt = Hardly ever vote

Glossary

Ainu: An indigenous ethnic group which resides largely on the Northern Island of Hokkaidô. They are Jômon people, one of the two main ethnic groups that comprise the Japanese population. Okinawans also are Jômon people.

Amae: Depend on one's kindness

Arigatô: Thank you

Aum Shinrikyô: Religion of the Truth; Japanese religious cult

Awase (culture): Culture that adjusts

Awase no bunka: Culture that adjusts

Bakufu: Shogunate

Bon: See Obon

Chiisakutomo kirai to hikarukuni: A small country with a bit of brilliant color emanating from within

Daiten-hô: Large Store Law

Dangô: Consultation

Enka: A popular song with a melody of traditional Japan, or ballad

Erabi (culture): Culture that selects

Gengenkai: deep, deep world

Genrô: Oligarchy of elder statesmen which governed Japan during the Meiji (1868-1912) period

Giin unei iinkai: Diet Steering Committee

Giri: Duty; obligation

Gosei: Fifth generation

Haiku: A seventeen-syllable poem

Hataraku: Work; labor

Heike monogatari: The Tale of Heike

Honjisuijyaku: Combining Buddhism and Shintôism

Honne: One's true motive or intention

Issei: First generation

Jigafukakujitsukan: Uncertain self

Jôruri: A ballad drama

Kabuki:Traditional Japanese theater in which all parts are played by men and the play is accompanied by Japanese musical instruments

Kaizen: Improve; make better

Kara gokoro: Chinese mind/spirit

Karôshi: Sudden death from overwork

Keiretsu: Company groupings

Kenminsei: Prefectural culture

Kojiki: Record of Ancient Matters

Kokinwakashû: Collection of aristocratic poetry compiled in the seventh century A.D.

Kokkaitaisaku iinkai (Kokutai iinkai): Diet Countermeasure Committee

Kokoro: Mind; heart

Kôshaku: Highest title of nobility

Kotoba: A word

Manyôshû: An anthology of 4,516 poems made between the beginning of the fifth century and 759 and compiled shortly after 759. It contains poems by males and females from all walks of life, from aristocrats to illiterate beggars.

Messhihôkô: War-time slogan exhorting "selfless devotion to the emperor"

Mochitsu motaretsu: Support and being supported; interdependence; a mutually dependent relationship

Monono aware: Literally "the sorrowful nature of things in the world." Motoori's (the foremost Japanologist) interpretation is that the ancient Japanese lived fully and freely unconstrained by Confucian ethical constraints. He tolerated Buddhist priests' yearnings for love and passion in being human while he urged people to know what is good and bad and to be sensitive to what is just and unjust.

Mujô: Subject to change

Naniwa-bushi: Chanting and reciting

Nihon Kokuminsei Chôsa: Japanese Culture Study Series

Nihon no Kokoro: Japanese Mind

Nihonjin no Kokuminsei: Japanese national character

Nihonjinron: Theory of Japanese culture

Nihonron: Literature on Japanese culture written prior to the rise of Nihonjinron literature in the 1970s

Ninjô: Human feelings

Nisei: Second generation

Obon: An annual event beginning in August during which Japanese remember their deceased relatives and loved ones. Derived from the Sanskrit ullambana, ("hanging upside down") obon refers to reversing the order of priority from self-centered "me-firstism" to being an integral part of all things in the world.

Ohajiki: Play beads/marbles

Omakase ryôri: Literally "leave-it-to-us dish;" a menu item in which the customer trusts the cook to prepare a meal.

Omiyage: Gifts or souvenirs that vacationing Japanese purchase for family, friends, and others

On: Obligation that one incurs to persons such as parents and teachers as one grows up

Oyabun-kobun: Boss-follower

Rashômon: Rashômon was the title of an award-winning film produced by Akira Kurosawa. Its theme is that there are multiple truths.

Rashomonesque: Rashômon-like

Sakura: Cherry blossoms; the national flower of Japan.

Sansei: Third generation

Seppuku: Ritual suicide

Shakai shisutemu kenkyûjo: Social System Research Institute

Shamisen: Traditional Japanese three-stringed instrument

Shinbutsujyushûgô: Learn to harmonize Shintôism, Buddhism, and Confucianism

Shinkô: Religious faith

Shiseiji: Single parent child

Shogyô: All things that are made or created

Shoshi: Single parent child

Showa: The current emperor Akihito's father, who reigned in Japan from 1926 through 1988. He is referred to in Japanese as Shôwa tennô, not "Hirohito" as he is known in the West.

Shutaisei: Positive and independent self

Soto: Outside

Tanka: Japanese short poems consisting of thirty-one syllables

Tatemae: Pretense

Uchi: Inside or home

Ukiyoe: Traditional Japanese painting style developed during the Tokugawa era

Wa: Harmony; "Wa" also refers to Japanese

Waka: A Japanese traditional poem of thirty-one syllables. Note that "wa" (peace or harmony) also refers Japanese, as well.

Wakon yôsai: A Meiji-era slogan meaning "Japanese spirit and western knowledge and technology"

Waza: An act, a work, a deed

Weltanschauung: Worldview

Yamato gokoro: Japanese mind/spirit

Yamazakura (bana): Mountain cherry blossom, wild cherry blossom

Yonsei: Fourth generation

Yûrikon-kankaku: The concept or sense of the mind's separation from the self/body

References

Araki, Hiroyuki. *Nihonjin no kôdôyôshiki*. Tokyo: Kôndansha, 1973.

Ashley, Richard K. "Living on Border Lines: Man, Post-structuralism, and War." In James Der Derian and Michael Shapiro eds. International/Inter-textual Relations. Lexington, Mass.: Lexington Books, 1989, 259–321.

Bachnik, Jane. "Introduction: *Uchi/Soto*: Challenging Our Conceptualizations of Self, Social Order, and Language." In Jane M. Bachnik and Charles J. Quinn, Jr. eds. *Situated Meaning*: *Inside and Outside in Japanese Self, Society, and Language*. Princeton: Princeton University Press, 1994, 3–37.

Banaji, Mahzarin R. and Debrorah A. Prentice. "The Self in Social Contexts." *Annual Review of Psychology*, Vol. 45, 1994, 297–332.

Beer, Lawrence W. "Law and Liberty." In Takeshi Ishida and Ellis Krauss eds. Democracy in Japan. Pittsbugh: University of Pittsburgh Press, 1989.

Bellah, Robert N., R. Madsen, W. M. Sullivan, A. Swidler, and S. M. Tipton. *Habits of the Heart*: *Individualism and Commitment in American Life*. Berkeley: University of California Press, 1985.

BenDasan, Isaiah (Shichihei Yamamoto). *Nihonjin to yudayajin*. Tokyo: Kadokawa-bunko, 1971.

Bendix, Regina. "National Sentiment in the Enactment and Discourse of Swiss Political Ritual." *American Ethnologist*, Vol. 19, 1992, 768–790.

Benedict, Ruth. *Patterns of Culture*. Boston, Mass.: Houghton Mifflin, 1934.

Benedict, Ruth. *The Chrysanthemum and the Sword*: *Patterns of Japanese Culture*. Boston, Mass.: Houghton Mifflin, 1944.

Benzécri, J. P., et al. *L'Analyses des Donnees 1,2*. Paris: Dunod, 1973.

Business Week, August 21, 1996, p. 40.

Cantril, Hadley. *Public Opinion*: *1935–1946*. Princeton, N.J.: Princeton University Press, 1951.

Caudill, William. "Patterns of Emotion in Modern Japan." In Robert J. Smith and Richard K. Beardsley, eds. *Japanese Culture*. New York: Wenner-Gren Foundation for Anthropological Research, 1962, 115–131.

Clemons, Steven C. "Japan Studies under Attack: How Rational Choice Theory Is Undermining America's Understanding of the World." Japan Policy Re-search Institute, Working Paper No. 1, August 1994.

Comte, Auguste. *System of Positive Polity*. London: Longmans Green, Vol. II, 1875, Vol. III, 1876, Vol. IV, 1877.

DeVos, George. "Dimensions of the Self in Japanese Culture." In Anthony J. Marsella, George DeVos, and Francis L. K. Hsu, eds. *Culture and Self: Asian and Western Perspectives*. New York: Tavistock Publications, 1985, 141–184.

Doi, Takeo. *Amae no kôzô*. Tokyo: Kobunsho, 1971.

Doi, Takeo. *The Anatomy of Dependence*. Tokyo: Kôdansha International Ltd., 1973.

Doi, L. Takeo. "Japanese Psychology, Dependency Need and Mental Health." Prepared for delivery at the Conference on Mental Health in Asia and the Pacific, East-West Center, Honolulu, Hawaii, March 28–April 1, 1966.

Doi, L. Takeo. "*Amae*: A Key Concept for Understanding Japanese Personality Structure." Reprinted in Takie Sugiyama Lebra and William P. Lebra, eds. *Japanese Culture and Behavior*. Honolulu: University of Hawaii Press, 1974, 121–129.

Dore, Ronald P. "Mobility, Equality, and Individuation in Modern Japan." In Ronald P. Dore, ed. *Aspects of Social Change in Modern Japan*. Princeton, N.J.: Princeton University Press, 1967, 113–150.

Dunn, L. C. and T. Dobzhansky. *Heredity, Race and Society*. New York: The New American Library, 1946.

Estudes Nipo-Brazilliros and contributors. *Burajurunikkeijin no ishiki chôsa*. Tokyo: Tôkei-suri kenkyûjo Research Report 74, 1993.

Etzioni, Amitai. *An Immodest Agenda: Rebuilding America before the Twenty-First Century*. New York: McGraw-Hill Book Company, 1983.

Etzioni, Amitai. *The Moral Dimension: Toward a New Economics*. New York: The Free Press, 1988.

Feldman, Ofer. "Political Psychology in Japan." *Political Psychology*, Vol. 11, No. 4, 1990, 787–804.

Frazer, James G. *The Golden Bough*, Vol. 1. New York: Macmillan, 1958.

Fukuyama, Francis. "The End of History." *The National Interest*, Summer 1989, 3–18.

Galtung, Johan and Fumiko Nishimura. "Structure, Culture and Languages: An Essay Comparing the Indo-European, Chinese and Japanese Languages." *Social Science Information*. London, Beverly Hills, and New York: Sage, Vol. 22, No. 6, 1983, 895–925.

Goethe, Johann Wolfgang von. *Faust: A Tragedy*. New York: The Modern Library, 1950.

Goldstone, Jack. *Revolution and Rebellion in the Early Modern World*. Berkeley: University of California Press, 1991.

Greenwald, Anthony G. and Anthony R. Pratkanis. "The Self." In Robert S. Wyer, Jr. and Thomas K. Srull, eds. *Handbook of Social Cognition*, Vol. 3. New York: McGraw-Hill, 1984, 129–178.

Hamaguchi, Eishun. *"Nihonrashisa" no Saihakken.* Tokyo: Nihonkeizaisha, 1977.

Hamaguchi, Eishun. *Kanjinshuginoshakai Nihon.* Tokyo: Nihonkeizai shimbun-sha, 1982.

Hayashi, Chikio. "On Prediction of Phenomena from Qualitative Data and the Quantification of Qualitative Data from the Mathmatico-statistical Point of View." *Annals of the Institute of Statistical Mathematics*, Vol. 8, 1952, 69–98.

Hayashi, Chikio. "Theory and Example of Quantification, II." *Proceedings of the Institute of Statistical Mathematics*, Vol. 4, No. 2, 1956, 19–30.

Hayashi, Chikio. "Multidimensional Quantification of the Data Obtained by the Method of Paired Comparison." *Annals of the Institute of Statistical Mathematics*, Vol. 16, 1964, 213–145.

Hayashi, Chikio, ed. *Hikakunihonjinron.* Tokyo: Chuôkôronsha, 1973.

Hayashi, Chikio. *Sûryôka no hôhô.* Tokyo: Keizai shimpô-sha, 1974a.

Hayashi, Chikio. "Minimum Dimensional Analysis MDA." *Behaviormetrika*, Vol. 1, 1974b, 1–24.

Hayashi, Chikio. "Minimum Dimension Analysis MDR-OR and MDA-UO." In S. Ikeda and Others, eds. *Essays in Probability and Statistics.* Tokyo: Shinkô Tsûsho Co. Ltd., 1976, 395–412.

Hayashi, Chikio. *Nihonjinkenkyûsanjyûnen.* Tokyo: Shiseidô, 1981.

Hayashi, Chikio. *Nihonjin no kokoro o hakaru.* Tokyo: Asahi shimbunsha, 1988.

Hayashi, Chikio. "Cultural Link Analysis for Comparative Research." *Survey Statistician, International Association of Survey Statisticians*, Vol. 21. Amsterdam: North-Holland, 1989, 625–632.

Hayashi, Chikio. "4.1 Nihonjin no kokuminseinitsuite." In Tôkeisûrikenkyûjo. *Daigo Nihonjin no kokuminsei.* Tokyo: Idemitsu shoten, 1992, 187–210.

Hayashi, Chikio. "Quantitative Social Research—Belief Systems, the Way of Thinking and Sentiments of Five Nations." *Behaviormetrika*, Vol. 19, No. 2, 1992a, 127–170.

Hayashi, Chikio. "Belief Systems and the Japanese Way of Thinking: Inter-chronological and International Perspectives." In H. Motoaki, J. Misumi and B. Wilpert, eds. *22nd International Congress of Applied Psychology, Kyoto, Japan, 22–27, July 1990: Proceedings Vol. 3.* Hove, UK: Lawrence Erlbaum Associates, 1992b, 3–34.

Hayashi, Chikio. "Nihonjin no kokuminsei." *Phase '93*, 1993, 64–96.

Hayashi, Chikio. "Nihonjin no kokoro no yukue." March 1995a.

Hayashi, Chikio. *Sûjikaramita nihonjin no kokoro.* Tokyo: Tokuma-shoten, 1995b.

Hayashi, Chikio, Hajime Ikeda, Yûzô Morita and Kazuo Terada, eds. *Keiryô-kenkyû.* Tokyo: Nansô-sha, 1974.

Hayashi, Chikio and Tatsuzô Suzuki. *Kokusaihikaku niokeru daeta kaiseki.* Tokyo: Iwanami-shoten, 1986.

Hayashi, Chikio, Tatsuzô Suzuki and Masamichi Sasaki. *Data Analysis for Comparative Social Research: International Perspective.* Amsterdam: North-Holland, 1992.

Hayashi, Ôki, ed. *Gensen.* Tokyo: Shôgaku-kan, 1986.

Hofstede, Geert. *Culture's Consequences: International Differences in Work-Related Values.* Beverly Hills, Calif.: Sage, 1980.

Holden, Nigel. "The Japanese Language: A Partial View from the Inside." *Multilingua,* Vol. 2, No. 3, 1983, 157–166.

Huntington, Samuel P. "The Clash of Civilizations." *Foreign Affairs,* Vol. 72, No. 3, Summer 1993a, 22–49.

Huntington, Samuel P. "If Not Civilization, What?" *Foreign Affairs,* Vol. 72, No. 5, November–December 1993b, 186–194.

Inkeles, Alex. "The American Character." *Center Magazine.* November–December, 1983, 25–39.

Inkeles, Alex and David H. Smith. *Becoming Modern: Individual Changes in Six Developing Countries.* Cambridge, Mass.: Harvard University Press, 1974.

Ishino, Iwao. "The Oyabun-Kobun: A Japanese Ritual Kinship Institution." *American Anthropologist,* Vol. 55, No. 5, 1953, 695–705.

Itzkoff, Seymour W. *Triumph of the Intelligent: The Creation of Homo Sapiens.* Ashfield, Mass.: Paideia, 1985.

Japan Economic Survey. Washington, D.C.: Japan Economic Institute, April 1989, 1–6.

Japan-Germany Collaborative Study. "Shinrin seitai ni kansuru tôkeiteki kenkykû" supported by Nihon Gakujjutsu Shinkô Kai [Japan Society for the Promotion of Science] and Shinrin Kankyô Kenkyûkai [Forest Environment Study Association]," headed by Tsunahide Shidei, 1977.

Johnson, Chalmers. *Japan: Who Governs?* New York: W.W. Norton & Company, 1995.

Johnson, Chalmers and E. B. Keehn. "A Disaster in the Making." *The National Interest,* No. 36, Summer 1994, 14–22.

Johnson, Frank. "The Western Concept of Self." In Anthony J. Marsella, George DeVos, and Francis L. K. Hsu, eds. *Culture and Self: Asian and Western Perspectives.* New York: Tavistock Publications, 1985, 91–138.

Kâgitçibasi, Cigdem. "A Critical Appraisal of Individualism and Collectivism: Toward a New Formulation." In Uichol Kim, Harry C. Triandis, Cigdem Kâgitçibasi, Sang-Chin Choi, and Gene Yoon, eds. *Individualism and Collectivism: Theory, Method, and Applications.* Thousand Oaks, Calif.: Sage, 1994, 52–65.

Kajimura, Noboru. *Nihonjin no Shinkô.* Tokyo: Chuôkôronsha, 1988.

Keene, Donald. *The Japanese Discovery of Europe—Honda Toshiaki and Other Discoverers.* London: Routledge and Kegan Paul, 1952.

Keller, Albert Galloway and Maurice R. Davie. Eds. *Essays of William Graham Sumner.* Vol. II. New York: Archon Books, 1969.

Kennedy, Paul M. *The Rise and Fall of the Great Powers.* London: Fontana, 1989.

Kim, Uichol, Harry C. Triandis, Cigdem Kâgitçibasi, Sang-Chin Choi, and Gene Yoon, eds. *Individualism and Collectivism: Theory, Method, and Applications*. Thousand Oaks, Calif.: Sage, 1994.

Kim, Uichol. "Individualism and Collectivism: Conceptual Clarification and Elaboration." In Uichol Kim, Harry C. Triandis, Cigdem Kâgitçibasi, Sang-Chin Choi, and Gene Yoon, eds. *Individualism and Collectivism: Theory, Method, and Applications*. Thousand Oaks, Calif.: Sage, 1994, 19–40.

Kindachi, Haruhiko. *The Japanese Language*. Tokyo: Charles E. Tuttle, 1978.

Kluckhohn, Clyde and W. H. Kelly. "The Concept of Culture." In Ralph Linton, ed. *The Science of Man in the World Crisis*. New York: Columbia University Press, 1945, 78–105.

Kluckhohn, Clyde. *Mirror for Man*. New York: Fawcett World Library, 1957.

Kobayashi, Hideo. *Motoori Norinaga*. Tokyo: Shinchôsha, 1977.

Koike, Seiji. *Nihongo wa ikani tsukuraretaka?* Tokyo: Chikuma shobô, 1989.

Koyasu, Nobukuni. *Motoori Norinaga*. Tokyo: Iwanami shinsho, 1992.

Kroeber, Alfred L. *Configurations of Cultural Growth*. Berkeley: University of California Press, 1944.

Kuroda, Yasumasa. "Protest Movements in Japan: A New Politics." *Asian Survey*, Vol. 12, No. 11, November 1972, 947–952.

Kuroda, Yasumasa. *Reed Town, Japan*. Honolulu: The University Press of Hawaii, 1974.

Kuroda, Yasumasa. "A Cross-National Analysis of the Japanese Character among Japanese-Americans in Honolulu." *Ethnicity*, Vol. 5, 1978, 42–59.

Kuroda, Yasumasa. "Japanese Perceptions of the Arab World: Their Nature and Scope." In Ronald Morse, ed. *Japan and the Middle East in Alliance Politics*. Washington, D.C.: The Wilson Center, 1986, 41–56.

Kuroda, Yasumasa. "Japanese Superiority Complex." *PHP Interact*, Vol. 3, No. 1, January 1987, 28–29.

Kuroda, Yasumasa. "Leadership Recruitment Patterns in the Japanese House of Representatives: General Elections 1–30, 1890–1963." *International Political Science Review*, Vol. 9, No. 2, April 1988, 119–130.

Kuroda, Yasumasa. "Japanese Patterns of Economic Development." *The Journal of Arab Affairs*, Vol. 10, No. 1, Spring 1991, 5–40.

Kuroda, Yasumasa. "Bush's New World Order: A Structural Analysis of Instability and Conflict in the Gulf." In Tareq Y. and J. S. Ismael eds. *The Gulf War and the New World Order*. Gainesville, Florida: University Press of Florida, 1994, 52–76.

Kuroda, Yasumasa. "Seijitekishikakukara mita nichi-bei kankei no tenbô." *Nomos*, No. 6, 1995, 8–15.

Kuroda, Yasumasa and Alice Kuroda. "Aspects of Community Political Participation in Japan: Sex, Education, Generation in the Process of Political Socialization." *Journal of Asian Studies*, Vol. 27, No. 2, 1968, 220–251.

Kuroda, Yasumasa, Alice K. Kuroda, Chikio Hayashi, and Tatsuzô Suzuki. "The End of Westernization and the Beginning of New Modernization in Japan: Attitudinal

Dynamics of the Japanese, 1953–1983." *The Arab Journal of the Social Sciences*, Vol. 2, No. 1, April 1987, 18–36.

Kuroda, Yasumasa and Chikio Hayashi. "Rashomonesque Yamazakura." Prepared for delivery at the Conference on Japanese Identity: Cultural Analysis, Teikyô Loretto Heights University, Denver, April 21–23, 1995.

Kuroda, Yasumasa, Chikio Hayashi, and Tatsuzô Suzuki. "The Role of Language in Cross-National Surveys: American and Japanese Respondents." *Applied Stochasitic Model and Data Analysis*, Vol. 2, No. 1, 1986, 69–86.

Kuroda, Yasumasa, Chikio Hayashi, Tatsuzô Suzuki, and Alice Kuroda. "The End of Westernization and the Beginning of New Modernization: The Attitudinal Dynamics of the Japanese, 1953–1978." *The Arab Journal of the Social Sciences*, Vol. 2, No. 1, 1987, 18–36.

Kuroda, Yasumasa and Tatsuzô Suzuki. "Language and Attitudes: A Study in Arabic, English, and Japanese on the Role of Language in Cross-cultural Thinking." In Donald M. Topping, Doris C. Crowell, and Victor N. Kobayashi, eds. *Thinking Across Cultures*. Hillsdale, N.J.: Lawrence Erlbaum Associates, 1989a, 147–161.

Kuroda, Yasumasa and Tatsuzô Suzuki. "A Comparative Analysis of Rationalism: Arab, American and Japanese Students." In *Urbanism in Islam: The Proceedings of the International Conference on Urbanism in Islam*, Vol. 3, 1989b, 65–96.

Kuroda, Yasumasa and Tatsuzô Suzuki. "Arab Students and English: The Role of Implicit Cultures." *Behaviormetrika*, No. 29, 1991a, 23–44.

Kuroda, Yasumasa and Tatsuzô Suzuki. "A Comparative Analysis of the Arab Culture: Arabic, English and Japanese Languages and Values." *Behaviormetrika*, No. 30, 1991b, 35–53.

Kuroda, Yasumasa and Tatsuzô Suzuki. "Tahalil Muqarin Thaqafa Al-Arabiye: Al-Lughat Wa Al-Queem Al-Arabiye Wa Al-Ankelizidyeh Wa Al-Yaban-iye." *Al Mustaqbal Al Arabi* [The Arab Future], No. 163, September 1992, 14–31.

Kuroda, Yasumasa, Tatsuzô Suzuki, and Chikio Hayashi. "A Comparative Analysis of Response Patterns: American and Japanese Respondents." Unpublished paper delivered at the Annual Meeting of the American Political Science Association, Chicago, 1987.

Kuwata, Tadachika. *Cha*. Tokyo: Davidosha, 1958.

Lebart, Ludovic, Alain Morineau and Kenneth M. Warwick. *Multivariate Descriptive Statistical Analysis*. New York: John Wiley & Sons, 1984.

Lebra, Takie Sugiyama. *Japanese Patterns of Behavior*. Honolulu: University of Hawaii Press, 1976.

Lerner, Michael. "Two More Years." *Tikkun*, Vol. 9, No. 6, November-December, 1994, 10-14.

Linnenberg, E. H. "Cognition and ethnolinguistics." *Language*, Vol. 29, 1953, 463–471.

Lowell, Percival. *The Soul of the Far East*. Boston, Mass.: Houghton Mifflin, 1888.

Markus, Hazel Rose and Shinobu Kitayama. "Culture and the Self: Implications for Cognition, Emotion, and Motivation." *Psychological Review*, Vol. 98, No. 2, 1991, 224–253.

Markus, Hazel Rose and Shinobu Kitayama, eds. *Emotion and Culture: Empirical Studies of Mutual Influence.* Washington, D.C.: American Psychological Association, 1994.

Marsella, Anthony J. "Culture, Self and Mental Disorder." In Anthony J. Marsella, George DeVos, and Francis C. K. Hsu, eds. *Culture and Self: Asian and Western Perspectives.* New York: Tavistock Publications, 1985, 281–307.

Maruyama, Saiichi. "Love and Eros in Literature: Contrasting Japanese and Chinese Tastes." *The Japan Foundation Newsletter.* Vol. 22, No. 2, November–December 1994, 1–6.

Marx, Karl. *Capital,* Vol. 1. New York: Modern Library, 1936.

Matsumoto, Scott Y. *Contemporary Japan.* Transactions of the American Philosophical Society, 1960, 50, Part 1.

McKean, Margaret A. "Equality." In Takeshi Ishida and Ellis S. Krauss, eds. *Democracy in Japan.* Pittsburgh: University of Pittsburgh Press, 1989, 201–224.

Miller, George A. and David McNeill. "Psycholinguistics." In Gardner Lindzey and Elliot Aronson, eds. *The Handbook of Social Psychology.* Vol. 3, Second ed. Reading Mass.: Addison-Wesley, 1969, 666–794.

Minami, Hiroshi. *Nihontekijiga.* Tokyo: Iwanami shinsho, 1983.

Minami, Hiroshi. *Psychology of the Japanese People.* Tokyo: University of Tokyo Press, 1971.

Minami, Hiroshi. *Nihonjinron—Meiji kara konnichi made.* Tokyo: Iwanimi shoten, 1994.

Mizuno, Kinji. "Kodomo—ie." In *Tôkeisûrikenkyûjo. Daigo Nihonjin no kokuminsei.* Tokyo: Idemitsu shoten, 1992, 99–106.

Moore, Charles A. "Concluding Remarks." In Charles A. Moore, ed. *The Status of the Individual in the East and West.* Honolulu: University of Hawaii Press, 1968, 547–576.

Moore, Wilbert E. *World Modernization: The Limits of Convergence.* New York: Elsevier, 1979.

Morgan, Lewis Henry. *Ancient Society, or Researches in the Lines of Human Progress from Savagery, through Barbarism to Civilization.* New York: H. Holt and Co., 1877.

Motoyama, Yukihiko. *Motoori Norinaga.* Tokyo: Shimizu shoin, 1978.

Muraoka, Noritsugu. *Motoori Norinaga Zenshû.* Vol. 1–6. Tokyo: Iwanami shoten, 1942–1944.

Mushakakoji, Kinhide. "The Cultural Premises of Japanese Diplomacy." *The Japan Interpreter,* Vol. 7, Summer-Autumn 1972, 282–292.

Nakamura, Hajime. *Ways of Thinking of Eastern Peoples.* Honolulu: East-West Center Press, 1964.

Nakamura, Hajime. "Consciousness of the Individual and the Universal among the Japanese." In Charles A. Moore, ed. *The State of the Individual in East and West.* Honolulu: University of Hawaii Press, 1968, 141–160.

Nakamura, Hajime, Mitsuji Fukunaga, Yoshirô Tamura, and Tôru Konno. *Bukkyô jiten.* Tokyo: Iwanami shoten, 1989.

Nakamura, Takashi. "3.6 Danjyo no sai." In *Tôkeisûrikenkyûjo. Daigo Nihonjin no kokuminsei.* Tokyo: Idemitsu shoten, 1992, 120–138.

Nakane, Chie. *Tateshakai no ningen kankei.* Tokyo: Kôdansha, 1967.

Nakane, Chie. *Japanese Society.* Berkeley and Los Angeles: University of California Press, 1970.

Nan-a, Yûkokushi. *Wasô bei.* Publisher unknown, 1774, as cited in Kokumin-bunko, ed. *Kokumin-bunko.* Tokyo: Kokumin-bunko Publishing Association, 1910, 3–4.

Newcomb, Theodore M. "An Approach to the Study of Communication Arts." *Psychological Review,* Vol. 60, 1953, 393–404.

Ochs, Terry. "'Why Can't We Speak Tagalog?' The Problematic Status of Multilingualism in the International School." *Journal of Multilingual and Multicultural Development,* Vol. 14, No. 6, 1993, 447–462.

Ôe, Kenzaburô. *Japan, the Ambiguous and Myself.* Tokyo: Kôdansha International, 1995.

Ogburn, William Fielding. *Social Change: With Respect to Cultural and Original Nature.* New York: B. S. Huebsch, 1922.

Ôno, Susumu. *Nihongo no sekai.* Tokyo: Asahi Shimbunsha, 1993.

Ôtsuki, Fumihiko. *Daigenkai.* Tokyo: Fuzanbô, 1956.

Ozawa, Ichirô. *Nihonkaizokeikaku.* Tokyo: Kôdansha, 1993.

Parrot, Vilified. *The Mind and Society.* Translated by A. Livingston. New York: Harcourt Brace Jovanovich, 1935.

Parsons, Talcott. *Structure and Process in Modern Societies.* Glencoe, Ill.: Free Press, 1960.

Putnam, Robert D. "Turning in, Turning out: The Strange Disappearance of Social Capital in America." *PS Political Science & Politics.* Vol. 28, No. 4, December 1995, 664–683.

Redfield, Robert. *Primitive World and Its Transformations.* Ithaca, N.Y.: Cornell University Press, 1953.

Reischauer, Edwin O. *The Japanese.* Cambridge, Mass.: Harvard University Press, 1977.

The Research Committee on the Study of Honolulu Residents. *Honolulu Residents and Their Attitudes in Multi-Ethnic Perspective: Toward A Theory of the American National Character.* Tokyo: The Institute of Statistical Mathematics, Monograph 1, 1980, Distributed by the University Press of Hawaii.

The Research Committee on the Study of Honolulu Residents. *Honolulu's Japanese Americans in Comparative Perspective.* Tokyo: The Institute of Statistical Mathematics, distributed through the University of Hawaii Press, 1984.

The Research Committee on the Study of Honolulu Residents. *The Third Attitudinal Survey of Honolulu Residents, 1983,* Monograph 3. Tokyo: The Institute of Statistical Mathematics, distributed through the University of Hawaii Press, 1986.

The Research Committee on the Study of Honolulu Residents, the Institute of Statistical Mathematics and the University of Hawaii at Manoa. *The Fourth Attitudinal Survey of Honolulu Residents, 1988*. Tokyo and Honolulu: The Institute of Statistical Mathematics and the University of Hawaii at Manoa, 1990.

The Research Committee on the Study of Japanese Americans in Honolulu, Hawaii. *A Study of Japanese-Americans in Honolulu, Hawaii*. The Annals of the Institute of Statistical Mathematics, Supplement 7, 1972.

Richardson, Bradley M. and Scott C. Flanagan. *Politics in Japan*. Boston: Little, Brown and Company, 1984.

Saeki, Shôichi and Tôru Haga, eds. *Gaikokujin-niyoru Nihonron no meicho*. Tokyo: Chûkoron-sha, 1987.

Sakaiya, Taichi. *Nihon to wa nanika*. Tokyo: Kôdansha, 1994.

Sakamoto, Hyakudai. "Japanese Philosophical Thought." *The Japan Foundation Newsletter*, Vol. 21, No. 2, September 1993, 11–17.

Sansom, Katherine Gordon Slingsby. *Living in Tokyo*. London: Chatto and Windus, 1936.

Sapir, Edward. *Language*. New York: Harcourt, Brace and World, 1921.

Sasaki, Masamichi and Tatsuzô Suzuki. "Changes in Religious Commitment in the United States, Holland, and Japan." *American Journal of Sociology*, Vol. 92, No. 5, March 1987, 1055–1076.

Schneider, Louis. *Classical Theories of Social Change*. Morristown, N.J.: General Learning Press, 1976.

Schroeder, Ralph. *Max Weber and the Sociology of Culture*. London: Sage Publications, 1992.

Sharabi, Hisham. *Neopatriachy: A Theory of Distorted Change in Arab Society*. New York: Oxford University Press, 1988.

Shidei, Tsunahide and Chikio Hayashi, eds. *Shinrin o mirukokoro*. Tokyo: Kyôritsu shuppan sha, 1984.

Shillony, Ben-Ami. *Goyakusareru Nihon*. Tokyo: Kôbunsha, 1986.

Shweder, Richard and Hazel Markus. "Culture, Identity and Conflict." *Items*, Vol. 49, No. 1, March 1995, 11–13.

Sibatani, Atuhiro. "The Japanese Brain: The Difference between East and West May Be the Difference between Left and Right." *Science*, December 1980, 22–27.

Skocpol, Theda. *States and Social Revolutions: A Comparative Analysis of France, Russia and China*. Cambridge, England: Cambridge University Press, 1979.

Smith, Adam. *The Wealth of Nations*. New York: Modern Library, 1937 (originally published 1776).

Sorokin, Pitirim A. *Social and Cultural Dynamics*. 4 vols. New York: American Book Company, 1937–1941.

Spencer, Herbert. *The Study of Sociology*. New York: Appleton, 1924.

Spengler, Oswald. *The Decline of the West*. Translated by Charles Francis Atkinson. New York: Alfred A. Knopf, Inc., 1932.

Suzuki, Tatsuzô. "Ways of Life and Social Milieus in Japan and the United States: A Comparative Study." *Behaviormetrika*, No. 15, 1984, 77–108.

Takahashi, Kôich and Ryôichi Shimizu. "Danjyo no sabetsu." In Tôkeisûri-kenkyûjyo kokuminseichôsa iinkai, ed. *Nihonjin no kokuminsei*. Tokyo: Shiseidô, 1961.

Takemura, Masayoshi. *Chiisakutomo kirari to hikarukuni, Nihon*. Tokyo: Kôbunsha, 1994.

Tilly, Charles. "Reflections on the History of European Statemaking." In Charles Tilly, ed. *The Formation of National States in Western Europe*. Princeton, N.J.: Princeton University Press, 1975, 3–83.

Tilly, Charles. *Coercion, Capital, and European States, AD 990–1990*. London/New York: Blackwell, 1992.

Tôkeisûrikenkyûjo. *Nihonjin no kokuminsei*. Tokyo: Shiseidô, 1961.

Tôkeisûrikenkyûjo. Daini *Nihonjin no kokuminsei*. Tokyo: Shiseidô, 1970.

Tôkeisûrikenkyûjo. *Daisan Nihonjin no kokuminsei*. Tokyo: Shiseidô, 1975.

Tôkeisûrikenkyûjo. *Daiyon Nihonjin no kokuminsei*. Tokyo: Idemitsu shoten, 1982.

Tôkeisûrikenkyûjo. *Daigo Nihonjin no kokuminsei*. Tokyo: Idemitsu shoten, 1992.

Tôkeisûrikenkyûjo. *Ishiki no kokusaihikakuhôhôron no kenkyû. Kenkyû Ripôto 71.* Tokyo: Tôkeisûrikenkyûjo, 1991.

Tôkeisûrikenkyûjo. *Burajirunikkeijin no ishikichôsa—1991–1992. Kenkyû ripôto 74.* Tokyo: Tôkeisûrikenkyûjo, 1993.

Toynbee, Arnold J. *A Study of History*, ed. D. C. Somerville. London: Oxford University Press, 1947–1957 (Abridgment of volumes I–X).

Triandis, Harry C. "Self and Social Behavior in Differing Cultural Contexts." *Psychological Review*, Vol. 96, 1989, 269–289.

Tsunoda, Tadanobu. *Japanese Brain: Uniqueness and Universality*. Tokyo: Taishûkan, 1985.

Umehara, Takeshi. "Shintô and Buddhism in Japanese Culture." *The Japan Foundation Newsletter*, Vol. 15, No. 1, July 1987, 1–7.

Varley, H. Paul. *Japanese Culture*, Third Edition. Honolulu: University of Hawaii Press, 1983.

Vico, Giambattista. *The New Science of Giambattista Vicco*. Translated by T. G. Bergin and M. Harold. Ithaca, N.Y.: Cornell University Press, 1968, 1744.

Waggoner, Hyatt H. *American Poets*. Baton Rouge: Louisiana State University Press, 1984.

Wakamori, Tarô. *Nihonshi no kyozô to jitsuzô*. Tokyo: Kadokawa shoten, 1974.

Weber, Max. *The Protestant Ethics and the Spirit of Capitalism*. London: Allen and Unwin, 1930.

Whorf, Benjamin L. *Language, Thought and Reality*, ed. J. B. Carroll. Cam-bridge Mass.: MIT Press, 1956.

Wierzbicka, Anna. "Cultural Scripts: A New Approach to the Study of Cross-Cultural Communication." In Martin Putz, ed. *Language Contact and Language Conflict*. Amsterdam: John Benjamins Publishing Company, 1994.

Wolferen, Karel van. *The Enigma of Japanese Power: People and Politics in a Stateless Nation.* New York: Alfred C. Knopf, 1989.

Wuthnow, Robert. "Cultural Change and Sociological Theory." In Hans Haferkamp and Neil J. Smelser, eds. *Social Change and Modernity.* Berkeley: University of California Press, 1992, 256–278.

Yamaori, Tetsuo. *Nihonjin no shinjô.* Tokyo: NHK Books, 1982.

Yang, K. S. "Will Societal Modernization Eventually Eliminate Cross-Cultural Psychological Differences?" In Michael H. Bond, ed. *The Cross-cultural Challenge to Social Psychology.* Newbury Park, Calif.: Sage, 1988, 67–85.

Yasuoka, Masahiro. *Nihonseishintsûgi: Nihon no "kokoro" o katsugakusuru.* Tokyo: Emôchio 21, 1993.

Yomikakinôryoku chôsa i-inkai. *Nihonjin no yomikakinôryoku.* Tokyo: Tôdai shuppankai, 1951.

Yoshino, Ryôzô. "3.3 Shûkyô." In Tôkeisûrikenkyûjo. *Daigo Nihonjin no kokuminsei.* Tokyo: Idemitsu shoten, 1992. 85–98.

Young, Pauline V. *Scientific Social Surveys and Research.* Third Edition. Englewood Cliff, N.J.: Prentice-Hall, Inc., 1956.

Yuasa, Yasuo. *Nihonkodai no seishinsekai.* Tokyo: Meichokankôkai, 1990.

Index

About the Authors

CHIKIO HAYASHI is Professor Emeritus at The Institute of Statistical Mathematics and President of the Japan Association for Public Opinion Research. He has had a long and distinguished career in statistical data analysis and survey research.

YASUMASA KURODA is Professor of Political Science at the University of Hawaii at Manoa. He has organized three major international conferences.

Both have published widely on comparative culture.

ISBN 0-275-95861-2

EAN

9 780275 958619

90000>

HARDCOVER BAR CODE